Title Withdrawn

ED-R

Junior
Worldmark
Encyclopedia of
World Cultures

Junior Worldmark Encyclopedia of

World Cultures

VOLUME

Afghanistan to
Bosnia Herzegovina

AN IMPRINT OF GALE

DETROIT · LONDON

JUNIOR WORLDMARK ENCYCLOPEDIA OF WORLD CULTURES

U•X•L Staff

Jane Hoehner, *U•X•L Senior Editor*
Carol DeKane Nagel, *U•X•L Managing Editor*
Thomas L. Romig, *U•X•L Publisher*
Mary Beth Trimper, *Production Director*
Evi Seoud, *Assistant Production Manager*
Shanna Heilveil, *Production Associate*
Cynthia Baldwin, *Product Design Manager*
Barbara J. Yarrow, *Graphic Services Supervisor*
Pamela A. E. Galbreath, *Senior Art Director*
Margaret Chamberlain, *Permissions Specialist (Pictures)*

Copyright © 1999
U•X•L
An Imprint of Gale

Library of Congress Cataloging-in-Publication Data
Junior worldmark encyclopedia of world cultures / Timothy L. Gall and
    Susan Bevan Gall, editors.
            p.   cm.
        Includes bibliographical references and index.
        Summary: Arranges countries around the world alphabetically,
    subdivides these countries into 250 culture groups, and provides
    information about the ethnology and human geography of each group.
        ISBN 0-7876-1756-X (set   :   alk. paper)
        1. Ethnology--Encyclopedias, Juvenile. 2. Human geography-
    -Encyclopedias, Juvenile. [1. Ethnology--Encyclopedias. 2. Human
    geography--Encyclopedias.]   I. Gall, Timothy L.   II. Gall, Susan B.
    GN307.J85   1999
    306' .03--dc21   98-13810
                                                                CIP
                                                                 AC

ISBN 0-7876-1756-X (set)
ISBN 0-7876-1757-1 (vol. 1)   ISBN 0-7876-1758-X (vol. 2)   ISBN 0-7876-1759-8 (vol. 3)
ISBN 0-7876-1760-1 (vol. 4)   ISBN 0-7876-1761-X (vol. 5)   ISBN 0-7876-1762-8 (vol. 6)
ISBN 0-7876-1763-6 (vol. 7)   ISBN 0-7876-1764-4 (vol. 8)   ISBN 0-7876-2761-5 (vol. 9)

Printed in the United States of America
10 9 8 7 6 5 4 3 2

Contents
Volume 1

Cumulative Contents

CUMULATIVE CONTENTS

CUMULATIVE CONTENTS

Volume 5

Volume 6

CUMULATIVE CONTENTS

CUMULATIVE CONTENTS

Volume 9

Contributors

Editors: Timothy L. Gall and Susan Bevan Gall

Senior Editor: Daniel M. Lucas

Contributing Editors: Himanee Gupta, Jim Henry, Kira Silverbird, Elaine Trapp, Rosalie Wieder

Copy Editors: Deborah Baron, Janet Fenn, Jim Henry, Patricia M. Mote, Deborah Ring, Kathy Soltis

Typesetting and Graphics: Cheryl Montagna, Brian Rajewski

Cover Photographs: Cory Langley

Data Input: Janis K. Long, Cheryl Montagna, Melody Penfound

Proofreaders: Deborah Baron, Janet Fenn

Editorial Assistants: Katie Baron, Jennifer A. Spencer, Daniel K. Updegraft

Editorial Advisors

P. Boone, Sixth Grade Teacher, Oak Crest Middle School, San Antonio, Texas

Jean Campbell, Foothill Farms Middle School, Sacramento, California

Kathy Englehart, Librarian, Hathaway Brown School, Shaker Heights, Ohio

Catherine Harris, Librarian, Oak Crest Middle School, San Antonio, Texas

Karen James, Children's Services, Louisville Free Public Library, Louisville, Kentucky

Contributors to the Gale Edition

The articles presented in this encyclopedia are based on entries in the *Worldmark Encyclopedia of Cultures and Daily Life* published in 1997 by Gale. The following authors and reviewers contributed to the Gale edition.

ANDREW J. ABALAHIN. Doctoral candidate, Department of History, Cornell University.

JAMAL ABDULLAH. Doctoral candidate, Department of City and Regional Planning, Cornell University.

SANA ABED-KOTOB. Book Review Editor, Middle East Journal, Middle East Institute.

MAMOUD ABOUD. Charge d'Affaires, a.i., Embassy of the Federal and Islamic Republic of the Comoros.

JUDY ALLEN. Editor, Choctaw Nation of Oklahoma.

HIS EXCELLENCY DENIS G. ANTOINE. Ambassador to the United States, Embassy of Grenada.

LESLEY ANN ASHBAUGH. Instructor, Sociology, Seattle University.

HASHEM ATALLAH. Translator, Editor, Teacher; Fairfax, Virginia.

HECTOR AZEVES. Cultural Attaché, Embassy of Uruguay.

VICTORIA J. BAKER. Associate Professor of Anthropology, Anthropology (Collegium of Comparative Cultures), Eckerd College.

POLINE BALA. Doctoral candidate, Asian Studies, Cornell University.

MARJORIE MANDELSTAM BALZER. Research Professor; Coordinator, Social, Regional, and Ethnic Studies Sociology, and Center for Eurasian, Russian, and East European Studies.

JOSHUA BARKER. Doctoral candidate, Department of Anthropology, Cornell University.

IGOR BARSEGIAN. Department of Sociology, George Washington University.

IRAJ BASHIRI. Professor of Central Asian Studies, Department of Slavic and Central Asian Languages and Literatures, University of Minnesota.

DAN F. BAUER. Department of Anthropology, Lafayette College.

JOYCE BEAR. Historic Preservation Officer, Muscogee Nation of Oklahoma.

SVETLANA BELAIA. Byelorussian-American Cultural Center, Strongsville, Ohio.

HIS EXCELLENCY DR. COURTNEY BLACKMAN. Ambassador to the United States, Embassy of Barbados.

BETTY BLAIR. Executive Editor, Azerbaijan International.

ARVIDS BLODNIEKS. Director, Latvian Institute, American Latvian Association in the USA.

ARASH BORMANSHINOV. University of Maryland, College Park.

HARRIET I. BRADY. Cultural Anthropologist (Pyramid Lake Paiute Tribe), Native Studies Program, Pyramid Lake High School.

MARTIN BROKENLEG. Professor of Sociology, Department of Sociology, Augustana College.

REV. RAYMOND A. BUCKO, S.J. Assistant Professor of Anthropology, LeMoyne College.

JOHN W. BURTON. Department of Anthropology, Connecticut College.

CONTRIBUTORS

DINEANE BUTTRAM. University of North Carolina-Chapel Hill.

RICARDO CABALLERO. Counselor, Embassy of Paraguay.

CHRISTINA CARPADIS. Researcher/Writer, Cleveland, Ohio.

SALVADOR GARCIA CASTANEDA. Department of Spanish and Portuguese, The Ohio State University.

SUSANA CAVALLO. Graduate Program Director and Professor of Spanish, Department of Modern Languages and Literatures, Loyola University, Chicago.

BRIAN P. CAZA. Doctoral candidate, Political Science, University of Chicago.

VAN CHRISTO. President and Executive Director, Frosina Foundation, Boston.

YURI A. CHUMAKOV. Graduate Student, Department of Sociology, University of Notre Dame.

J. COLARUSSO. Professor of Anthropology, McMaster University.

FRANCESCA COLECCHIA. Modern Language Department, Duquesne University.

DIANNE K. DAEG DE MOTT. Researcher/Writer, Tucson, Arizona.

MICHAEL DE JONGH. Professor, Department of Anthropology, University of South Africa.

GEORGI DERLUGUIAN. Senior Fellow, Ph.D., U. S. Institute of Peace.

CHRISTINE DRAKE. Department of Political Science and Geography, Old Dominion University.

ARTURO DUARTE. Guatemalan Mission to the OAS.

CALEB DUBE. Department of Anthropology, Northwestern University.

BRIAN DU TOIT. Professor, Department of Anthropology, University of Florida.

LEAH ERMARTH. Worldspace Foundation, Washington, DC.

NANCY J. FAIRLEY. Associate Professor of Anthropology, Department of Anthropology/Sociology, Davidson College.

GREGORY A. FINNEGAN, Ph.D. Tozzer Library, Harvard University.

ALLEN J. FRANK, Ph.D.

DAVID P. GAMBLE. Professor Emeritus, Department of Anthropology, San Francisco State University.

FREDERICK GAMST. Professor, Department of Anthropology, University of Massachusetts, Harbor Campus.

PAULA GARB. Associate Director of Global Peace and Conflict Studies and Adjunct Professor of Social Ecology, University of California, Irvine.

HAROLD GASKI. Associate Professor of Sami Literature, School of Languages and Literature, University of Tromsø.

STEPHEN J. GENDZIER.

FLORENCE GERDEL.

ANTHONY P. GLASCOCK. Professor of Anthropology; Department of Anthropology, Psychology, and Sociology; Drexel University.

LUIS GONZALEZ. Researcher/Writer, River Edge, New Jersey.

JENNIFER GRAHAM. Researcher/Writer, Sydney, Australia.

MARIE-CÉCILE GROELSEMA. Doctoral candidate, Comparative Literature, Indiana University.

ROBERT GROELSEMA. MPIA and doctoral candidate, Political Science, Indiana University.

MARIA GROSZ-NGATÉ. Visiting Assistant Professor, Department of Anthropology, Northwestern University.

ELLEN GRUENBAUM. Professor, School of Social Sciences, California State University, Fresno.

N. THOMAS HAKANSSON. University of Kentucky.

ROBERT HALASZ. Researcher/Writer, New York, New York.

MARC HANREZ. Professor, Department of French and Italian, University of Wisconsin-Madison.

ANWAR UL HAQ. Central Asian Studies Department, Indiana University.

LIAM HARTE. Department of Philosophy, Loyola University, Chicago.

FR. VASILE HATEGAN. Author, *Romanian Culture in America*.

BRUCE HEILMAN. Doctoral candidate, Department of Political Science, Indiana University.

JIM HENRY. Researcher/Writer, Cleveland, Ohio.

BARRY HEWLETT. Department of Anthropology, Washington State University.

SUSAN F. HIRSCH. Department of Anthropology, Wesleyan University.

MARIDA HOLLOS. Department of Anthropology, Brown University.

HALYNA HOLUBEC. Researcher/Writer, Cleveland, Ohio.

YVONNE HOOSAVA. Legal Researcher and Cultural Preservation Officer, Hopi Tribal Council.

HUIQIN HUANG, Ph.D. Center for East Asia Studies, University of Montreal.

ASAFA JALATA. Assistant Professor of Sociology and African and African American Studies, Department of Sociology, The University of Tennessee, Knoxville.

STEPHEN F. JONES. Russian Department, Mount Holyoke College.

THOMAS JOVANOVSKI, Ph.D. Lorain County Community College.

A. KEN JULES. Minister Plenipotentiary and Deputy Head of Mission, Embassy of St. Kitts and Nevis.

GENEROSA KAGARUKI-KAKOTI. Economist, Department of Urban and Rural Planning, College of Lands and Architectural Studies, Dar es Salaam, Tanzania.

EZEKIEL KALIPENI. Department of Geography, University of Illinois at Urbana-Champaign.

CONTRIBUTORS

DON KAVANAUGH. Program Director, Lake of the Woods Ojibwa Cultural Centre.

SUSAN M. KENYON. Associate Professor of Anthropology, Department of History and Anthropology, Butler University.

WELILE KHUZWAYO. Department of Anthropology, University of South Africa.

PHILIP L. KILBRIDE. Professor of Anthropology, Mary Hale Chase Chair in the Social Sciences, Department of Anthropology, Bryn Mawr College.

RICHARD O. KISIARA. Doctoral candidate, Department of Anthropology, Washington University in St. Louis.

KAREN KNOWLES. Permanent Mission of Antigua and Barbuda to the United Nations.

IGOR KRUPNIK. Research Anthropologist, Department of Anthropology, Smithsonian Institution.

LEELO LASS. Secretary, Embassy of Estonia.

ROBERT LAUNAY. Professor, Department of Anthropology, Northwestern University.

CHARLES LEBLANC. Professor and Director, Center for East Asia Studies, University of Montreal.

RONALD LEE. Author, *Goddam Gypsy, An Autobiographical Novel.*

PHILIP E. LEIS. Professor and Chair, Department of Anthropology, Brown University.

MARIA JUKIC LESKUR. Croatian Consulate, Cleveland, Ohio.

RICHARD A. LOBBAN, JR. Professor of Anthropology and African Studies, Department of Anthropology, Rhode Island College.

DERYCK O. LODRICK. Visiting Scholar, Center for South Asian Studies, University of California, Berkeley.

NEIL LURSSEN. Intro Communications Inc.

GREGORIO C. MARTIN. Modern Language Department, Duquesne University.

HOWARD J. MARTIN. Independent scholar.

HEITOR MARTINS. Professor, Department of Spanish and Portuguese, Indiana University.

ADELINE MASQUELIER. Assistant Professor, Department of Anthropology, Tulane University.

DOLINA MILLAR.

EDITH MIRANTE. Project Maje, Portland, Oregon.

ROBERT W. MONTGOMERY, Ph.D. Indiana University.

THOMAS D. MORIN. Associate Professor of Hispanic Studies, Department of Modern and Classical Literatures and Languages, University of Rhode Island.

CHARLES MORRILL. Doctoral candidate, Indiana University.

CAROL A. MORTLAND. Crate's Point, The Dalles, Oregon.

FRANCIS A. MOYER. Director, North Carolina Japan Center, North Carolina State University.

MARIE C. MOYER.

NYAGA MWANIKI. Assistant Professor, Department of Anthropology and Sociology, Western Carolina University.

KENNETH NILSON. Celtic Studies Department, Harvard University.

JANE E. ORMROD. Graduate Student, History, University of Chicago.

JUANITA PAHDOPONY. Carl Perkins Program Director, Comanche Tribe of Oklahoma.

TINO PALOTTA. Syracuse University.

ROHAYATI PASENG.

PATRICIA PITCHON. Researcher/Writer, London, England.

STEPHANIE PLATZ. Program Officer, Program on Peace and International Cooperation, The John D. and Catherine T. MacArthur Foundation.

MIHAELA POIATA. Graduate Student, School of Journalism and Mass Communication, University of North Carolina at Chapel Hill.

LEOPOLDINA PRUT-PREGELJ. Author, *Historical Dictionary of Slovenia.*

J. RACKAUSKAS. Director, Lithuanian Research and Studies Center, Chicago.

J. RAKOVICH. Byelorussian-American Cultural Center, Strongsville, Ohio.

HANTA V. RALAY. Promotions, Inc., Montgomery Village, Maryland.

SUSAN J. RASMUSSEN. Associate Professor, Department of Anthropology, University of Houston.

RONALD REMINICK. Department of Anthropology, Cleveland State University.

BRUCE D. ROBERTS. Assistant Professor of Anthropology, Department of Anthropology and Sociology, University of Southern Mississippi.

LAUREL L. ROSE. Philosophy Department, Carnegie-Mellon University.

ROBERT ROTENBERG. Professor of Anthropology, International Studies Program, DePaul University.

CAROLINE SAHLEY, Ph.D. Researcher/Writer, Cleveland, Ohio.

VERONICA SALLES-REESE. Associate Professor, Department of Spanish and Portuguese, Georgetown University.

MAIRA SARYBAEVA. Kazakh-American Studies Center, University of Kentucky.

DEBRA L. SCHINDLER. Institute of Arctic Studies, Dartmouth College.

KYOKO SELDEN, Ph.D. Researcher/Writer, Ithaca, New York.

ENAYATULLAH SHAHRANI. Central Asian Studies Department, Indiana University.

ROBERT SHANAFELT. Adjunct Lecturer, Department of Anthropology, The Florida State University.

TUULIKKI SINKS. Teaching Specialist for Finnish, Department of German, Scandinavian, and Dutch, University of Minnesota.

JAN SJÅVIK. Associate Professor, Scandinavian Studies, University of Washington.

CONTRIBUTORS

MAGDA SOBALVARRO. Press and Cultural Affairs Director, Embassy of Nicaragua.

MICHAEL STAINTON. Researcher, Joint Center for Asia Pacific Studies, York University.

RIANA STEYN. Department of Anthropology, University of South Africa.

PAUL STOLLER. Professor, Department of Anthropology, West Chester University.

CRAIG STRASHOFER. Researcher/Writer, Cleveland, Ohio.

SANDRA B. STRAUBHAAR. Assistant Professor, Nordic Studies, Department of Germanic and Slavic Languages, Brigham Young University.

VUM SON SUANTAK. Author, *Zo History.*

MURAT TAISHIBAEV. Kazakh-American Studies Center, University of Kentucky.

CHRISTOPHER C. TAYLOR. Associate Professor, Anthropology Department, University of Alabama, Birmingham.

EDDIE TSO. Office of Language and Culture, Navajo Division of Education.

DAVID TYSON. Foreign Broadcast Information Service, Washington, D.C.

NICOLAAS G. W. UNLANDT. Assistant Professor of French, Department of French and Italian, Brigham Young University.

GORDON URQUHART. Professor, Department of Economics and Business, Cornell College.

CHRISTOPHER J. VAN VUUREN. Professor, Department of Anthropology, University of South Africa.

DALIA VENTURA-ALCALAY. Journalist, London, England.

CATHERINE VEREECKE. Assistant Director, Center for African Studies, University of Florida.

GREGORY T. WALKER. Associate Director, Office of International Affairs, Duquesne University.

GERHARD WEISS. Department of German, Scandinavian, and Dutch, University of Minnesota.

PATSY WEST. Director, The Seminole/Miccosukee Photographic Archive.

WALTER WHIPPLE. Associate Professor of Polish, Germanic and Slavic Languages, Brigham Young University.

ROSALIE WIEDER. Researcher/Writer, Cleveland, Ohio.

JEFFREY WILLIAMS. Professor, Department of Anthropology, Cleveland State University.

GUANG-HONG YU. Associate Research Fellow, Institute of Ethnology, Academia Sinica.

RUSSELL ZANCA. Department of Anthropology, College of Liberal Arts and Sciences, University of Illinois at Urbana-Champaign.

Reader's Guide

Junior Worldmark Encyclopedia of World Cultures contains articles exploring the ways of life of over 290 culture groups worldwide. Arranged alphabetically by country in nine volumes, this encyclopedia parallels the organization of its sister set, *Junior Worldmark Encyclopedia of the Nations*. Whereas the primary purpose of *Nations* is to provide information on the world's nations, this encyclopedia focuses on the traditions, living conditions, and personalities of many of the world's culture groups.

Defining groups for inclusion was not an easy task. Cultural identity is shaped by such factors as history, geography, nationality, ethnicity, race, language, and religion. Sometimes the distinctions are subtle, but important. Most chapters in this encyclopedia begin with an article on the people of the country as a nationality group. For example, the chapter on Kenya begins with an article entitled "Kenyans." This article explores the national character shared by all people living in Kenya. However, there are separate articles on the Gikuyu, Kalenjin, Luhya, and Luo—four of the largest ethnic groups living in the country. They are all Kenyans, but each group is distinct. Many profiled groups—like the Kazaks—inhabit lands that cross national boundaries. Although profiled in the chapter on Kazakstan, Kazaks are also important minorities in China, Uzbekistan, and Turkmenistan. In such cases, cross-references direct the student to the chapter where the group is profiled.

The photographs that illustrate the articles show a wonderfully diverse world. From the luxury liners docked in the harbor at Monaco to the dwellings made of grass sheltering the inhabitants of the rain forest, people share the struggles and joys of earning a living, bringing children into the world, teaching them to survive, and initiating them into adulthood. Although language, customs, and dress illustrate our differences, the faces of the people pictured in these volumes reinforce our similarities. Whether on the streets of Tokyo or the mountains of Tibet, a smile on the face of a child transcends the boundaries of nationality and cultural identity to reveal something common in us all. Photographer Cory Langley's images on pages 93 and 147 in Volume 6 serve to illustrate this point.

The picture of the world this encyclopedia paints today will certainly differ from the one painted in future editions. Indigenous people like the Jivaro in Ecuador (Volume 3, page 77) are being assimilated into modern society as forest lands are cleared for development and televisions and VCRs are brought to even the most remote villages. As the global economy expands, traditional diets are supplemented with Coke, Pepsi, and fast food; traditional storytellers are replaced by World Cup soccer matches and American television programs; and cultural heroes are overwhelmed by images of Michael Jordan and Michael Jackson. Photographer Cynthia Bassett was fortunate to be among a small group of travelers to visit a part of China only recently opened to Westerners. Her image of Miao dancers (Volume 2, page 161) shows a people far removed from Western culture . . . until one looks a little closer. Behind the dancers, in the upper corner of the photograph, is a basketball hoop and backboard. It turns out that Miao teenagers love basketball!

ORGANIZATION

Within each volume the chapters are arranged alphabetically by country. A cumulative table of contents for all volumes in the set follows the table of contents to each volume.

Each chapter covers a specific country. The contents of the chapter, listing the culture group articles, follows the chapter title. An overview of the composition of the population of the country appears after the contents list. The individual articles follow, and are organized according to a standard twenty-heading outline explained in more detail below. This structure allows for easy comparison between cultures and enhances the accessibility of the information.

Articles begin with the **pronunciation** of the group's name, a listing of **alternate names** by which the group is known, the group's **location** in the world, its **population**, the **languages** spoken, and the **religions** practiced. Articles are illustrated with maps showing the primary location of the group and photographs of the culture group being profiled. The twenty standard headings by which the articles are organized are presented below.

1 ● INTRODUCTION: A description of the group's historical origins provides a useful background for understanding its contemporary affairs. Information relating to migration helps explain how the group arrived at its present location. Political conditions and governmental structure(s) that affect members of the profiled ethnic group are also discussed.

2 ● LOCATION: The population size of the group is listed. This information may include official census data from various countries and/or estimates. Information on the size of a group's population located outside the traditional homeland may also be included, especially for those groups with large scattered populations. A description of the homeland includes information on location, topography, and climate.

3 ● LANGUAGE: Each article lists the name(s) of the primary language(s) spoken by members. Descriptions of linguistic origins, grammar, and similarities to other languages may also be included. Examples of common words, phrases, and proverbs are listed for many of the profiled groups, and some include examples of common personal names and greetings.

4 ● FOLKLORE: Common themes, settings, and characters in the profiled group's traditional oral and/or literary mythology are highlighted. Many entries include a short excerpt or synopsis of one of the group's noteworthy myths, fables, or legends. Some entries describe the accomplishments of famous heroes and heroines or other prominent historical figures.

5 ● RELIGION: The origins of traditional religious beliefs are profiled. Contemporary religious beliefs, customs, and practices are also discussed. Some groups may be closely associated with one particular faith (especially if religious and ethnic identification are interlinked), while others may have members of diverse faiths.

6 ● MAJOR HOLIDAYS: Celebrations and commemorations typically recognized by the group's members are described. These holidays commonly fall into two categories: secular and religious. Secular holidays often include an independence day and/or other days of observance recognizing important dates in history that affected the group as a whole. Religious holidays are typically the same as those honored by people of the same faith worldwide. Some secular and religious holidays are linked to the lunar cycle or to the change of seasons. Some articles describe customs practiced by members of the group on certain holidays.

7 ● RITES OF PASSAGE: Formal and informal events that mark an individual's procession through the stages of life are profiled. These events typically involve rituals, ceremonies, observances, and procedures associated with birth, childhood, the coming of age, milestones in education or religious training, adulthood, and death.

8 ● RELATIONSHIPS: Information on greetings, body language, gestures, visiting customs, and dating practices is included. The extent of formality to which members of a certain ethnic group treat others is also addressed, as some groups may adhere to customs governing interpersonal relationships more or less strictly than others.

9 ● LIVING CONDITIONS: General health conditions typical of the group's members are cited. Such information includes life expectancy, the prevalence of various diseases, and access to medical care. Information on urbanization, housing, and access to utilities is also included. Transportation methods typically utilized by the group's members are also discussed.

10 ● FAMILY LIFE: The size and composition of the family unit is profiled. Gender roles common to the group are also discussed, including the division of rights and responsibilities relegated to male and female group members. The roles that children, adults, and the elderly have within the group as a whole may also be addressed.

11 ● CLOTHING: Many entries include descriptive information (design, color, fabric, etc.) regarding traditional clothing (or national costume) for men and women, and indicate the frequency of its use in contemporary life. A description of typical clothing worn in modern daily life is also provided, especially if traditional clothing is no longer the usual form of dress. Distinctions between formal and work attire and descriptions of clothing preferences of young people are described for many groups as well.

12 ● FOOD: Descriptions of items commonly consumed by members of the group are listed. The frequency and occasion for meals is also described, as are any unique customs regarding eating and drinking, special utensils and furniture, and the role of food and beverages in ritual ceremonies. Many entries include a recipe for a favorite dish.

13 ● EDUCATION: The structure of formal education in the country or countries of residence is discussed, including information on primary, secondary, and higher education. For some groups, the role of informal education is also highlighted. Some articles include information regarding the relevance and importance of education among the group as a whole, along with parental expectations for children.

14 ● CULTURAL HERITAGE: Since many groups express their sense of identity through art, music, literature, and dance, a description of prominent styles is included. Some articles also cite the contributions of famous individual artists, writers, and musicians.

15 ● EMPLOYMENT: The type of labor that typically engages members of the profiled group is discussed. For some groups, the formal wage economy is the primary source of earnings, but for other groups, informal agriculture or trade may be the usual way to earn a living. Working conditions are also highlighted.

16 ● SPORTS: Popular sports that children and adults play are listed, as are typical spectator sports. Some articles include a description and/or rules to a sport or game.

17 ● RECREATION: Listed activities that people enjoy in their leisure time may include structured pastimes (such as public musical and dance performances) or informal get-togethers (such as meeting for conversation). The role of popular culture, movies, theater, and television in everyday life is also discussed where it applies.

18 ● CRAFTS AND HOBBIES: Entries describe arts and crafts commonly fabricated according to traditional methods, materials, and style. Such objects may often have a functional utility for everyday tasks.

19 ● SOCIAL PROBLEMS: Internal and external issues that confront members of the profiled group are described. Such concerns often deal with fundamental problems like war, famine, disease, and poverty. A lack of human rights, civil rights, and political freedom may also adversely affect a group as a whole. Other problems may include crime, unemployment, substance abuse, and domestic violence.

20 ● BIBLIOGRAPHY: References cited include works used to compile the article, benchmark publications often recognized as authoritative by scholars, and other reference sources accessible to middle school researchers. Website addresses are provided for researchers who wish to access the World Wide Web. The website citation includes the author and title of the website (if applicable). The address begins with characters that follow "http://" in the citation; the address ends with the character preceding the comma and date. For example, the citation for the website of the German embassy appears as follows:

German Embassy, Washington, D.C. [Online]
Available http://www.germany-info.org/, 1998.

To access this site, researchers type:
www.germany-info.org

A glossary and an index of groups profiled appears at the end of each volume.

ACKNOWLEDGMENTS

The editors express appreciation to the members of the U•X•L staff who were involved in a number of ways at various stages of development of the *Junior Worldmark Encyclopedia of World Cultures.*

SUGGESTIONS ARE WELCOME: We appreciate any suggestions that will enhance future editions. Please send comments to:

Editors
Junior Worldmark Encyclopedia of World Cultures
U•X•L
27500 Drake Road
Farmington Hills, MI 48331-3535
(800) 877-4253

Junior Worldmark
Encyclopedia of World Cultures

Afghanistan

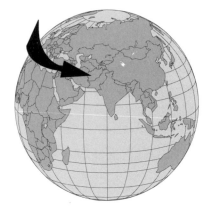

The people of Afghanistan are called Afghanis. The Pashtun make up about 43 percent of the population and are often referred to as "true Afghans." The Tajiks comprise nearly 25 percent of the population, the Uzbeks, 6 percent, and the Hazaras, about 5 percent. For more information on the Tajiks, see the chapter on Tajikistan in Volume 9; for more information on the Uzbeks, see the chapter on Uzbekistan, also in Volume 9.

Afghanis

PRONUNCIATION: af-GHAN-eez
LOCATION: Afghanistan
POPULATION: 22 million
LANGUAGE: Dari; Pashto; Turkish
RELIGION: Islam (Sunni Muslim, 80–90 percent; Shi'ite Muslim, 10–20 percent)

1 ● INTRODUCTION

Afghanistan became an independent nation in 1919. In the sixty years that followed, the leaders tried to establish a government based on parliamentary democracy. In April 1978, the government was overthrown in a coup d'état. The Soviet Union (a powerful communist country at the time) sent its army into Kabul, the capital of Afghanistan, to support the government established after the coup. The troops stayed for ten years. During that time, thousands of Afghanis became refugees, fleeing their homes to escape the practices of the new government. Many settled in the neighboring countries of Pakistan and Iran. By the late 1990s, at least one out of every four Afghanis was living outside of Afghanistan as a refugee.

2 ● LOCATION

Afghanistan is a remote, mountainous, land-locked country in southwestern Asia. It is about the same size as the state of Texas. The mountain ranges known as the Hindu Kush cover most of the country. Afghanistan's climate features little rainfall. To cultivate crops in Afghanistan, farmers must use irrigation systems.

The total population is about 22 million. In the mid-1990s, about 3 million were nomads (people who move frequently, living in dwellings that can be easily transported), and millions were refugees living

AFGHANIS

0   250   500   750 Miles

0 250 500 750 1000 Kilometers

RUSSIA

Caspian Sea

Aral Sea

KAZAKSTAN

Zaysan

UZBEKISTAN

Almaty (Alma-Ata)

TURKMENISTAN

Tashkent

KYRGYSTAN

Ashkhabad   Tejen

Dushanbe

TAJIKISTAN

IRAN

AFGHANISTAN

CHINA

Kabul

Zaranj

Islāmābād

Saindak

PAKISTAN

Pasni

New Delhi

NEPAL

BHUTAN

Kathmāndu

Arabian Sea

Lakhpat

INDIA

Dhaka

BANGLADESH

Surat

Gulf of Oman

outside Afghanistan. The five major cities in Afghanistan are Kabul, Kandahar, Herat, Mazar-e-Sharif, and Kunduz. The major ethnic groups in Afghanistan are Pashtun and Hazara. (Until recently, the terms *Afghan* and *Pashtun* were interchangeable. Today, however, *Afghan* denotes all citizens of Afghanistan.)

3 ● LANGUAGE

There are two principal languages spoken in Afghanistan: Dari, a form of Persian; and Pashto (also spelled Pashtu), which is also spoken in some areas of the neighboring country, Pakistan. Both Dari and Pashto are official languages of Afghanistan. Most educated Afghanis can speak both. Most Afghani names are Islamic. Afghanis have only recently begun to use surnames (last names).

4 ● FOLKLORE

Afghanis love to tell stories. Stories for children usually teach about foolish people who get what they deserve, such as "The Smell and the Jingle." According to this story, there was once a beggar who lingered near the property of a wealthy merchant, smelling the wonderful smells from a barbecue the merchant was hosting. Not one of the guests offered the beggar even a morsel to eat. The next day, the merchant accused the beggar of ruining his picnic by lingering nearby. (The merchant felt his guests were offended when the beggar "stole" the wonderful smells of the barbecue.) The merchant took the beggar to court, where the beggar told the Amir (ruler) he was innocent of any crime. The Amir wanted to win favor with the wealthy merchant (and didn't care much about the beggar), so he sentenced the beggar to pay the merchant ten dinars. The beggar had no money to pay the fine, so he went to Abu Khan (a local philosopher) for advice. Abu Khan pondered for a moment, and shook his head knowingly. "Don't worry, my friend. Allah will help you. Meet me at the Amir's court tomorrow, and—God willing—the debt will be settled." The next day, the Amir asked the merchant, "Are you ready to receive payment of the fine?" The merchant replied impatiently, "Yes, I am waiting." Abu Khan handed the ten dinars to the beggar and said, "Now throw them down." The beggar did so, and the coins jingled as they scattered on the marble floor. "Did you hear the jingle?" Abu Khan asked the merchant. "That is the part of the dinars that belongs to you. If a man can spoil a barbecue by merely smelling the wonderful aroma, then a man can well be paid by hearing the jingle of money." The Amir smiled, knowing that he had to agree with Abu Khan. The merchant had received a fair payment.

5 ● RELIGION

Afghanistan is one of the most solidly Muslim countries in the world. The majority follow the main branch of Islam, the Sunni tradition. About 10 to 20 percent of Afghanis follow the Shi'ite branch of Islam. There are also sufis (or dervishes), members of the mystical branch of Islam. Religious folk traditions are generally more important to Afghanis than the scholarly study of Islam. Local religious leaders are usually not highly educated. Mostly, they are peasants who do other part-time work.

6 ● MAJOR HOLIDAYS

Probably the most important annual holiday in Afghanistan is the ancient Persian New Year celebration. Called *Nawruz*, meaning "new day," it occurs at the beginning of spring on March 21. Special foods are eaten, including a dessert called *samanak*. Fairs and carnivals brighten Nawruz. So does the custom of dyeing farm animals— green chickens and purple sheep abound.

Most major holidays in Afghanistan are Islamic holy days, which are reckoned by a lunar calendar. One of the most important is Ramadan (pronounced Rah-mah-zan in Afghanistan), a month of fasting from dawn to dusk each day.

Secular (nonreligious) holidays in Afghanistan include Revolution Day on April 27; Workers' Day (similar to Labor Day) on May 1; and Jeshn, or Independence Day, on August 18.

7 ● RITES OF PASSAGE

Weddings are the most festive occasions in Afghanistan, with ceremonies traditionally spread over a three-day period. The groom's family pays for the wedding, which involves much feasting and dancing. In the official ceremony *(nikah-namah),* the marriage contract is signed in front of witnesses. The *mullah* (local religious leader) reads from the Koran (the sacred text of Islam), and sugared almonds and walnuts are tossed onto the bridegroom.

The birth of a first child is the occasion for a day-long celebration, which is most elaborate if the child is a boy. Children are named on the third day after birth. Boys are usually circumcised at about the age of seven. Afterward they begin wearing turbans.

In the year following a death, memorial dinners take place several times.

8 ● RELATIONSHIPS

Most Afghanis only use their given (first) names in public. Within the privacy of the home, they call each other by nicknames, or *laqubs*. All nicknames consist of the same few words—including "candy," "flower," "lion," "uncle," and "dear"—in combinations such as "Lion Uncle" or "Flower Dear."

Afghanis are very physically expressive. They use exaggerated gestures and facial expressions to communicate. Physical affection is openly expressed between members of the same sex. However, the laws of Islam forbid members of the opposite sex who are not close relations to touch each other.

Afghani men greet friends and acquaintances by clasping both hands in a firm handshake, hugging, and kissing each other on the cheeks. They often walk together, arm in arm. Business contracts are sealed with a nod of the head.

Interpersonal relations among Afghanis are largely ruled by *Pashtunwalli*, a set of unwritten laws and codes. Pashtunwalli includes such concepts as *milmastia*, being a good and generous host; and *nanawati*, providing shelter to anyone who needs it.

9 ● LIVING CONDITIONS

Afghanistan is one of the poorest countries in the world. Constant warfare has prevented the Afghanis from developing effective irrigation systems, which are required for farming. Most of the few major roadways in the country have been destroyed in the wars. Afghanistan has one of the highest infant mortality rates in the world.

Afghanistan is one of the few countries of the world that still has a sizable number of nomads. Nomadic Afghanis, called *kochis*, live in tents. There are about two million nomads in Afghanistan. They move from place to place to find grazing grounds for their herds of camel and sheep. Settled Afghanis mostly live in small villages of a few hundred to a few thousand people. Some wealthier Afghanis live in *qalas,* or country forts, with other farmers working their land.

Village houses are made of bricks plastered with a mixture of mud and straw. Most are flat-roofed, but in some regions domed roofs are preferred. Households have the bare minimum of furniture, with mattresses

AP/Wide World Photos

The woman on the right is in traditional dress, while the other woman and child wear Western-style attire. In large cities, particularly Kabul, Western-style clothing is becoming increasingly popular for both men and women.

spread on the floor at night for beds. The mattresses are then stacked in a corner during the day.

High-rise brick buildings are found in cities to house the ever-growing urban population. Though the standard of living is better than in rural areas, modern comforts such as plumbing are not always available.

10 ● FAMILY LIFE

Most marriages are arranged by the parents and relatives, often when children are still very young. Men generally marry between the ages of eighteen and twenty, and women between the ages of sixteen and eighteen.

Marriage between cousins, especially paternal ones, is preferred.

Afghani life revolves around the family, including the extended family. Extended families often live together in the same household, or in separate households clustered together. Even large cities are made up of small "villages" of extended family units. The women of the family households form a single work group, and care for and discipline the children. The senior male member, usually the grandfather, controls all spending. The grandmother organizes all domestic chores.

Women have a great deal of power in the home, but little authority in public. Islamic tradition requires that they be veiled and kept separate from men in public.

Divorce is fairly simple in Islamic law. To divorce his wife, a man merely has to say "I divorce you" three times in front of witnesses. A woman has to appear before a judge with reasons for divorcing her husband. However, few Afghanis end their marriages.

Children are cherished in Afghani society, especially boys. Girls are not mistreated, but their brothers' needs always come first. Children are expected to grow up quickly and learn to take care of themselves.

11 ● CLOTHING

The ordinary clothing of Afghani men is a rather baggy pair of trousers with a drawstring at the waist, and a loose, long-sleeved shirt reaching about to the knees. When it is cool, a vest is also worn. Brightly striped, quilted coats are worn in rural areas. Afghanis' turbans were traditionally white but are now any color.

Women generally wear pleated trousers under a long dress, and cover their heads with a shawl. Some urban women continue to wear the *chadri,* a traditional ankle-length cloth covering, which was officially banned in 1959. It is like a sack over the whole body, with a mesh insert over the eyes and nose.

In large cities, especially Kabul, Western-style clothing is becoming increasingly popular with both men and women.

12 ● FOOD

Afghani cuisine has been influenced by the peoples who have occupied their country throughout history. The strongest influences are India and Iran. Staple foods are rice, a flatbread known as *naan,* and dairy products. A variety of fruits and vegetables are also available. The main feature of a big meal is a rice *pilau,* which is rice cooked with meats or vegetables.

Bread is eaten at every meal. It often serves as a utensil for scooping up food, since Afghanis generally eat with their fingers. The typical beverage is tea, usually drunk without milk. Alcohol and pork are forbidden by Islam. In rural Afghanistan, regular meals are not eaten between breakfast and supper, but people carry nuts and dried fruit to eat during the day for energy.

A special soup served only on *Nawruz,* the Persian New Year, is *haft miwa.* This soup is made of seven fruits and nuts to symbolize spring. In the recipe that follows, peaches are substituted for a locally grown Afghani fruit known as *sanje.*

Recipe

Haft Miwa
(Seven Fruits)

Ingredients

1 cup blanched almonds (unsalted)
1 cup shelled walnuts (unsalted)
1 cup shelled pistachios (unsalted)
1 cup dried peaches
1 cup raisins
1 cup golden raisins
1 cup dried apricots
6 cups water

Directions

1. If using salted nuts, rinse off the salt with water. Combine all the nuts in one bowl. Combine all the fruits in another bowl.

2. Add 3 cups of cold water to each bowl. Stir, cover the bowls, and refrigerate.

3. After two days, combine the ingredients from the two bowls into one large bowl. Stir, cover the bowl, and refrigerate for two or three more days. Serve cold.

Adapted from Ansary, Mir Tamim. *Afghanistan: Fighting for Freedom.* New York: Dillon Press, 1991.

13 ● EDUCATION

Western-style education has never been widely accepted in Afghanistan. Relatively few people are literate (can read and write). With the constant warfare, formal education has not always been available. Before the communist takeover in 1978, there were 3,404 schools with 83,500 teachers. Two decades later, there were only 350 schools left, with 2,000 teachers—and nearly 400,000 children. That means there are two hundred students per teacher.

The educational system of Afghanistan consists of six years of primary school, and six years of *lycee,* or high school. When the University of Kabul was founded in 1946, there were separate programs for men and women. By 1960, its curriculum had become coeducational (including men and women together).

13 ● CULTURAL HERITAGE

Nearly constant warfare since the seventeenth century has prevented the Afghanis from giving their attention to the arts. There has been little original art, literature, or architecture produced in Afghanistan.

Afghanis write little fiction or other prose. The Islamic reverence for poetry, however, continues to inspire poetry recitals. The most popular theme in Afghani poetry is war, followed by love, jealousy, and religion.

Most painting is in the form of calligraphy (decorative lettering) and other functional decoration. Graceful Muslim architecture can be seen in the design of mosques and other buildings.

14 ● EMPLOYMENT

Most Afghanis (about 70 percent) are farmers and herders. The army and government administration are the only major types of employment other than agriculture. Only the few large cities, including the capital, Kabul, have modern businesses.

15 ● SPORTS

Afghanis are very competitive and take their sports seriously. Winning is a question of personal and family honor. Afghani sports also tend to be violent, although injuries are rare. A favorite Afghani sport is called *buzkashi,* or "goat pulling." Two teams compete for possession of a headless animal carcass (usually a calf). Teams have been known to number up to 1,000 players.

Another popular Afghani sport is wrestling, or *pahlwani*. Modern sports introduced in the twentieth century include tennis, golf, cricket, basketball, soccer, and field hockey.

16 ● RECREATION

In war-torn Afghanistan, families do not have money to buy toys, and few are available. Children play simple games with basic toys made from natural objects, such as slingshots. *Buzul-bazi* is a game like marbles or dice, played with sheep's knucklebones. Girls play a game very similar to hopscotch.

Boys enjoy kite-fighting *(gudi-paran jungi)* with kites made from tissue paper stretched over bamboo sticks. The point of the game is to cross strings with another kite-flyer and saw your string back and forth against his to cut the string and set his kite loose. To make their strings sharper, boys "glass" them by soaking them in a mixture of ground glass and paste.

Adults love to sing and dance, and do so often. Afghanis do not dance with partners; instead, they either dance alone or in circles. Men spend time in teahouses listening to music, drinking tea, and talking. They also indulge in a more violent entertainment—animal-fighting, usually with cocks (roosters). The two animals fight to the death, and men bet on the outcome.

17 ● CRAFTS AND HOBBIES

The main folk art is carpet-weaving. The weaving is done mostly by young girls and women. Patterns are passed down from generation to generation and are considered family secrets. For the finest work, it takes four weavers three months to finish a rug that measures six square meters (about seven squares yards).

Embroidery is widely practiced. Skullcaps, shirts, vests, and coats may be embroidered—especially ones worn on special occasions. Metalworking has produced silver jewelry and elaborately designed dagger handles, as well as trays and bowls. Afghanistan is the world's leading producer of the stone lapis lazuli, which is made into jewelry.

18 ● SOCIAL PROBLEMS

Continual warfare is the biggest social problem facing the Afghanis. The fighting has severely disrupted education, health care, employment opportunities, and even the provision of basic needs such as food and shelter.

19 ● BIBLIOGRAPHY

Ali, Sharifah Enayat. *Cultures of the World: Afghanistan*. New York: Marshall Cavendish, 1995.

Ansary, Mir Tamim. *Afghanistan: Fighting for Freedom*. New York: Dillon Press, 1991.

Clifford, Mary Louise. *The Land and People of Afghanistan*. Portraits of the Nations. New York: Lippincott, 1989.

WEBSITES

Echo of Islam. [Online] Available http://chuma.cas.usf.edu/~rfayiz/afghani.htm, 1998.

Investor's Business Journal. Afghanistan. [Online] Available http://www.afghan-web.com/, 1998.

World Travel Guide. Afghanistan. [Online] Available http://www.wtgonline.com/country/af/gen.html, 1998.

Hazaras

PRONUNCIATION: huh-ZAH-ruhz
LOCATION: Afghanistan
POPULATION: 1.5– 4.3 million (estimate)
LANGUAGE: Dari (Khorasani Persian); Pashtu; Baluchi; Turkic
RELIGION: Islam (Shi'ite Muslim)

1 ● INTRODUCTION

The Hazaras live in Afghanistan. Local legends and some native historians trace their ancestry to the biblical figure Yafith (or Japheth), the son of Noah. The Hazaras believe themselves to be descendants of the Turko-Mongol tribes of Asia. However, there is little precise knowledge about their ethnic origins and their history in Afghanistan.

2 ● LOCATION

Most of the Hazaras are concentrated in the mountainous central region of Afghanistan. The area that serves as their homeland is known as Hazarajat. Hazaras are also found scattered in other areas of the country in smaller numbers. There is also a Hazara population in Baluchistan, Pakistan.

The exact number of Hazaras is not known because there has never been a com-plete national census taken in Afghanistan. Estimates of the Hazara population range from about 1.5 million to 4.3 million people (or 7 to 20 percent of the total Afghani population).

3 ● LANGUAGE

Most Hazaras today speak Dari, a form of Persian, also called Khorasani Persian. In addition to Persian, some Hazaras also speak Pashtu, Baluchi, and Turkic.

4 ● FOLKLORE

Hazaras believe in common rural superstitions, such as the evil eye, ghosts, and superstitions involving animals and night-time. Hazaras enjoy storytelling, sharing tales of their history, ancestors, and heroes.

Hazaras also have many proverbs, including the following examples:

> If your father owns the mill, you still must wait your turn to grind your flour. (In business, the customer comes first.)

> The sons of wolves will be wolves. (Children will be like their parents.)

> Two people are afraid of an empty rifle: the one with the rifle, and the one without it. (A person being threatened feels afraid. But the person doing the threatening is also afraid if he knows he can't follow through on the threat.)

5 ● RELIGION

The Hazaras are Shi'ite Muslims, one of the world's two major Islamic sects. Muslims celebrate their religious holidays by going to the mosque for group prayers. Then they return home to large meals with family and visiting relatives.

HAZARAS

0   250   500   750 Miles

0   250 500 750 1000 Kilometers

RUSSIA

Caspian Sea

KAZAKSTAN

Aral Sea

Zaysan

UZBEKISTAN

Almaty (Alma-Ata)

TURKMENISTAN

Tashkent

KYRGYSTAN

Ashkhabad

Tejen

Dushanbe

TAJIKISTAN

IRAN

AFGHANISTAN

CHINA

Kabul

Zaranj

Islāmābād

Saindak

PAKISTAN

Indus

Pasni

New Delhi

NEPAL

BHUTAN

Kathmandu

Ganges

Gulf of Oman

Arabian Sea

Lakhpat

INDIA

Dhaka

BANGLADESH

Surat

6 ● MAJOR HOLIDAYS

As Shi'ite Muslims, Hazaras celebrate the two major Islamic holidays, *Eid al-Fitr* and *Eid al-Adha*. Eid al-Fitr is a three-day celebration that comes after a month of fasting called Ramadan. Eid al-Adha commemorates the willingness of Abraham to obey God's command and sacrifice his son, Isaac. People making a pilgrimage (religious journey) are expected to sacrifice a goat or sheep and offer the meat to the poor. One other holiday celebrated among Hazaras is *Nawruz*, the Persian New Year.

7 ● RITES OF PASSAGE.

Special celebrations involving passages to a new stage of life include circumcision for young boys, weddings, and funerals. Once girls reach puberty, they are required to cover their hair with scarves and to spend more of their time indoors. Marriages are arranged by the families of the bride and groom. When a daughter is married, she moves in with her husband's family.

8 ● RELATIONSHIPS

The Hazara people are very hospitable and friendly to guests. They prepare special food for their guests, who are honored with the best seats at mealtime. Most Hazaras eat with their hands, rarely using utensils such as forks and knives.

9 ● LIVING CONDITIONS

Generally speaking, Hazaras are poor people with few economic opportunities. However, their living conditions vary depending on their location. Conditions are more harsh for those living in cold climates, where shelter is a greater concern, travel is difficult, and agriculture is poor.

10 ● FAMILY LIFE

It is customary for extended families to live together in one house, including grandparents and women married to the sons of the household. Newborn babies are usually named by the older people of the household. Grandparents are actively involved in raising their grandchildren. After the death of the grandparents, especially the grandfather, the sons usually begin living in separate households of their own.

11 ● CLOTHING

The most common clothing among the Hazaras is *perahan-u-tunban*, a type of clothing that resembles pajamas. Men wear turbans, vests, overcoats, and sweaters over their perahan-u-tunbans. Their clothing is usually made from wool or cotton. Unlike the men, who wear plain-colored clothes, the women usually wear clothes with bright colors and designs. Women usually wear lighter-weight clothes because they remain indoors more of the time. Hazaras do not own large amounts of clothing.

12 ● FOOD

The Hazaras' diet includes a large proportion of high-protein food such as meat and dairy products. They use plenty of oil when cooking. Usually a meal consists of one type of food, rather than a wide selection. However, a variety of foods may be served at meals when guests are present, or may be served in wealthier Hazara households.

13 ● EDUCATION

Hazaras have two systems of education. The traditional system provides religious instruction and informal home education in practical tasks, according to whether the student is a girl or a boy. The formal education system is that found in schools administered by the government. Most students attend these schools only through the sixth grade. A few of the best students are then sent to Kabul to continue their education.

14 ● CULTURAL HERITAGE

Hazara social gatherings include music and dancing. Women and men dance separately, each having different styles. Poetry is read and the *dambura* is played. The dambura is a bowl lute with a long neck and two strings that are plucked. The dambura is also used

PhotoEdit

Afghani women have a great deal of power in the home, but little authority in public.

to accompany the recitation of poetry, epics, and love stories.

Hazaras have many different *dubaitis* (folk songs). The following is an example:

The stars shone and I lay awake
I was behind the broken wall
As the cock began to crow
I was still waiting for my love.

15 ● EMPLOYMENT

In rural areas, Hazara men generally work in the fields growing crops. In Kabul, they usually have low-paying, menial jobs such as janitorial work. Most women spend their time inside their homes, tending to household tasks and the needs of their children.

16 ● SPORTS

Due to a lack of leisure time, Hazaras do not spend a great deal of time playing sports. Hazaras in some areas take part in the national Afghani game, *buzkashi*. This is a sport in which as many as 1,000 men on horseback compete for possession of a dead goat or calf. Other sports played by Hazaras include hunting, wrestling, archery, and horse racing.

17 ● RECREATION

Hazaras in rural areas have more time for recreation in the winter, when there is less work to do. They tell stories, visit with each other, and drink tea in the evenings.

18 ● CRAFTS AND HOBBIES

Hazaras produce handmade coats, overcoats, sweaters, jackets, shoes, hats, gloves, and scarves. These are mostly made by the women and are sold in shops in Kabul and other cities.

19 ● SOCIAL PROBLEMS

The Hazaras are generally poorer and less educated than other Afghanis. As Shi'ite Muslims, they are in the minority in the largely Sunni population of Afghanistan. These differences create tensions between the Hazaras and other Afghanis.

20 ● BIBLIOGRAPHY

Ali, Sharifah Enayat. *Cultures of the World: Afghanistan.* New York: Marshall Cavendish, 1995.

Clifford, Mary Louise. *The Land and People of Afghanistan.* New York: Lippincott, 1989.

Nyrop, Richard F., and Donald M. Seekins, eds. *Afghanistan: A Country Study.* Washington, D.C.: U.S. GPO, 1986.

WEBSITES

Echo of Islam. [Online] Available http://chuma.cas.usf.edu/~rfayiz/afghani.htm, 1998.

Investor's Business Journal. Afghanistan. [Online] Available http://www.afghan-web.com/, 1998.

World Travel Guide. Afghanistan. [Online] Available http://www.wtgonline.com/country/af/gen.html, 1998.

Pashtun

PRONUNCIATION: PASH-toon
ALTERNATE NAMES: Pushtun; Pakhtun; Pashtoon; Pathan; Afghan
LOCATION: Southeastern Afghanistan; northwestern Pakistan
POPULATION: 8–9 million
LANGUAGE: Pashtu
RELIGION: Islam (Sunni Muslim)

1 ● INTRODUCTION

Pashtun (also spelled Pushtun, Pakhtun, Pashtoon, Pathan) are a people who live in southeastern Afghanistan and the northwestern province of Pakistan. They are one of the largest ethnic groups in Afghanistan. There is no true written history of the Pashtun in their own land. Pashtun are traditionally pastoral nomads (herders who move frequently to find grazing land) with a strong tribal organization. Each tribe is divided into clans, subclans, and patriarchal families.

2 ● LOCATION

Pashtun have lived for centuries between Khurasan and the Indian subcontinent, at the crossroads of great civilizations.

Pashtun are made up of about sixty tribes of varying sizes. Each one occupies its own

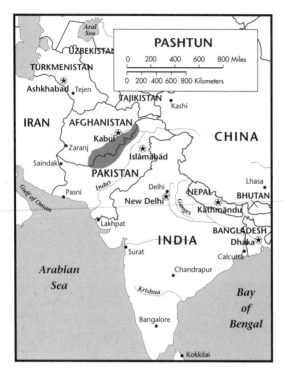

territory. Pashtun are the major ethnic group in Afghanistan. In Pakistan, Pashtun predominate north of the town of Quetta and between the Sulaiman Mountain Ranges and the Indus River.

3 ● LANGUAGE

Pashtu is the language of the Pashtun and one of the two official languages of Afghanistan. It is also the language of twelve million Pashtun in Pakistan. Pashtu belongs to the North-Eastern group of languages within the Iranian branch of Indo-European. Pashtu is written in the Perso-Arabic script.

Some typical examples of the Pashtu language are the words used for parts of the Pashtun code of morals and manners, called *Pashtunwalli*. These include *milmastia* (hospitality); *tureh* (courage; also the word

for sword*)*; *badal* (revenge); and *ghayrat* (protection of one's honor). A Pashtun tribal council is called a *jirga*.

4 ● FOLKLORE

Pashtun have many traditional stories, both in their own language and in Persian. One story tells of a man who wanted to discover how to change his luck. According to the story, a man may be given the opportunity to experience luck, but he must have the intelligence to take advantage of it.

A man asked his lucky brother, "Where is good luck?" "In the forest," his brother replied. So the unlucky man set out for the forest. On the way he met a lion. When the lion heard where the man was going, he begged him to ask why he was ill, and why nothing made him feel better. When the man had gone a little farther, he found a horse lying down, too weak to stand. Next he came upon a tree, who asked the man, "Please, enquire on my behalf, why am I leafless?" When the man reached the place where he found his good luck, he seized it. His good luck said, "You may have good luck, but you still do not have intelligence." The man asked the questions he carried for the lion, the horse, and the tree. His fortune replied, "Tell the lion that he should devour a fool and he will recover his health. Tell the horse that he should take a master who will ride him and he will grow strong. And tell the tree that under its roots lies the treasure of seven kings. If the treasure is dug up, the tree's roots will flourish." On his way home, the man stopped first by the tree. He told the tree, and the tree begged him to dig the treasure from his roots. The man replied, "What good are riches, since I

Afghanis in Kabul read news about the conflict between government forces and the Pashtun-dominated Taliban movement which seeks to turn Afghanistan into a fundamentalist Islamic state.

have my fortune." When he reported to the horse, the animal begged, "Please, sir, become my master!" But the man replied, "I have my fortune now, so look for someone else to be your master." Finally, he reported to the lion that he should devour a fool—and he told the lion all about the tree and the horse, too. When the story was finished, the lion said, "You yourself are a superlative fool!" And, with that, the lion devoured the man.

He was a man of no cleverness, who could not recognize his opportunities, so his fortune did him no good.

5 ● RELIGION

Islam was introduced to the Pashtun in the eighth century. All but a few Pashtun tribes are followers of the Sunni Muslim sect.

6 ● MAJOR HOLIDAYS

Pashtun celebrate the two major festivals of the Islamic lunar calendar year: *Eid al-Fitr* and *Eid al-Adha*. They also observe the tenth of Muarram, which commemorates the martyrdom of the prophet Muhammad's grandson.

7 ● RITES OF PASSAGE

Pashtun are automatically considered Muslims (followers of Islam) at birth. When a baby is born, Pashtun whisper the call for prayer in the baby's ear. The male circumcision ceremony is held at the same time as the birth celebration (at about the age of one week). Children officially join in the rituals of prayers and fasting when they reach sexual maturity, but in practice they begin much earlier.

8 ● RELATIONSHIPS

Pashtun society is largely communal (group-oriented) and attaches great importance to an unwritten code, called *Pashtunwalli.* This code defines the way members should behave to keep the tribe together. Hospitality *(milmastia)* is important, as is the use of the tribal council *(jirga)* to resolve conflicts and make decisions. Other Pashtun virtues include courage *(tureh);* taking revenge *(badal);* and protecting one's honor *(ghayrat).* Another part of the Pashtun code of conduct is *nanawati,* a way of resolving differences through the group's elders.

9 ● LIVING CONDITIONS

Generally, the Pashtun of Afghanistan do not have very high living standards. Many groups of Pashtun along the border between Afghanistan and Pakistan live as nomads (people who move frequently, carrying their dwelling with them).

10 ● FAMILY LIFE

The eldest male holds complete authority over the extended family. Married sons live in their fathers' households, rather than establishing homes of their own. The household normally consists of a man and his wife, his unmarried children, and his married sons and their wives and children. When young women marry, they join their husbands' households and transfer their loyalty to their husbands' families.

Economically, the Pashtun family is a single unit. Wealthy family members contribute to the support of those who are poorer. Old people depend on their children for care and support. The whole family shares the expense of having a child away at school.

11 ● CLOTHING

Traditional male dress is *qmis,* a loose-fitting shirt that reaches to the knees, and *shalwar,* full trousers tied at the waist with a string. A vest is usually worn over the shirt. Footwear consists of *chaplay,* thick leather shoes. Most Pashtun adult males wear *pagray,* turbans. Long strips of cotton cloth are wound around the head, leaving the forehead exposed because it is touched during prayer. The turban is fastened so that one end dangles. The loose end is used as a typ of washcloth for wiping the face. Usually men also wear a long, wide piece of cloth called a *chadar* on their shoulders.

Rural women wear baggy black or colored trousers, a long shirt belted with a sash, and a length of cotton over the head. City women wear the same type of trousers, a qmis (long shirt), and a cotton cloth to cover their heads. Over their clothing, they also usually wear a *burqa*—a veil that covers them from the head to below the knees.

Recipe

Quabili Pulaw Dampukht
(Rice with Carrots and Raisins)

Ingredients

2 to 3 Tablespoons vegetable oil
1 onion, chopped
1 pound lean beef stew meat
2 cups water
½ teaspoon each cinnamon, cloves, cumin,
  and cardamom
2 medium carrots, cut into small, match-
  stick-sized pieces
1 teaspoon sugar
1 cup seedless raisins
pinch of saffron
2 Tablespoons blanched almonds
2 Tablespoons blanched pistachios
2 to 3 cups rice, cooked in broth from
  cooking meat

Directions

1. Heat oil and brown onion. Add beef
   stew meat and brown on all sides.
2. Add water and spices. Cover pan and
   simmer mixture until meat is tender
   (about one hour).
3. Remove meat and set aside. Save the
   broth to use for cooking rice.
4. Heat small amount of oil in a small pot
   and add carrots and almonds. Cook until carrots and almonds are lightly
   browned.
5. Remove carrots and almonds, and add
   them to the meat. Put raisins in the
   saucepan with about ¼ cup water. Simmer for 5 minutes until raisins are puffy.
6. Remove raisins and add them to the
   meat mixture. Cook the rice according
   to package directions, using the broth
   from step 3 for the liquid, adding more
   water if necessary.
7. Combine all ingredients and mix. Place
   mixture in a large casserole and bake at
   300°F for 20 to 30 minutes.

Adapted from McKellar, Doris. *Afghan Cookery*. Kabul, Afghanistan: Kabul Uni-versity, 1967.

12 ● FOOD

Religious prohibitions prevent Pashtun (and all Muslims) from eating pork and drinking alcoholic beverages. Staples of the Pashtun diet include bread, rice, vegetables, milk products, meat, eggs, fruits, and tea. A favorite dish is *pulaw,* a rice dish flavored with coriander, cinnamon, and cardamom that has many variations.

13 ● EDUCATION

Education throughout Afghanistan has been disrupted, first by the Russian invasion and occupation (1978), and since then by con-tinuing civil warfare. Traditionally, educa-tion took place in religious institutes and mosque (religious) schools (called *madrassa* or *maktab*). As of the late 1990s, there were boys' and girls' schools for Pashtun children in almost in every village.

14 ● CULTURAL HERITAGE

Choral singing is part of the Pashtun cul-ture. Pashtun have a folk song tradition that includes special songs for marriages and funerals. Poems known as *matal* are very popular. *Atan* is a famous group folk dance of the Pashtun.

15 ● EMPLOYMENT

Pashtun work at a variety of occupations in agriculture, business, and trade. Women and children also play roles in agricultural work. Many Pashtun of Afghanistan are poor agricultural workers. Working conditions are generally better for Pashtun living in Pakistan than for those in Afghanistan.

16 ● SPORTS

Naiza bazi, a game involving riding horses and throwing spears, is a sport enjoyed among the Pashtun. Some Pashtun also have rock-throwing competitions. Pashtun in the northern regions of Afghanistan enjoy *buzkashi,* or "goat pulling," a game in which men on horseback compete for possession of a dead goat or calf.

17 ● RECREATION

Social get-togethers are the major form of entertainment.

18 ● CRAFTS AND HOBBIES

The Pashtun in the city sew unique designs on their clothes and wear small hats made of silk.

19 ● SOCIAL PROBLEMS

Differences among Pashtun clans and families have led to much violence and killing, both in Afghanistan and in Pakistan.

20 ● BIBLIOGRAPHY

Ali, Sharifah Enayat. *Cultures of the World: Afghanistan.* New York: Marshall Cavendish, 1995.

Clifford, Mary Louise. *The Land and People of Afghanistan.* New York: Lippincott, 1989.

Nyrop, Richard F., and Donald M. Seekins, eds. *Afghanistan: A Country Study.* Washington, D.C.: U.S. GPO, 1986.

WEBSITES

Echo of Islam. [Online] Available http://chuma.cas.usf.edu/~rfayiz/afghani.htm, 1998.

Investor's Business Journal. Afghanistan. [Online] Available http://www.afghan-web.com/, 1998.

World Travel Guide. Afghanistan. [Online] Available http://www.wtgonline.com/country/af/gen.html, 1998.

Albania

The people of Albania are called Albanians. About 98 percent of the population trace their descent to Albania. There are two ethnic groups—the Ghegs, who live in the northern half of the country, and the Tosks, who live in the south. The remaining 2 percent of the population is made up primarily of Greeks and Macedonians. For information on the Greeks, consult the chapter on Greece in Volume 4. Information on the Macedonians can be found in the chapter on Macedonia in Volume 5.

Albanians

PRONUNCIATION: al-BAY-nee-uhns
ALTERNATE NAMES: Shqipëtarë, Shqipëria
LOCATION: Albania; Macedonia; Greece
POPULATION: 3.5 million
LANGUAGE: Albanian
RELIGION: Evangelical Christianity (Seventh-Day Adventist, Jehovah's Witness); Roman Catholicism; Islam; Eastern Orthodox

1 ● INTRODUCTION

The name "Albania" is derived from an ancient Illyrian tribe, the Albanoi, who inhabited part of modern-day Albania from around 1225 BC to AD 200. Albanians call their country Shqipëri (Skip-AIR-ee), "Land of the Eagle."

For almost 500 years, Albania was controlled by the Turks of the Ottoman Empire. The Albanians fought to resist being controlled by the Turks. Their national hero,

Skanderbeg, led the Albanian people's resistance to the Ottoman Empire in the 1400s in at least twenty-five fierce battles. It was only after Skanderbeg died in 1468 that the Turks were able to claim victory. They then ruled for 445 years. The Turks were Muslims, and a majority of Albanians became Muslims during this period.

Albania won independence from the Ottoman Empire in 1912. Its present-day boundaries were confirmed following World War I (1914–18) at the Paris Peace Conference in 1919.

There are two major ethnic groups in Albania—the Ghegs and the Tosks. The main difference between the two groups is the dialect (variation on a language) of Albanian that they speak. The Ghegs live in the northern half of the country, and the Tosks live in the south.

As of the late 1990s, there were as many Albanians living just outside of Albania's

ALBANIANS

| 0 | 100 | 200 | 300 Miles |
| 0 | 100 | 200 | 300 Kilometers |

Along the coast the summers are hot and dry, while the winters are rainy.

Away from the coast, most of Albania is covered with mountains. The North Albanian Alps reach 8,500 feet (2,590 meters) above sea level. There is more rainfall in the mountains than along the seacoast.

Albania's population numbers approximately 3.5 million, and is projected to reach 3.6 million by 2000. In 1950, almost 80 percent of the population lived on farms. By the mid-1990s, many farmers had moved to the cities, leaving only about 60 percent of the population living in rural areas.

3 ● LANGUAGE

Albanian (*Shqip*) is one of Europe's oldest languages. It is one of the nine Indo-European languages. Albanian has seven vowel sounds: *a* (ah), *e* (eh), *i* (ee), *o* (oh), *u* (oo), *ë* (uh), and *y* (ew). When *ë* appears at the end of a word, it is sometimes silent.

Albanian uses the same alphabet as English, and adds the letter ç, representing the *ch* sound.

ENGLISH	ALBANIAN	PRONUNCIATION
one	një	nyUH
two	dy	dEW
three	tre	trEH
four	katër	KAHT-uhr
five	pesë	pEHS
six	gjashtë	JASH-tuh
seven	shtatë	sh-TAHT
eight	tetë	tEHt
nine	nënd	nUHnd
ten	dhgetë	duh-YEHT

The two main Albanian groups—the Ghegs in the north and the Tosks in the south—both speak Albanian but use different pronunciations. For example, when

borders as there were within it. Observers often describe Albania as a country completely surrounded by itself.

2 ● LOCATION

Albania is one of the Balkan countries that form a peninsula bordered by the Adriatic, Aegean, and Black Seas. The word "Balkan" means mountain in Turkish, and the Balkan countries take their name from the Balkan Mountains.

Albania is about the same size as the state of Maryland. Albania's dimensions are 230 miles (370 kilometers) long by about 90 miles (144 kilometers) at its widest point. Albania's western edge borders the Adriatic Sea, about 50 miles (80 kilometers) from the "boot" of Italy. The coastline features some areas of scenic white sandy beaches.

Cory Langley

Many Albanian young people, especially in the capital of Tiranë, understand some English.

speaking the word *është* (is), a Tosk would say EH-shtah, but a Gheg would say AH-sht. Until World War II (1939–45), Gheg was the dominant dialect. After 1945, most political leaders were Tosks, and the government tried to make the Tosk dialect the standard. Many writers and political activists spoke the Gheg dialect, and they kept it alive in the north of the country.

Many Albanians speak Italian because Italian television programs are broadcast in Albania. Southern Albania is near Greece, so many Albanians there speak and understand Greek. Young people, especially in the capital of Tiranë, understand some English.

4 ● FOLKLORE

Fairies, snakes, and dragons are among the main figures in Albanian mythology. Characters in Albanian folklore include the *kucedër* (a snake or dragon with many heads), the *shtrigë* or *shpriga* (witch), and the *stuhi* (a flame-throwing winged being that guards treasures). *Zana* are mythical female figures who help mountain folk in distress. To call someone a *kukudh* is the ultimate insult, since it means "a dwarf with seven tails who can't find rest in his grave."

5 ● RELIGION

Albania has no official state religion. The communist government (in power from

1946 to 1992) outlawed religion in 1967, and confiscated (took away) all church property. Freedom of religion in Albania was not restored until 1989–90. More than 70 percent of Albanians are Muslims. Muslims are followers of the religion known as Islam.

Islam has five "pillars," or practices, that must be observed by all Muslims: (1) praying five times a day; (2) giving alms (money or food), or *zakat,* to the poor; (3) fasting from dawn to dusk during the month of Ramadan; (4) making the pilgrimage, or *hajj,* to Mecca; and (5) reciting the *shahada* (*"ashhadu an la illah ila Allah wa ashhadu in Muhammadu rasul Allah"*). This phrase means "I witness that there is no god but Allah and that Muhammad is the prophet of Allah."

About 20 percent of Albanians follow Christianity as members of Evangelical, Eastern Orthodox, and Roman Catholic churches.

6 ● MAJOR HOLIDAYS

Albanian Muslims observe Ramadan and the holy days of Islam. Ramadan, a month of fasting from dawn to dusk, occurs in early January. Albanian Christians celebrate traditional holidays such as Christmas and Easter. Another holiday, *Dita e Verës* (Spring Day), comes from an ancient pagan holiday and is still celebrated in mid-March. Albanians throughout the world commemorate November 28 as Albanian Independence Day (*Dita e Flamurit*).

7 ● RITES OF PASSAGE

Most Albanians mark the major life events, including birth, marriage, and death, within either the Muslim or Christian religious tradition.

Albania has no funeral parlors. Wakes for the deceased are generally held at home for a period of two or three days before burial.

8 ● RELATIONSHIPS

The Albanians are very expressive people. They commonly emphasize their statements by gesturing with their hands, shrugging their shoulders, and rolling their eyes upwards. When they want to respond "no" to a question, Albanians might nod their heads or shake their index fingers. To answer "yes," they might shake their head.

When two Albanian men meet, they embrace (hug) and kiss each other on the cheeks. It is common for them to walk along together with their arms linked. Men and women limit their greetings to a handshake; kissing in public is considered scandalous.

There is a greeting ritual when entering the home of an Albanian family. A female member of the host family serves the guest a *qerasje* (kehr-AHS-jeh) or treat. This consists of *liko* (LEEK-oh), a jam-like sweet, and a drink, such as Turkish coffee. It is considered rude to refuse these refreshments. However, it is acceptable to refuse the offer of a cigarette. The visitor then inquires about the health of each member of the host's family. Then the hostess inquires about the visitor's family. Only after this exchange is completed do people relax and begin normal conversation.

Common Greetings

English	Albanian	Pronunciation
Hello	Tungjatjeta	tune-jat-YET-ah
Good morning	Mirëmëngjes	meer-mihn-JEHS
Good afternoon	Merëdita	meer DEE tah
Yes	Po	pOH
No	Jo	jOH
Thank you	Faleminderit	FA-leh-meen-DEH-reet
Do you speak English?	A flisni anglisht?	ah FLEAS-nee ahn-GLEESHT?

When an Albanian gives the *besa* (BEH-sah)—pledged word or promise—it is considered sacred. Here are some greetings in Albanian:

9 ● LIVING CONDITIONS

Under communist rule from 1946 to 1992, many Albanians were forced to live in large, poorly constructed apartment buildings that provided only a couple of rooms for a family of four or more people. Many dwellings still lack central heating. There is a shortage of water, and there are frequent electric power outages in the larger cities. There is no regular rubbish collection, and cities are littered with trash.

There are no regulations against smoking in Albania. People feel free to smoke anywhere, including in public buildings, restaurants, and when visiting someone's home.

10 ● FAMILY LIFE

Albanian families tend to be small, with the average being two children. The Albanian husband does not generally do housework.

Both husband and wife believe that the household is the wife's responsibility. Elderly parents often live with their children, where they are treated with honor and respect. From the time he is born, the oldest son is trained to become the head of family when his father dies.

11 ● CLOTHING

The *fustanella,* or Albanian kilt, was common dress for men until the 1400s. Common villagers and rural people wore a fustanella made from coarse linen or wool; more affluent men wore silk.

When Albania was ruled by the Ottoman Empire (1468–1912), many aspects of Turkish culture were adopted by Albanians. In rural areas, men may still wear the *fez,* a traditional Turkish cap, and a colorful cloth belt. Women may wear embroidered blouses in the Turkish style, with loose pants.

Traditional costume for women of southern Albania features a blouse with wide cuffs in fabric to match an embroidered vest. A pleated petticoat is worn under a full skirt, and an elaborately embroidered apron and sash complete the outfit. Gold chains cascade from the neckline, are gathered into the sash, and are tucked into a pocket at the right side of the skirt. A kerchief covers the woman's hair.

In the north, the sleeves of the blouse are wide, with lace embroidery along the edges. Embroidery on the apron is elaborate, but distinct from the style of southern Albanian women. Gold coins are worn on a headband

Traditional costume for women of southern Albania (left) features an embroidered apron and gold chains attached to a sash. In the north, the traditional costume (center) also features embroidery on the apron, with gold coins worn on a headband and necklace. The fustanilla *(kilt) and* fez *(hat) are both part of the traditional men's costume (right), seen today only at festivals.*

and on several strands of necklace that adorn the bodice (upper part) of the dress.

In cities, conservative Western-style dress is more common. Albanians are modest, however. Neither men nor women wear shorts or other revealing clothing. Traditional clothing is seen mostly at theatrical or folk dance performances in cities.

12 ● FOOD

Albanian cooking is influenced by the years of Turkish rule. Lamb, rather than beef or pork, is the most common meat. *Lakror* (LAHK-roar), a typical dish, is a mixture of eggs, vegetables or meat, and butter wrapped in thin, many-layered pastry sheets. Another popular food is *fërgesë*

(FUHR-ges), a dish usually made with minced meat, eggs, and ricotta cheese. Bread is a major staple of the Albanian diet. In fact, the word for bread, *bukë* (bew-KUH), is the normal word for "meal." Many Albanians enjoy *raki* (rah-KEE), a clear, colorless brandy made from grapes.

13 ● EDUCATION

About 88 percent of Albanians can read and write. This is one of the highest literacy rates in the Balkan region. School is mandatory from age seven through fifteen. The rulers of the Ottoman Empire forbade the teaching of the Albanian language until 1887; the first school (*Mësonjtorja*) that

AP/Wideworld Photos

School is mandatory for students between the ages of seven and fifteen. Until 1887, all school lessons were taught in Turkish or Persian rather than Albanian.

taught it was opened that year. Before then, all teaching was done in Turkish or Persian.

14 ● CULTURAL HERITAGE

Albanians love music, and there are many symphony orchestras performing in cities in Albania. Albanian folk instruments include the *civility* (a long-necked two-stringed mandolin); the *gërnetë* (guhr-NET-uh), a type of clarinet; the *gajda* (gahj-dah) and *bishnica* (bish-NICK-ah), wind instruments; and the *sharkia* (shar-KEY-ah) and *lahuta* (la-HOO-tah), stringed instruments.

Ismail Kadarë is Albania's most famous writer. Kadarë's novel *The General of the*

Dead Army was made into an Italian film in 1982.

15 ● EMPLOYMENT

Since the end of the communist era (1946–92), a new spirit of enterprise has developed. Albanians have been quick to form their own businesses. Since 1992, Albanians have had a five-day work week, in contrast to the six-day work week under communism. Women make up over 40 percent of the labor force.

16 ● SPORTS

Albania's favorite sport is soccer (commonly called "football" in Europe). Second to football is volleyball, in which both men's and women's teams have become regional champions. Basketball and tennis are becoming more and more popular. Chess continues to gain favor, especially with children.

17 ● RECREATION

After a late afternoon nap, Albanians enjoy a leisurely stroll along their wide streets on their way to meet friends and relatives for a late dinner.

Albanians love storytelling. In coffee shops throughout the country, men can be found entertaining each other with humorous stories or heroic tales. Television programs broadcast from Italy are also very popular.

Classical music performances are well attended in Albania, and discos (dance clubs) are popular with teenagers and young adults.

18 ● CRAFTS AND HOBBIES

Albanian women and girls are known for *qëndisje* (kuhn-DIS-jeh), elaborate embroidery created to decorate their dwellings. Using a small loom known as a *vegël* (VEH-guhl), they weave colorful rugs. Albanians produce sweaters, socks, gloves, and other items, using wool, cotton, acrylics, and fur. Lace-making, *ounë me grep* (WEE-nuh MEH-grehp), is another traditional folk art.

Men usually work with metals such as copper, brass, and aluminum to craft decorative plates, wall hangings, and utensils. Women are increasingly involved with pottery, creating unique useful and sculptural pieces.

19 ● SOCIAL PROBLEMS

The democratically elected government of President Sali Berisha has been accused of using some of the same dictatorial methods as the former communist government. It has been accused of silencing political dissent, restricting freedom of the press, and rigging the national elections. Journalists who strongly criticize the government can be heavily fined or imprisoned. Human rights groups charge that some have even been tortured.

Albanian television and radio programming reflects the official positions of the government.

20 ● BIBLIOGRAPHY

Albania—In Pictures. Minneapolis: Lerner Publications, 1995.

Hall, Derek R. *Albania and the Albanians.* New York: St. Martin's Press, 1994.

Hutchins, Raymond. *Historical Dictionary of Albania.* Lanham, Md.: Scarecrow Press, Inc., 1996.

Sherer, Stan. *Long Life to Your Children!: A Portrait of High Albania.* Boston: University of Massachusetts Press, 1997.

Wright, David K. *Albania.* Chicago: Children's Press, 1997.

Zickel, Raymond E., and Walter R. Iwaski. *Albania: A Country Study.* 2nd ed. Washington, D.C.: U.S. Govt. Printing Office, 1994.

WEBSITES

Albanian.com. [Online] Available http://www.albanian.com, 1998.

Encyclopaedia Britannica. [Online] Available http://www.albania.co.uk/, 1998.

Frosina Information Network. [Online] Available http://www.frosina.org, 1998.

World Travel Guide. [Online] Available http://www.wtgonline.com/country/al/gen.html, 1998.

Algeria

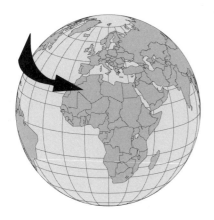

Algerians are sometimes referred to as Berbers, descendents of North African peoples related by language and the Islamic faith. In fact, Algerians do not call themselves "Berbers," preferring instead to refer to themselves according to their tribe or the region where they live. There are about one million Europeans and 140,000 Jews living in Algeria.

Algerians

PRONUNCIATION: al-JEER-ee-uhns
LOCATION: western north Africa (the Maghrib)
POPULATION: 28 million
LANGUAGE: Arabic; Berber; French
RELIGION: Islam (Sunni Muslim)

1 ● INTRODUCTION

Algeria is one of the countries forming the Maghrib (the western part of north Africa). Its known history can be traced as far back as 30,000 BC. The original inhabitants of the area were called Maghrib. They later became known as Berbers.

The invasion of Arab Muslims (people who practice the religion of Islam) between AD 642 and 669 led to conversion of the Berbers to Islam. The Muslim Ottoman Empire, based in present-day Turkey, spread its influence over northern Africa (including what is today Algeria). The Ottomans protected the region from invasion by the major European powers until the nineteenth century.

In 1830, France invaded Algeria. The French annexed Algeria (claimed the country as part of their territory) and turned it into a colony. The people were forced to leave their land, and it was sold at low prices to immigrants from France and other European countries. In spite of uprisings by the Algerian people, France retained control of Algeria through both World War I (1914–18) and World War II (1939–45).

In 1954, the Algerians began a bloody war for independence that lasted almost a decade. Nearly a million people were killed between 1956 and 1962, one-tenth of the Algerian population. Finally, a French withdrawal was negotiated, and Algeria was declared an independent nation on July 5, 1962.

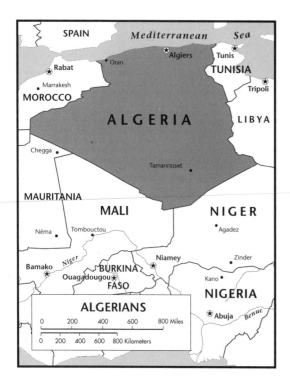

2 ● LOCATION

Algeria is located in north Africa on the Mediterranean Sea. The north is relatively fertile and mountainous. The south includes part of the Sahara desert. In all, more than four-fifths of the country is desert.

Algeria has a population of almost 28 million people. Most people in Algeria live in urban areas. The desert regions are almost completely uninhabited.

3 ● LANGUAGE

Arabic is the national language of Algeria. Because of 130 years of French domination, the French language is also widely understood. Algerians speak their own Arabic dialect (variation on a language) that includes many slang terms from French. The dialect also includes many Berber words, including place names and names of plants.

Many Arabic expressions used in Algeria are religious in nature. When promising to do something, an Algerian Muslim says, *Insha Allah* (If God wills it). Before any action, a religious Muslim will say *Bismillah* (In the name of God).

Common Algerian female names are *Nafisa, Aysha,* and *Farida.* Common male names are *Abd al-Haq, Hamid,* and *Abd al-Latif.*

4 ● FOLKLORE

Most folklore in Muslim countries concerns important figures in religious history, such as Muhammad. One such story describes an event known as *al-Isra wa al-Miraj.* The Prophet Muhammad is said to have traveled at night from Mecca in Saudi Arabia to

Different factions within Algeria have continued to fight for political and social freedom, even after their country gained independence from France. In 1988, the government allowed new political parties to form, and the Islamic Salvation Front (FIS) was born. FIS preached a return to traditional Islamic values and quickly grew in popularity. The government was afraid that FIS would win the elections and decided to cancel the elections in 1991 and exiled (sent out of the country) 10,000 FIS members. In response, a civil war erupted. As many as 30,000 Algerians are believed to have died in the war between the country's military rulers and those who opposed them. As of the late 1990s, there continue to be violent conflicts between the government and its opposition.

Cory Langley

About 80 percent of Algeria is desert.

Jerusalem in Israel. From there, he rode his wondrous horse, al-Burak, on a nocturnal (nighttime) visit to heaven.

Algeria has many legends based on the exploits of Muslim leaders called *marabouts* who either resisted the Crusaders (Christian soldiers) or the French colonizers. They are believed to have *baraka,* a blessing or divine grace, that allowed them to perform miracles. Their burial sites are destinations of pilgrimages (religious journeys). Many regard marabouts as saints.

5 ● RELIGION

The overwhelming majority of Algerians are Muslims. Muslims are followers of the religion known as Islam. The practice of Islam, however, varies. Most Algerians belong to the Sunni school of Islam, which was brought to Algeria by the original conquering Arabs.

Islam has five "pillars," or practices, that must be observed by all Muslims: (1) praying five times a day; (2) giving alms, or *zakat,* to the poor; (3) fasting from dawn to dusk during the month of Ramadan; (4) making the pilgrimage (religious journey), or *hajj,* to Mecca; and (5) reciting the *shahada ("Ashhadu an la illah ila Allah wa ashhadu in Muhammadu rasul Allah")*. This phrase means, "I witness that there is no god but Allah and that Muhammad is the prophet of Allah."

6 ● MAJOR HOLIDAYS

Algeria celebrates both secular (nonreligious) and Muslim holidays. The two major Muslim holidays are *Eid al-Fitr* and *Eid al-Adha*. Eid al-Fitr is a three-day celebration that takes place after the month of fasting called Ramadan. Eid al-Adha commemorates the willingness of Abraham to obey God's command and sacrifice his son, Isaac. People making a pilgrimage (religious journey) are expected to sacrifice a goat or sheep and offer the meat to the poor.

Muslims celebrate their religious holidays by going to the mosque for group prayers. Afterward, they return home to large meals with family and visiting relatives. They also exchange gifts on religious holidays.

Algerian secular holidays include New Year's Day (January 1); Labor Day (May 1), which commemorates worker solidarity around the world; and Independence Day (July 5). Most businesses, banks, and government offices are closed on these holidays.

7 ● RITES OF PASSAGE

Algerian families celebrate births, baby-namings, male circumcisions, and weddings. Weddings are joyous affairs paid for by the groom's family. The celebration lasts several days. After days of singing and eating, the bride and groom are united in marriage. Their union is followed by another week of celebrations.

8 ● RELATIONSHIPS

Algerians shake hands during greetings. It is common for good friends of the same sex

to kiss each other on the cheek. Religious men and women do not shake hands with persons of the opposite sex.

Most socialization revolves around the family. Guests are treated with great hospitality and are served pastries and sweets.

Algerian men and women do very little socializing together. The sexes are separated at most gatherings. Dating is not allowed, and marriages are arranged by the families or by matchmakers.

9 ● LIVING CONDITIONS

Algerian houses and gardens are surrounded by high walls for privacy. Inside, most homes have a central, open area or patio surrounded by the rooms of the house. Homes have a receiving room, kitchen, bathroom, bedrooms, and, if the family is wealthy, a second patio. The outside of the house is usually whitewashed brick or stone.

Algeria has a severe housing shortage. It is common for more than one family to live together in the same house.

10 ● FAMILY LIFE

Over a century of French rule and the long Algerian war for independence led to a breakdown of the traditional extended family unit. Before the French began to occupy their country, Algerians lived with their extended families in tightly knit communities. A mother and father would live in one home with their children, including grown sons and their wives. The grandparents would usually live with them. If a daughter became divorced or widowed, she, too,

Cory Langley

Algerian men do business in a busy city marketplace. Many Algerians combine modern Western-style and traditional clothing.

would live with the family. Children were raised by the entire extended family.

Beginning in the mid-1800s, French rule led to changes in the family unit. In cities, the nuclear family became more common as wealthier Algerians began to imitate the lifestyle of the French colonizers.

The war for independence changed the role of women in Algerian society. Women were actively involved in military battles and other political activities. After the war, women held on to much of the freedom they had gained during the war. Algerian women can vote and run for office.

11 ● CLOTHING

Many Algerians, especially in the cities, dress in modern Western-style clothing. Many others, however, dress in traditional clothes. Village men wear a *burnous* (a long, hooded robe) and baggy pants. Women wear a *haik* (a long piece of cloth draped over the entire body and head). The *hijab* (a long, loose dress and hair covering) is an Islamic garment worn by many women.

12 ● FOOD

Couscous, Algeria's national dish, is made from steamed semolina wheat. The wheat is

Recipe

Chicken Stuffed with Dried Fruit

Ingredients

5 Tablespoons olive oil
1 onion, chopped
¼ cup pine nuts or chopped almonds
1 cup mixed dried fruit (apricots, apples, pears, prunes, and raisins), soaked in water, drained, and chopped
salt to taste
3½ pounds chicken
Package of couscous

Directions

1. Preheat oven to 325°F.
2. Heat 2 tablespoons of olive oil in a frying pan, and cook the onion in the oil until the onion is pale gold.
3. Stir in the nuts and cook for 2 to 3 minutes. Add the fruits and salt.
4. Let cool.
5. Place chicken in pan, breast side up.
6. Stuff the chicken with the fruit mixture and tie the legs together with twine.
7. Place the casserole or roasting pan on the burner and brown the chicken in the remaining 3 tablespoons of oil. Place the chicken on its side.
8. Cover and cook in the oven for 1½ hours, turning the chicken every 30 minutes. Leave chicken breast side up for the last 30 minutes.
9. While the chicken is roasting, prepare the couscous according to instructions on the package. Serve chicken and couscous.

Adapted from Walden, Hilaire, *North African Cooking.* Edison, N.J.: Chartwell Books, 1995.

formed into tiny particles that can be combined with other ingredients to make a main course. Couscous can be served surrounded by meat, such as lamb or chicken, or mixed with vegetables. Algerians enjoy combining three favorites: couscous, meat, and fruit.

Spices are used generously in Algerian cooking, especially cumin, coriander, and cinnamon. Dried fruits are also a favorite, both in main courses and desserts.

Pork and alcoholic beverages are forbidden by the laws of Islam. Algeria does, however, produce wine for export to Europe.

13 ● EDUCATION

Children between the ages of five and fifteen are required by law to attend school. After that, they choose general, technical, or vocational secondary education. Before they graduate from secondary school, teenagers take exams to determine what kind of college or university they may attend.

In 1962, when Algeria won its independence from France, only 10 percent of Algerians were literate (could read and write). Education has since been supported by the Algerian government. As a result, in 1990, nearly 60 percent had achieved literacy.

14 ● CULTURAL HERITAGE

One of the most famous French-language Algerian writers is Albert Camus (1913–60), an essayist, playwright, and novelist. In 1957, Camus won the Nobel Prize for literature.

15 ● EMPLOYMENT

About one-third of Algerian workers are employed in industrial jobs. Algerian laborers manufacture electronics, building materials, plastics, fertilizer, paper, clothing, leather goods, and food products. Another 30 percent are farm workers, mostly on small, privately owned farms. Algerians who do not find work at home often find employment in Europe, especially in France. As of the late 1990s, many Algerian workers lived in Europe.

Most women who work outside the home hold jobs such as secretary, teacher, nurse, and technician.

16 ● SPORTS

Algeria's national sport is soccer, known as "football." Soccer is popular as both a spectator and a participant sport. In cities, boys play outside housing developments. Algeria has a national soccer team that participates in matches held by the African Football Confederation. Algerians also enjoy horseback riding and swimming. Clubs that specialize in water activities are found along the Algerian coast of the Mediterranean Sea.

17 ● RECREATION

Algerians are beach-goers. Swimming, water-skiing, and tennis are offered at Mediterranean resorts that are popular with Algerians of the middle class. The country has movie theaters, but not enough of them to meet the demands of its population. In most cities and villages, there are few swimming pools, and almost no Western-style dance halls and clubs. Television shows are produced in both Arabic and French.

18 ● CRAFTS AND HOBBIES

Algerian handicrafts include rugs, pottery, embroidery, jewelry, and brass. Handwoven baskets are sold at *suqs* (markets) and used by customers to carry the goods they purchase.

19 ● SOCIAL PROBLEMS

The greatest problems facing Algeria today stem from the civil war. Tens of thousands of civilians (people not in the military) have been murdered by both sides in the conflict. A side effect of political violence is that buildings, roads, parks, and other structures are either destroyed. The civil war has also distracted citizens and building owners from taking care of their property, so many parts of the country are becoming run-down from lack of attention.

In the capital, Algiers, certain districts are controlled by the military, and the rest are run by the resistance. Neither side has the time or interest to maintain roads and buildings.

Between 1962 and 1992 there were significant improvements in women's rights, human rights, and education. By the mid-1990s, these causes were forgotten as the political conflict heated up.

20 ● BIBLIOGRAPHY

Brill, M. *Algeria*. Chicago: Children's Press, 1990.

Kagda, Falaq. *Algeria*. New York: Marshall Cavendish, 1997.

Metz, Helen Chapin, ed. *Algeria: A Country Study*. Washington, D.C.: Federal Research Division, Library of Congress, 1993.

Walden, Hilaire. *North African Cooking: Exotic*

Delights from Morocco, Tunisia, Algeria, and Egypt. Edison, N.J.: Chartwell Books, 1995.

WEBSITES

AfricaNet. [Online] Available http://www.africa-net.com/africanet/country/algeria/, 1998.

ArabNet. Algeria. [Online] Available http://www.arab.net/algeria/algeria_contents.html, 1998.

Andorra

Andorrans make up only about 30 percent of the population of Andorra. More than half of the population is Spanish, and the remaining population is French (less than 10 percent). To learn more about the Spanish, refer to the chapter on Spain in Volume 8. Information on the French can be found in the chapter on France in Volume 3.

Andorrans

PRONUNCIATION: an-DOHR-uhns
LOCATION: Andorra (between France and Spain)
POPULATION: 60,000
LANGUAGE: Catalan; French; Spanish; some English
RELIGION: Roman Catholicism; Protestantism; Judaism

1 ● INTRODUCTION

Andorra, a tiny, mountainous nation in western Europe, is an autonomous (self-governing) principality (territory ruled by a prince). This isolated rural region was almost unknown to the outside world until the middle of the twentieth century. Since then, Andorra has grown to be a popular tourist site for vacationers from Spain, France, and other European countries.

Since the late thirteenth century, Andorra has been under joint French and Spanish rule. France's leaders (including all its pres-idents since 1870) have had the title of Prince of Andorra.

Andorra became a parliamentary democracy in 1993, when it adopted its first constitution. It retained the nation's relationship to its French and Spanish princes but limited their powers. Andorra became a member of the United Nations in July 1993.

2 ● LOCATION

Andorra is located on the southern slopes of the Pyrenees Mountains, which form the border between France and Spain. With a total area of 175 square miles (453 square kilometers), Andorra is one of the world's smallest nations—about 2.5 times the size of Washington, D.C. The land includes picturesque mountains, meadows, fields, and lakes. Andorra has one of the highest population densities in Europe: 337 people per square mile (130 people per square kilometer.) Less than one-third of Andorra's residents were born there.

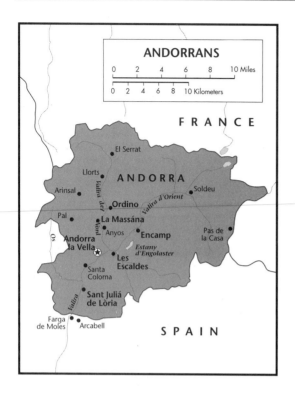

ANDORRANS

0   2   4   6   8   10 Miles

0 2 4 6 8 10 Kilometers

rounded by flowers. Finally, it was decided that the statue was meant to remain in that spot. Then a church was built to house it. The statue became Andorra's most important religious symbol and a popular destination for pilgrimages (journeys to a sacred place).

A famous character from secular lore is Andorra's "White Lady" (also known as Our Lady of Meritxell or the Virgin of Meritxell). According to tradition, she was a princess abused by a wicked stepmother. After surviving her stepmother's attempt to have her killed, she married a man who headed a rebellion against her father and stepmother, and the two became Andorra's most famous couple. The "White Lady" is part of all major festivals.

3 ● LANGUAGE

Andorra's official language is Catalan, a Romance language spoken in Catalonia, a region in Spain. Most Andorrans also speak French and Spanish, and some speak English.

4 ● FOLKLORE

Andorra's most famous religious shrine is the church at Meritxell. It houses a statue of the Virgin of Meritxell, which is the subject of a popular legend. People believe that hundreds of years ago the statue was found on a snowy hillside, surrounded by blooming plants. Travelers who found the statue tried repeatedly to move it to a covered area in town. Each time, it disappeared, only to be found once again on the hillside sur-

5 ● RELIGION

More than 90 percent of Andorrans are Roman Catholic, and Catholicism influences many aspects of Andorran life. All public records are kept by the Roman Catholic Church, and only Catholic marriages are officially recognized in Andorra.

6 ● MAJOR HOLIDAYS

Andorra's holidays include New Year's Day (January 1), Good Friday and Easter Monday (in March or April), Andorran National Day (September 8), and Christmas (December 25), as well as other holy days of the Christian calendar. The National Day is observed by making a pilgrimage to the shrine of the Virgin of Meritxell, Andorra's most important religious site.

7 ● RITES OF PASSAGE

Baptism, first communion, and marriage are considered rites of passage for Andorrans, as they are for most Roman Catholics.

8 ● RELATIONSHIPS

Life centers around the family for most Andorrans, and fathers traditionally exert strict control over their wives and children.

9 ● LIVING CONDITIONS

Many Andorrans still live in traditional, slate-roofed, stone farmhouses, often built against mountainsides to leave stretches of level land free for planting. Most of these rural houses have livestock areas or toolsheds on the ground floor, a kitchen and family area on the second floor, and bedrooms on the third. Andorra also has modern multistory apartment buildings. However, due to the scarcity of flat land, it is difficult to find space on which to build.

10 ● FAMILY LIFE

Family loyalty and togetherness are central to life in Andorra. However, the strict control traditionally exercised by fathers has declined over the past half-century due to the social changes brought about by the opening of Andorra to tourism and commerce. Exposure to Western ways has encouraged women and men to become more equal.

11 ● CLOTHING

Andorrans wear modern Western-style clothing. Traditional costumes are still worn for folk dancing and on special occasions. The traditional costume for women features a full, flowered skirt over a white petticoat;

© Corel Corporation

A view of the Andorran countryside.

a blouse (sometimes covered by a flowered shawl); long, black, fingerless net gloves; and black espadrilles (cloth sandals) with white stockings. The traditional costume for men is a white shirt, dark knee-length pants, white stockings, and black shoes. They may also wear broad red sashes tied at the waist.

12 ● FOOD

Favorite Andorran recipes are often based on farm produce and freshly caught game. Common entrees (main dishes) include *trinxat* (boiled potatoes and cabbage), grilled trout, and omeletts made with wild mushrooms. Andorra also has distinctive regional desserts, most notably *coques,* flat cakes made with grape syrup, brandy, and other flavorings.

13 ● EDUCATION

Schooling is compulsory between the ages of six and sixteen. About half of Andorra's primary schools teach in French; the other half offer instruction in Spanish or Catalan. Andorrans who attend college usually do so in France or Spain.

14 ● CULTURAL HERITAGE

Andorra has an old and rich folk heritage that is perpetuated in its folk dances. One of the most popular dances is the *sardana,* which is also the national dance of Catalonia in northeastern Spain. The dancers form a circle or a long line, holding their clasped hands high in the air to perform this slow, graceful dance. In addition to the sardana, various regions have their own dances, including the *marratxa,* the *contrapas,* and the *Bal de Santa Ana.*

15 ● EMPLOYMENT

About 25 percent of the work force is employed in commerce; 20 percent in restaurants and hotels; 20 percent in manufacturing and construction; 10 percent in public administration; 1 percent in agriculture; and the remainder in other areas.

16 ● SPORTS

Andorra has the perfect climate for skiing. It is snow-covered for six months of the year, but its skies are clear and sunny. Once the ski season is over, Andorra's mountains are still frequented by hikers, mountaineers,

and rock climbers. Competitive sports include rugby, soccer, tennis, and golf.

17 ● RECREATION

Andorrans receive both television and radio broadcasts from neighboring countries. Twenty-one uninhabited cabins in the mountains are open to the hikers for use as overnight shelters.

18 ● CRAFTS AND HOBBIES

Traditional Andorran crafts include fancy, carved pinewood furniture, pottery, and ironwork. A regional specialty is a class of products known as *musicatures,* which are carved in a distinctive style with a knife point. These designs are found on many types of items, including wooden, leather, and metal handicrafts.

19 ● SOCIAL PROBLEMS

Tourism has aided Andorra's economy, but it has also had a negative effect on the country's beautiful landscape. Towns have been overrun with tourist shops and restaurants. Heavy automobile traffic has led to the growth of Andorra's police force from four officers in the 1950s to 150 in the 1990s.

20 ● BIBLIOGRAPHY

Carrick, Noel. *Andorra.* New York: Chelsea House, 1988.

Deane, Shirley. *The Road to Andorra.* New York: Morrow, 1961.

Taylor, Carry. *Andorra.* Santa Barbara, Calif.: Clio Press, 1993.

WEBSITES

World Travel Guide. Andorra. [Online] Available http://www.wtgonline.com/country/ad/gen.html, 1998.

Angola

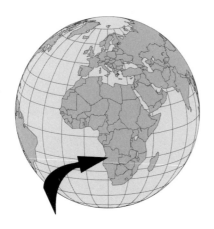

The people of Angola are called Angolans. More than 95 percent of the population of Angola speaks one of the many Bantu languages. The largest Bantu-speaking groups are the Ovimbundu (37 percent), the Mbundu (22 percent), and the Bakongo (13 percent). To learn more about Bakongo, see the chapter on the Republic of Congo in Volume 2. The mestizo (mixed-heritage) population is about 200,000, and there are about 10,000 whites, mostly of Portuguese descent.

Angolans

PRONUNCIATION: an-GOH-luhns
LOCATION: Angola
POPULATION: 11 million
LANGUAGE: Portuguese; Ovimbundu; Mbundu, Kongo; Chokwe; other Bantu languages
RELIGION: Christianity (Roman Catholicism and Protestantism); indigenous religious beliefs

1 ● INTRODUCTION

In 1482 the Portuguese established forts and missions along the west coast of the Republic of Angola. King Alphonso of the Kongo converted to Christianity and established friendly relations with Portugal. In 1575, the Portuguese sent convicted criminals to Angola, where they founded a settlement at Luanda, the present-day capital of Angola.

In 1483, slave trading began and continued for almost 400 years, even though there were many attempts to ban it. The Portu-guese formally abolished slavery in 1875, but it was not until 1911 that the slave trade really ended.

In 1900 the Portuguese settlers began cacao and palm oil plantations. Diamond mining began in 1912. In 1951 the Portuguese made Angola an overseas territory and an integral part of Portugal. A year later, the first *colonatos* (planned settlements) were settled by Portuguese immigrants. The Portuguese had a policy known as *assimilado*. This policy permitted only culturally assimilated Angolans (those who had adopted European ways) to enjoy the privileges of Portuguese citizenship. As of 1960, only about 80,000 of 4.5 million people in Angola qualified as citizens.

Many in Angola were not happy with the Portuguese control of their country. These Angolans organized resistance movements. After years of struggle, Angola gained its independence from Portugal on November

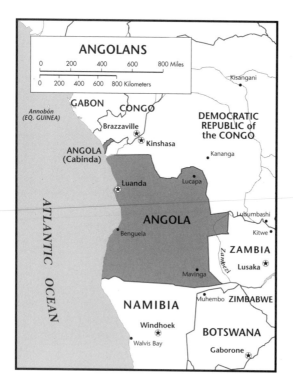

who move often during part of the year, transporting their households with them). Until around 1900, these people hunted and gathered, but now they herd animals and grow food crops.

2 ● LOCATION

The population of Angola is estimated to be more than 11 million people; it is projected to reach over 20 million people by the year 2015.

Angola is bordered by the Democratic Republic of the Congo to the north, Zambia to the east, and Namibia to the south. To the west lies the Atlantic Ocean. The total area is 481,354 square miles (1,246,700 square kilometers). The capital is Luanda.

The Bié Plateau lies in the center of the country. This plateau is the source of several major rivers, including the Cunene River, flowing to the south and west; the Kuanza River, flowing northwest to the Atlantic; the Kwango River, flowing northward; and the Zambezi River, flowing to the east.

The tallest mountains (serra) are found in the region of the Bié Plateau. In the southwest, in the mountain range known as Serra Xilengue, Mt. Moco rises to 8,594 feet (2,578 meters).

3 ● LANGUAGE

Portuguese is the official language, although 95 percent of Angolans speak Ovimbundu, Mbundu, Kongo, Chokwe, and other languages. Portuguese remains important because it is the language of government, national media, and international relations. Since Angola became indepen-

11, 1975. With independence came conflict between different factions of society. There has been constant civil unrest in Angola since 1975, and hundreds have lost their lives in the conflict. In 1995, the United Nations sent peacekeepers to monitor an agreement among rival leaders to try to end twenty years of fighting.

The largest ethnic group is the Ovimbundu, comprising 37 percent of the population. The Mbundu are second at 22 percent. These two groups adapted well to European ways introduced by the Portuguese, and are successful traders. The third largest group is the Bakongo at 13 percent, followed by the Luimbe-Nganguela and the Nyaneka-Humbe at a little over 5 percent each. Scattered in the arid (hot and dry) southern third of Angola are seminomadic peoples (people

dent in 1975, African languages have been taught in school.

4 ● FOLKLORE

The first president of Angola, Antonio Agostinho Neto, is a national hero. His birthday, September 17, is celebrated as National Hero's Day. He belonged to a group responsible for shaping Angola when it became independent from Portugal. His group's battle cry in the early 1950s was "Let us discover Angola." The group also coined the term *angolidade* (Angolinity), to describe national identity.

5 ● RELIGION

About 90 percent of Angolans are Christian, with Catholics representing 70 percent, and Protestants, 20 percent. Traditional religion is practiced by about 10 percent of Angolans.

6 ● MAJOR HOLIDAYS

Public holidays include *Inicio de Luta Armada* (Commencement of Armed Struggle Day) on February 4; Victory Day on March 27; Youth Day on April 14; Armed Forces Day on August 1; National Hero's Day (anniversary of the birth of Antonio Agostinho Neto, first Angolan president) on September 17; Independence Day on November 11; Pioneers' Day on December 1; and Foundation of the MPLA Workers' Party Day on December 10.

On Christmas and New Year's Day, friends assume godmother *(madrinha)* and godfather *(padrinho)* relationships. They take turns giving gifts to each other; one offers the other a gift on Christmas and the other returns the gesture on New Year's

Day. In the capital, young people are likely to spend New Year's Eve with their families until midnight, just long enough to taste some champagne. Then they head for the discos with friends until early morning. Angolans celebrate *carnival* (Mardi Gras) on the Tuesday preceding the Christian holiday of Ash Wednesday, which begins the period of Lent leading up to Easter.

7 ● RITES OF PASSAGE

Many of the rites of passage are marked by Christian ceremonies. Birth, baptism, marriage, and funeral ceremonies are all celebrated by church rites. To celebrate a birth, people drink champagne and give gifts. To mark a death, friends and relatives join the family of the person who has died for a meal after the burial ceremony. A widow often wears black for a month, and stays inside for a week after the funeral.

8 ● RELATIONSHIPS

The most common greeting is the Portuguese *Ola* (OH-lah, Hello), followed by *Como esta?* (ko-mo ess-TAH) or *Como vai?* (ko-mo VA-ee), both of which translate to "How are you?" Depending on the time of the day, one might hear *Bom dia* (bone JEE-ah, Good morning), *Boa tarde* (bow-ah TAR-day, Good afternoon), or *Boa noite* (bow-ah NWAH-tay, Good night). Shaking hands is common. A kiss on each cheek is becoming an accepted greeting among friends in urban life, although older people prefer to shake hands. Pointing is considered rude.

Dating rules depend on the family. Young people usually choose their own

Cory Langley

Houses are typically made from local materials, with walls of mud and sticks with thatched roofs. Sometimes, the roof is made of galvanized iron, and the walls of cinderblock.

spouses. Dating in the cities is common and usually involves going out to a movie, eating in a restaurant, or attending parties. When a couple becomes engaged to be married, a ring is offered by the young man. The two families then meet to discuss matters such as bride price. Bride price, which is paid to the father of the bride, may involve gifts of clothing, perfume, and jewelry. The custom of payment of bride price is more common in the rural areas, where traditional practices are more common in all aspects of life. In towns and cities, social customs have changed more rapidly to reflect Western ways.

9 ● LIVING CONDITIONS

Living conditions have worsened as a result of the civil war that has been going on since 1975. Health care and medical facilities have gotten worse, especially in those parts of the country where neither the government nor the rebels are in control.

The civil unrest has forced people to leave their homes to search for safe places to live. Millions of these refugees cannot find adequate food, water, and sanitary services. They are at risk of infectious and parasitic diseases and starvation. Land mines are buried all over Angola, and as many as 50,000 people—including women and children—have lost arms or legs in land-mine explosions. There are not enough doctors to care for the population. It is estimated that there is only one doctor per 10,000 people, a low ratio even for Africa. Private medical facilities exist, providing a higher standard of medical care. But the refugees who are in the greatest need of food, water, and medical care cannot afford to go to private hospitals or clinics.

Houses are typically made out of local materials, with mud or cinderblock walls and thatched or galvanized iron roofs. In Luanda, where space is limited, apartment living is becoming more common. Electricity in Luanda is fairly dependable. However, water is irregular in some zones, and families who can afford it install their own reserve water tanks.

10 ● FAMILY LIFE

In rural Angola, women till the fields, gather wood and water, and do domestic chores. Polygyny (when a husband has more than one wife) is practiced in both rural and urban areas, but men must have enough wealth to support more than one wife. Co-wives live separately from each other in their own houses. Abortion is legal only to save a woman's life.

In Angolan villages, women typically raise between six and twelve children. However, women's rights groups such as the Organization of Angolan Women are helping to establish literacy programs and health units.

In larger towns, women have fewer children and compete for male-dominated jobs. Women drive cars, study at universities, vote, occupy non-combat positions in the army, and serve as traffic policewomen. As of the late 1990s, five women ministers held government cabinet posts in such areas as oil, fisheries, and culture. Five women were Public Ministry magistrates, and there were three women judges. One woman headed a political party and was a candidate in the 1992 elections.

In traditional families, extended kin relationships are common. Ovimbundu children inherit from both their mother and their father. In most other ethnic groups boys inherit from their mother's brother. In the Mbundu ethnic group, a daughter joins her husband in his village, and a son joins his uncle's (mother's brother's) village.

11 ● CLOTHING

In the towns and cities, Western-style clothing is common, though some people still wear traditional clothing. The villages remain more traditional, where women wear *panos,* African wraparound batik garments. Dressing up for parties and special occasions in the cities almost certainly means wearing Western-style outfits. Angolan youth prefer casual jeans and T-shirts, except for special occasions. There are a few groups, such as the Mukubao in the southern Angolan province of Kuando Kubango, who do not wear any clothing.

12 ● FOOD

Whenever possible, Angolans eat three meals a day. A breakfast consists of bread, eggs, and tea or coffee. Sometimes mothers may prepare a special breakfast treat of sweet rice *(arroz doce).*

Jason Lauré

Classroom in Luanda, Angola. Schools continue to struggle against social instability, low investment, and teacher shortages.

The staple foods include cassava (a plant with an edible root), corn, millet (a small-seeded grain), sorghum (a grassy plant that yields a grain used alone or to make syrup), beans, sweet potatoes, rice, wheat, and bananas. Typical midday meals consist of a ball of manioc dough (cassava flour mixed with boiling water), with fish, chicken, or meat. People in the north and in the capital enjoy pounded cassava leaves *(kisaka)*. Specialty dishes include *mwamba de galinha,* a palm-nut paste sauce in which chicken, spices, and peanut butter are cooked, creating a delightful aroma. A recipe adapted for Western cooks follows. Angolans make use of their abundant fresh and saltwater fish.

One dish, *calulu*, combines fresh and dried fish. A favorite dish among Angolans is *cabidela,* chicken's blood eaten with rice and cassava dough.

13 ● EDUCATION

When Angola was a colony of Portugal, all schools were operated by the Catholic Church. High schools were for a small number of students from elite (wealthy and powerful) families. Only a few of those who attended high school actually completed their studies and graduated. Education at the primary level was of low quality, and only about 10 percent of the population could read and write when Angola won independence from Portugal in 1975.

Since then, the civil war has made improving the education system difficult, but the government has worked to improve the literacy rate. By the late 1990s, 42 percent of Angolans could read and write, but males still have far greater educational opportunity. Overall, 56 percent of males are literate, compared with only 28 percent of females. About three times as many men as women continue their studies beyond the tenth grade. The United Nations Children's Fund (UNICEF) was providing funding in the late 1990s to support education for poor and rural children. It is difficult for Angolan schools to operate in a society that is constantly at war, and where there are not enough funds or teachers to meet the students' needs. Private schooling exists but is costly.

The Agostinho Neto University, the public university in Luanda, has three campuses but has been devastated by poor economic conditions resulting from the war. Many students decide to go to college outside Angola. Many go to Cuba or Russia. Some even travel to study in the United States.

14 ● CULTURAL HERITAGE

Percussion, wind, and string instruments are found throughout Angola. Maracas *(saxi)* are made by drilling a few small holes in dried gourds and placing dried seeds or glass beads inside. The box lute *(chilhumba)* is played during long journeys by nomads in southern Angola. Musical performances often include dancing. Members of the Luimbe-Ngangela ethnic group in eastern Angola wear masks when they dance.

Recipe

Mwamba de Galinha (Chicken Mwamba)

Ingredients

1 teaspoon red pepper flakes
1 onion, chopped
3 cloves of garlic, chopped
½ cup lemon juice
½ cup creamy peanut butter (natural style works best); in Angola, palm hash, made from palm oil, would be used
2 cups water
3 Tablespoons vegetable oil
8 to 10 chicken breasts (may use skinless and boneless if preferred; other chicken parts, such as drumsticks, wings, and thighs, may also be substituted)

Directions

1. Prepare marinade. Combine all ingredients except chicken in a bowl and mix well.
2. Place chicken in a single layer in a casserole dish. Pour marinade over chicken, cover with plastic wrap, and refrigerate at least 3 hours.
3. Remove chicken from marinade. Pour off the marinade and save it. Pat the chicken dry.
4. Heat about 2 tablespoons of oil in a skillet over medium heat. Add chicken, a few pieces at a time, and brown on all sides. Return the browned pieces to the casserole.
5. Pour the marinade from step 3 over the chicken, cover with a lid or foil, and bake at 350°F for 30 to 40 minutes.

Serve with rice.

Traditional music has strongly influenced popular music. Young people prefer to dance, holding each other close, to *kizumba,* a style of upbeat rhythmic music. The discos play imports such as the samba from Brazil, and popular music from the United States and the Democratic Republic of the Congo.

Storytelling is an important foundation of Angolan literature. It is generally agreed that written literature began in 1850 with a book of verse by José de Silva Maia Ferreira. Since 1945 the liberation struggle has developed strong links between literature and political activism. Many MPLA (Worker's Party) leaders and members, including Agostinho Neto, took part in this movement. From 1975 until the early 1990s, Angolan writers had to be affiliated with some kind of governmental organization in order to be published.

Angola's cultural heritage also is tied to the Portuguese language. Angola shares its past as a Portuguese colony with four other African countries—Mozambique, Guinea Bissau, Sao Tomé and Principe, and Cape Verde.

15 ● EMPLOYMENT

Angola is recovering from a severe reduction in its work force, which began in 1975 with the abrupt departure of more than 90 percent of the white settlers. Many of the 300,000 departing Portuguese took their skills with them, and deliberately destroyed factories, plantations, roads, and transportation systems. The prolonged civil war chased away skilled Angolans and foreign money. Angolans currently are undertaking a national recovery program to rebuild and diversify their economy and to retrain their people.

16 ● SPORTS

Soccer is the most popular participant and spectator sport, played by both girls and boys. The "Citadel" in Luanda is one of Africa's largest stadiums.

In the 1990s, basketball gained popularity in Angola after the Angolan men's national basketball team won three consecutive All-African championships. Backboards and baskets are now seen on street corners in most villages, towns, and cities. Handball, volleyball, and track and field round out the most popular sports.

Chess is a popular pursuit in Angola. The country has nearly a dozen international chess masters. Children enjoy a traditional game, *ware,* which is a *mancala* game. Mancala games, played in many variations throughout Africa, involve two players who move stones around a playing surface. The surface may be a board with carved indentations or a patch of ground with indentations dug out of the soil.

Ware

Equipment

Playing board with two rows of six small pits or indentations. (An empty styrofoam egg carton works well.)

48 seeds, small shells, or pebbles

Players face each other with the board between them.

Directions

1. Distribute 48 seeds, small shells, or pebbles by placing them randomly into each receptacle on the playing board.

2. Players decide who will take the first turn. The first player picks up all the seeds from one receptacle on his side of the board and distributes them ("sows"), one at a time, in a counterclockwise direction, into the receptacles. If the last seed falls into an empty receptacle, his turn is over. If the last seed falls into a receptacle occupied by one or three seeds, he captures those seeds. If the last seed falls into a receptacle that contains an even number of seeds, he must continue playing by lifting out all the pebbles and sowing them.

3. He continues in this way until he "captures" an odd number of seeds or sows a seed into an empty receptacle.

4. The other player now repeats this procedure. For their second turns, the players must begin by emptying the receptacle immediately to the right of the one used for the previous turn. If there are only two seeds left on the board, the first player to have them both on his side of the board may claim them.

5. When all the seeds have been captured and none remains on the board, the player who has won the most seeds subtracts his opponent's winnings from his own.

6. The winner records the difference between his/her winnings and his/her opponent's, and another round is played.

7. The game continues until one player reaches a total of sixty.

17 ● RECREATION

The advent of the satellite dish has made television an increasingly popular form of entertainment in Luanda and other urban centers. The dishes are status symbols and allow Angolans to increase their options from the one government-run station to an array of channels from all over the world. Angolans connect with the world's popular culture by watching Brazilian shows (in Portuguese), MTV, and American movies with Portuguese subtitles. Residents in apartment buildings lower their costs by sharing the same satellite dish. While movie theatres remain popular, video rental stores are growing in popularity in Luanda, and videos are part of an urban trend toward home entertainment.

18 ● CRAFTS AND HOBBIES

Luanda's three museums, including the Museum of Anthropology, contain a fine collection of African art and handicrafts. Noncommercial masks and sculptures vary according to ethnic group. They symbolize rites of passage or changes in seasons, and play important roles in cultural rituals. Artisans work with wood, bronze, ivory, malachite, and ceramics.

In the 1980s, the Ministry of Culture stifled art by controlling all art production and marketing. Recent deregulation (the removal of government restrictions) has made handicraft production a blossoming cottage industry (small business often operated from the home). Stylized masks, statuettes, and trinkets ("airport art") now flood the popular Futungo tourist market on the outskirts of Luanda. This art may not reflect the deep cultural beliefs of the people, but it provides work and a source of income for people with artistic skills. Shoppers at the Futungo market are treated to musicians playing traditional instruments such as *marimbas* (xylophones), *xingufos* (big antelope horns), and drums, giving the feeling of a village festival.

19 ● SOCIAL PROBLEMS

An underdeveloped economy resulting from thirty years of civil war is the cause of much social upheaval. The refugee squatter settlements on Luanda's outskirts have created new urban problems and changed family structure. Despite the significant income from the sale of oil products to foreign countries, political instability has slowed economic growth in Angola. Jobs that pay adequate salaries require a diploma from a foreign university and are hard to find without special connections. Low salaries discourage Angolans with technical skills from staying in their country.

Drug addiction is not widespread, though cigarette smoking is. No age limit exists on the purchase or consumption of alcohol, but social mores (customs or values) discourage alcohol abuse. Burglary and petty thievery, however, are common. Minor crimes are often punishable on the streets. For example, thieves in the public market are immediately identified by a shout of *ladron!* (thief!) and are then chased and punished on the spot if caught.

20 ● BIBLIOGRAPHY

Africa on File. New York: Facts on File, 1995.

Africa South of the Sahara. London, Eng.: Europa Publishers, 1997.

Broadhead, Susan H. *Historical Dictionary of Angola*. Metuchen, N.J., and London: The Scarecrow Press, Inc., 1992.

Sommerville, Keith. *Angola: Politics, Economics, and Society*. Marxist Regimes Series. Boulder, Colo.: Lynne Rienner, 1986.

WEBSITES

Internet Africa Ltd. Angola. [Online] Available http://www.africanet.com/africanet/country/angola/, 1998.

Republic of Angola. [Online] Available http://www.angola.org, 1998.

World Travel Guide. [Online] Available http://www.wtgonline.com/country/ao/gen.html, 1998.

Antigua and Barbuda

Approximately 95 percent of Antiguans and Barbudans descended from African slaves. The rest are of European, Asian, Arab, and mixed descent.

Antiguans and Barbudans

PRONUNCIATION: an-TEE-gahns and bar-BYEW-dahns
LOCATION: Antigua and Barbuda
POPULATION: 75,000
LANGUAGE: English; Creole dialect
RELIGION: Anglican; other Protestant Christian groups; Roman Catholicism

1 ● INTRODUCTION

The nation of Antigua and Barbuda consists of two islands located in the Caribbean Sea. Christopher Columbus sighted Antigua in 1493 and gave it its original name, Santa María de la Antigua. Spanish, French, British, and Dutch colonizers avoided Antigua and Barbuda. However, in 1632 a group of British settlers sailed from the nearby island of St. Kitts and established tobacco and ginger plantations.

Except for a brief period of French rule in 1666, Antigua and neighboring Barbuda remained under British control for over 300 years. The islands became major producers of sugar, with the work done mostly by slaves brought to the islands from Africa.

The slaves were emancipated (freed) in 1834 but their living conditions were little better than they had been under slavery, since they had no way to get food and shelter. Antigua and Barbuda won the right to self-govern, with no control by the British, in 1967. Full independence followed in 1981. Some residents of Barbuda wanted to separate from Antigua. They were convinced to remain united with Antigua with the promise that Barbuda could control its own affairs. Barbudans continue to feel they have been ignored by both the British (before independence) and the majority on Antigua (after independence). A Barbudan proverb expresses this feeling: "Barbuda is behind God's back."

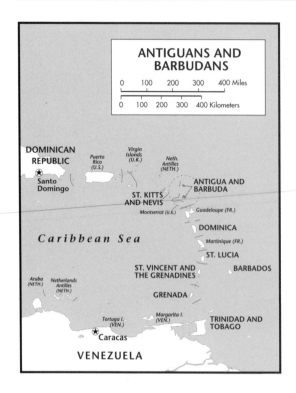

ANTIGUANS AND BARBUDANS

| 0 | 100 | 200 | 300 | 400 Miles |
| 0 | 100 | 200 | 300 | 400 Kilometers |

The population of Antigua and Barbuda is just under 75,000, of whom 1,200 live on Barbuda. St. John's, the country's capital and economic center, has an estimated population of 35,000 to 40,000 people.

3 ● LANGUAGE

English is the official language of Antigua and Barbuda, but most inhabitants speak a dialect that is based on standard English combined with African expressions and local slang. Standard English pronunciation and grammar are also modified.

One of the most noticeable differences is in the form of pronouns used as the subject of a sentence, as in "Her my friend." Antiguans and Barbudans also omit the helping verb "to be." The standard English version of the previous sentence is, "She is my friend."

2 ● LOCATION

Antigua and Barbuda—close to the mid-point of the island chain known as the Lesser Antilles—is located at the outer curve of the Leeward Islands, between the Atlantic Ocean and the Caribbean Sea. Antigua is 404 miles (650 kilometers) southeast of Cuba. With an area of 108 square miles (281 square kilometers), it is the second-largest of the Leeward Islands and about two-thirds the size of New York City. Barbuda lies about 31 miles (50 kilometers) northeast of Antigua and is about half its size.

Barbuda has sandy beaches and a large lagoon and mangrove swamp on its western side. The island was leased to a single British family for nearly 200 years and has only one village, Codrington.

4 ● FOLKLORE

Obeah, a collection of beliefs and practices from Africa, has followers in Antigua and Barbuda, even though it has been declared illegal. Believers say it can heal the sick, harm one's enemies, and even be used for such common purposes as "fixing" a court case. Its features include a belief in spirits (of which the best-known are *jumbies*) and the use of herbal potions.

A number of proverbs are shared among Antiguans and Barbudans to reflect on aspects of daily life. Examples are:

> Better man belly bus' than good food waste.
> Every dog is lion in he own backyard.
> Mout' open, story jump out.
> Stone under water na know when sun hot.
> No fisherman ever say he fish stink.
> De worse o' livin' better than de bes' o' dead.

The award-winning design for the national costume, featuring madras plaid fabric.

5 ● RELIGION

About 45 percent of the population belongs to the Anglican Church, also known as the Church of England. The Anglican Cathedral overlooking the capital city of St. John's is one of Antigua's oldest landmarks. Other Christian groups account for about 42 percent of the population, and about 8 percent are Roman Catholic.

6 ● MAJOR HOLIDAYS

Public holidays in Antigua and Barbuda include New Year's Day (January 1), Labor Day (first Monday in May), CARICOM Day (July 3), Independence Day (November 1), Christmas (December 25), and Boxing Day (December 26). The Christian holidays of Good Friday, Easter Monday, and Whit Monday are celebrated, and occur on different dates each year. (CARICOM Day commemorates the founding in 1973 of the Caribbean Community and Common Market.)

The nation of Antigua and Barbuda is particularly known for its Carnival celebration, held in late July through the first Tuesday in August. Most of the festivities take place in the capital city of St. John's, including street parades led by revelers wearing elaborate glittering costumes, calypso and steel drum music, street dancing ("jump-up"), and contests. The climax of the festival is *J'Ouvert* on the first Monday in August. Then, thousands of celebrants pour into the streets at 4:00 AM in a frenzy of dancing accompanied by steel drum and brass bands. The island of Barbuda holds its own, more modest, Carnival celebration, Caribana, in June.

7 ● RITES OF PASSAGE

Most young men and women go through the Christian ceremony of religious confirmation, performed around age thirteen. Other major life transitions, such as birth, marriage, and death, are also marked by Christian ceremonies.

8 ● RELATIONSHIPS

"Aunty" and "Uncle" are sometimes used as terms of respect in addressing anyone older than the person speaking. A woman may be addressed with "Mistress" before her last name. A handshake is a customary greeting among business associates.

9 ● LIVING CONDITIONS

Most Antiguans and Barbudans live in houses constructed of concrete and wood, with at least two bedrooms, a living/dining room, a kitchen, and a bathroom. Most homes on both islands now have indoor plumbing and electricity.

10 ● FAMILY LIFE

Couples in Antigua and Barbuda follow customs similar to those on other English-speaking islands in the Caribbean. They may be legally married or may live together without being married. Another arrangement is called a "visiting union." This is where a man and woman consider themselves a couple, but live apart. In this arrangement, the woman raises the children. Many children are raised by relatives other than their parents. Some children grow up in a succession of different households. Where a child lives depends on the family situation, including the parents' financial situa-

Recipe

Pepperpot Soup

This is an Antiguan and Barbudan recipe. It is served with fungi (cornmeal pudding) or dumplings, but cornbread can be used instead.

Ingredients

1 pound salt beef or other fresh meat, cut up (optional)
1 pound salt pork
2 pig's feet (¼ pound ham or Canadian bacon may be substituted)
1 pig snout (1 Tablespoon ketchup may be substituted)
2 teaspoons oil
¼ pound fresh spinach, cut into large pieces
1 large eggplant, chopped
2 teaspoons margarine
4 okras, diced
2 onions, chopped
1 pound chopped spinach
2 tomatoes, diced
1 cup pumpkin, diced
1 cup squash, diced
2 cups green peas, cooked
1 Tablespoon fresh chives or ½ teaspoon dried
1 Tablespoon fresh thyme or ½ teaspoon dried
Salt and pepper to taste

Directions

1. Heat the oil in a large soup pot over medium heat.
2. Fry the meat, stirring occasionally, until it is almost cooked. Remove the meat to a plate.
3. Add all of the vegetables (except peas) and about 1 cup of water to the soup pot. Cook until vegetables are tender, about 7 to 10 minutes.
4. Mash about a third of the vegetables with a potato masher or spoon.
5. Add the meat back into the pot. Add the peas, chives, and thyme. Add salt and pepper to taste.
6. Cook until thick. For a thicker soup, more vegetables may be mashed.

tion and employment, and whether there are grandparents to care for.

Couples may have children whether they are legally married or not. A 1987 law made it illegal to discriminate against children born out of wedlock. Children inherit from their parents, whether or not the mother and father were married.

Antigua and Barbuda is a popular tourist destination, and many women work in the tourist industry. The lack of child care can make it complicated for Antiguan mothers and fathers to raise their children.

11 ● CLOTHING

The people of Antigua and Barbuda wear modern Western-style clothing. Colorful costumes are worn by many during the Carnival celebration in August.

In 1992, a competition to select a national costume was held as a part of the islands' eleventh anniversary of independence. The winning design was submitted by native Antiguan Heather Doram. The costume has versions for men and women, and is worn by many Antiguans and Barbudans on Heritage Day, the last business day before Independence Day, November 1. The costume features madras fabric, introduced from India after Antigua won independence.

12 ● FOOD

The Creole food of Antigua and Barbuda is similar to that of other West Indian nations and includes such basics as rice and peas, pumpkin soup, and pepperpot soup. Fish and shellfish are an important part of the diet. The regional species of spiny lobster is especially popular, as are crabs and conch. *Fungi,* a sort of cornmeal pudding made with boiled okra, is another staple on the islands. It is usually served with salt fish.

Breadfruit (originally introduced to the region from the East Indies) is another staple. Meat-filled pastries ("pasties") are sold by street vendors. The country's most distinctive fruit is the Antigua black pineapple, which is exceptionally sweet.

13 ● EDUCATION

Primary and secondary education is mandatory between the ages of five and sixteen. Pre-primary schooling is available from the age of three. The educational system in Antigua and Barbuda is based on the British system, which has grade levels called "forms." There are forty-five primary schools and twelve secondary schools on the islands. Although the nation has a literacy rate of 90 percent, there are serious problems in the educational system. These include a shortage of qualified teachers and inadequate facilities and supplies.

14 ● CULTURAL HERITAGE

The music of the Fife Band is an important part of the islands' musical heritage. The band is made up of a stringed guitar, drum, and fife (or flute).

Internationally famous author Jamaica Kincaid was born and grew up on the island of Antigua and now lives in the United States. Her novels, short stories, and essays provide a vivid portrait of the Antiguan people and way of life. Kincaid has been a staff writer for *The New Yorker* magazine since the 1970s, and her 1988 book-length essay, *A Small Place,* harshly criticizes British colonialism, the tourist industry, and government corruption and neglect in Antigua.

Antiguan playwright Dorbrene "Fats" Omarde is known for dramas that address the social and political issues confronting his country.

15 ● EMPLOYMENT

The majority of people in Antigua and Barbuda are employed by the government. About 11 percent of the people work in agriculture; industry employs the remaining 7 percent. Since tourism-related jobs are seasonal, it is a common practice to have ore than one source of income. This may require people to take on such part-time agricultural pursuits as keeping livestock or selling produce from backyard farming. Fishing is an important source of income on Barbuda, as are government employment and tourism.

© Corel Corporation

A view of the Atlantic Ocean from the Leeward Islands. Antigua and Barbuda is located at the outer curve of the Leeward Islands between the Atlantic Ocean and the Caribbean Sea.

16 ● SPORTS

Cricket, a left-over from the British rule, is the national sport of Antigua and Barbuda. The country has produced some of the world's best players. Antiguans play on the West Indies cricket team, which has been one of the world's best since the 1970s. Soccer is another popular sport.

17 ● RECREATION

The Caribbean's most popular male pastime of dominoes is enjoyed in Antigua and Barbuda. A game called *warri*, a *mancala*-type game brought from Africa, is also popular.

Cricket, soccer, and basketball are all played for recreation.

Favorite types of music include calypso, reggae, and religious hymns. *Benna* is a type of calypso music that comes from the song-dance of African slaves. It was sung by "Quarkoo," who were Antiguan street vendors and entertainers. The Quarkoo were somewhat like street rappers in America. They made up Benna songs on the spot, using repeating lyrics and "call and response" with the audience. Their lyrics were often satirical or controversial, sometimes landing a Quarkoo in jail.

18 ● CRAFTS AND HOBBIES

Antiguan artisans are known for the exceptional quality of their handthrown pottery. Striking items, both decorative and functional, are also crafted from handwoven sea cotton adorned with dyes and embroidery. Other handicrafts include woodcarving and basketry.

19 ● SOCIAL PROBLEMS

Antigua and Barbuda has serious environmental problems. Since there is no central sewage system, contamination by raw sewage and other forms of household waste poses a serious threat to the water supply. This is especially dangerous because the country does not have permanent natural lakes or year-round rivers. Also, the removal of sand for construction purposes threatens the nation's beaches, which are the basis of its tourist industry.

Problems in the educational system have contributed to a shortage of skilled workers, and the tourist industry, while using a large number of workers, creates work that is in most cases unskilled and low-paid. The government's abolition of personal income taxes and its reliance on foreign borrowing have left the country with a massive foreign debt.

20 ● BIBLIOGRAPHY

Cameron, Sarah, and Ben Box, eds. *Caribbean Islands Handbook.* Chicago: Passport Books, 1995.

Luntta, Karl. *Caribbean Handbook.* Chico, Calif.: Moon Publications, 1995.

Schwab, David, ed. *Insight Guides. Caribbean: The Lesser Antilles.* Boston: Houghton Mifflin, 1996.

Walton, Chelle Koster. *Caribbean Ways: A Cultural Guide.* Westwood, Mass.: Riverdale, 1993.

WEBSITES

Antigua and Barbuda Department of Tourism. [Online] Available http://www.interknowledge.com/antigua-barbuda/, 1998.

Argentina

The people of Argentina are called Argentines. Most Argentines are of European origin (principally from Spain and Italy). About 3 percent are Amerindian (native people). The Amerindian population has been increasing slightly through immigration from neighboring Bolivia and Paraguay. Argentina has the eighth-largest population of Jews in the world. There are about 400,000 Jews living in Argentina.

Argentines

PRONUNCIATION: AHR-jen-tines
LOCATION: Argentina
POPULATION: 32.3 million
LANGUAGE: Spanish (official); Italian; English; Quechua; other native languages
RELIGION: Roman Catholicism (official); Evangelical Protestantism

1 ● INTRODUCTION

Argentina gets its name from the Latin word for silver, *argentum,* and this is what drove the Spanish, the colonial rulers of Argentina, to explore the land during the sixteenth century. Ever since, the country has attracted European immigrants, including Welsh, Basque, English, Italians, and Ukranians. When these immigrants encountered indigenous (native) peoples, they simply removed them from the land, claiming it as their own.

During the 1820s, a series of independence movements throughout South America combined to pry control of the continent away from the hands of Spain. Under the leadership of General José de San Martín and others, the United Provinces of the River Plata (the first name of the present-day Argentina) declared independence in 1816. Argentina's Constitution was established in 1853.

After decades of military dictatorships, today the country is ruled by a parliamentary democracy. During the 1970s and 1980s, the military government waged what has come to be known as the "Dirty War" against its own people. In the name of protecting the country from Communists, the military murdered thousands of innocent civilians whom they labeled as "subversives." This violent period has had a lasting impact on the character of the Argentines.

2 ● LOCATION

Geographically, Argentina is the world's eighth-largest country, only slightly smaller than India. It has a total area of about 1.1 million square miles (2.8 million square

ARGENTINEANS

0	250	500	750 Miles
0	250	500	750 Kilometers

La Paz • Trinidad
Arequipa
Arica
Antofagasta •
PARAGUAY BRAZIL
Asunción
Curitiba •
San Miguel de Tucumán
Resistencia
Paraná
CHILE
Córdoba • Pôrto Alegre
Salto
Valparaíso Rosario • URUGUAY
Santiago Mendoza • Montevideo
Buenos Aires
Concepción ARGENTINA
Bahía Blanca • Mar del Plata
Puerto Montt
ATLANTIC OCEAN
Rawson •
Comodoro Rivadavia
Stanley
Estrecho de Magallanes Falkland Islands (UK)
Punta Arenas
Ushuaia

areas. More than 33 percent live in Gran Buenos Aires, which includes the Capital Federal and its suburbs in the Buenos Aires province. The majority of people (85 percent) come from European stock, including about four hundred thousand Jews. Argentina is the world's eighth-largest Jewish community. Approximately 15 percent of the population are Mestizo—people of mixed Indian and European blood.

3 ● LANGUAGE

The official language of Argentina is Spanish, but a number of other European-descended communities still maintain their own languages. Italians, for instance, constitute the largest immigrant group. As a result, Italian is widely understood, as is English, another significant immigrant language. Some seventeen native languages still survive, though some are spoken by very few individuals.

COMMON PHRASES

English	Spanish	Pronunciation
Hello.	Hola.	OH-lah
Good day.	Buenos días.	BWAY-noss DEE-ahs
Goodbye.	Adiós.	ah-dee-OHSS
please	por favor	PORE fah-VORE
thank you	gracias	GRAH-see-ahs

4 ● FOLKLORE

Despite the fact that Argentina considers itself cultured and European, spiritualism and the worship of the dead play an important part in the lives of the people. A famous novelist, Tomás Eloy Martínez, has pointed out that the country's national heroes, such

kilometers), excluding the South Atlantic island and the part of Antarctica it claims as national territory. From north to south (from Quiaca on the Bolivian border to Ushuaia in Tierra del Fuego), it is nearly 2,175 miles (3,500 kilometers) in length. This is about the same distance as from Havana, Cuba, to the Hudson Bay in Canada, or from the Sahara Desert in Africa to Scotland.

Approximately 80 percent of the population of 32.3 million people live in urban

as San Martín, are honored not on the anniversary of their birth but of their death. This is the way that saints' days are celebrated. Pilgrims regularly visit the Recoleta and Chacarita cemeteries in Buenos Aires, where personal prayers are said and ritual offerings are left, especially at the tombs of political and popular culture figures.

During the 1800s, the *gaucho,* the Argentine cowboy, came to represent a free-spirited symbol for the country. He was seen as a rebel who challenged authority in order to preserve his freedom. Legends about him grew, and he became the inspiration for many writers.

5 ● RELIGION

The official state religion is Roman Catholicism, but Evangelical Protestant movements are making converts among traditional Catholic believers. The Catholic religion also faces challenges where popular folklore conflicts with official church teaching.

6 ● MAJOR HOLIDAYS

The main Christian festivals such as Easter and Christmas are celebrated throughout the country. There are also national celebrations of historical times and heroes such as the May Revolution of 1810; Malvinas Day on June 10, which celebrates the establishment of the "Comandancia Política y Militar de las Malvinas" in 1829; Independence Day on July 9; and Día de San Martín, the anniversary of Saint Martin's death on August 17.

7 ● RITES OF PASSAGE

Baptism, first communion, and saints' days are major events, important to both individ-

Cynthia Bassett

The coastline of Argentina features rugged mountainous terrain. The majority of Argentines live in urban areas.

uals and families. Because of the strong Spanish and Italian heritage and the continuing influence of the Catholic Church, these occasions are used as important family get-togethers. Younger people, however, no longer feel obliged to get married in church. Civil marriages have become popular. There is a growing trend toward divorce and remarriage.

8 ● RELATIONSHIPS

Argentines are extremely outgoing and eagerly invite visitors to participate in their activities. One famous pastime is drinking

Cynthia Bassett

Major cities in Argentina have a European look to them. Middle class families live in modern apartment buildings or in bungalows with small gardens.

with a bulbous filter at its lower end that prevents the leaves from entering the tube.

Argentines are quite formal in public and are very aware of proper civilities. Even when asking a stranger for directions in the street, one is expected to approach the person with a greeting such as *buenos días* or *buenas tardes,* "good day" or "good afternoon."

9 ● LIVING CONDITIONS

The major cities in Argentina have a European look to them. The middle classes live in tall, modern apartment buildings or in bungalows with small gardens. Since the 1930s, rural workers have flocked to the big cities and a number of slums have sprouted on the outskirts, where the workers live in shacks. Rural houses are often built of adobe, with earth floors and roofs of straw and mud.

10 ● FAMILY LIFE

The strong Catholic and Spanish heritage has meant that the family plays a central role in Argentine life. There is still a strong belief in the nuclear family, which also extends to grandparents, uncles and aunts, and other close relatives.

mate, a Paraguayan tea made from holly leaves. This is more than a simple drink like tea or coffee. It is an elaborate ritual, shared among family, friends, and colleagues. For those taking part, the sharing of the tea-making process seems to be the whole point of the *maté* ritual.

During the process, one person is responsible for filling a gourd almost to the top with the tea. Meanwhile, water is heated, but not boiled, in a kettle. The hot water is then poured into the gourd vessel. Everyone sips the liquid from a silver tube

Much social life is family-centered, and occasions such as birthdays, First Communions, weddings, and funerals are of major importance. Meals are also important occasions for families and are often elaborate, and quite long. A favorite family get-together is the barbecue.

11 ● CLOTHING

Most city-dwellers wear Western-style clothes, and many enthusiastically follow the fashions of Europe, particularly those of Italy.

In the rural areas, however, many workers on the *estancias* (ranches) wear at least part of the *gaucho* costume—a wide-brimmed hat and loose trousers tucked into the boots—as part of their outfit. In the northwest, the Indians wear ponchos, colorful skirts, and bowler hats.

12 ● FOOD

There are enormous cattle ranches in the Pampas region in Argentina. So it is not surprising that the Argentine diet is meat-oriented. A recipe for a popular beef main dish follows.

There is a surprising ethnic and regional variety to Argentine cooking. The Italian presence has resulted in a great popularity for pasta dishes such as spaghetti, lasagna, cannelloni, and ravioli. Beef, though, is the center of most meals. The most popular form is the *parrillada,* a mixed grill of steak and other cuts.

Some regions have very distinctive food. The Andean northwest offers very spicy dishes. It is common to find Middle Eastern food in the Mendoza north.

13 ● EDUCATION

With a 94 percent literacy rate, Argentina is one of Latin America's most literate countries. From the ages of five to twelve, education is free and compulsory.

Recipe

Argentine Beef Sauté

Ingredients

1 pound lean beef stew meat (beef chuck or sirloin)
1½ cups chopped onions
1 cup chopped green pepper
1 teaspoon salt
½ teaspoon pepper
1 teaspoon crumbled dried basil
1 teaspoon crumbled dried oregano
1 teaspoon sugar
Pinch of hot pepper flakes
3 large garlic cloves, pressed through a garlic press
2 Tablespoons parsley, chopped
1 8-ounce can of red kidney beans
1 8-ounce can polenta
Cooked rice as an accompaniment

Directions

1. Brown meat in a large frying pan over medium heat.
2. Add onion and green peppers and sauté until limp.
3. Stir in salt, pepper, basil, sugar, oregano, red peppers, garlic, and parsley.
4. Drain beans and reserve ¼ cup liquid.
5. Add beans and polenta and simmer, uncovered, adding about ¼ cup liquid bean liquid.
6. Cook for 10 minutes, stirring occasionally. Keep warm.
7. Cook rice according to instructions on package.

Serve with cooked rice.

Adapted from Sarvis, Shirley. *Woman's Day Home Cooking Around the World.* New York: Simon and Schuster, 1978.

Universities are traditionally free and open, but the courses tend to be rigidly specialized. With so much higher education available, the system has turned out many people with professional qualifications, such as doctors and lawyers. Unfortunately, not of all of these people can easily find work in the capital city, Buenos Aires. Despite this, few of them are willing to move to the provinces.

14 ● CULTURAL HERITAGE

During the early nineteenth and twentieth centuries, Buenos Aires adopted French trends in art, music, and particularly architecture. This can be seen in many of the buildings constructed in the capital in the early 1900s.

Argentine writers of the twentieth century are some of the most famous writers in the world. They include Jorge Luis Borges, Julio Cortázar, Ernesto Sábato, Manuel Puig, Osvaldo Soriano, and Adolfo Bioy Casares. Most of their work is available in English translation.

In Buenos Aires, the Teatro Colón opera house is one of the finest of its kind in the world. Classical music and ballet, as well as modern dance, are staged here. The capital also has a lively theater circuit, as rich as any major city elsewhere in the world. Even in the provinces, live theater is an important part of cultural life.

15 ● EMPLOYMENT

Despite its abundant natural resources and its well-educated and cultured population, Argentina has failed to live up to its potential. Earlier in the twentieth century, Argentina was seen to be on a par with prosperous countries such as Canada and Australia. Yet not only has it failed to keep up with them, it has continually fallen behind them.

Like other Latin American countries, one of Argentina's fundamental problems lies in the poverty of its rural areas. Control of the richest agricultural lands of the Pampas is in the hands of a small number of wealthy families. Most rural people are reduced to scratching out a living on marginal lands or laboring as poorly paid workers on the big estates.

16 ● SPORTS

The country is soccer-crazed. Argentina won the World Cup at home in 1978, and again in 1986. The country has produced a number of internationally known players such as Diego Maradona and Daniel Passarella, who now coaches the national team. There are more first-division soccer teams in Buenos Aires than anywhere else in the world. Of the country's twenty teams, eight are based in the capital, while five are in the nearby suburbs.

Several Argentine tennis players have also become world-famous, such as Guillermo Vilas and Gabriela Sabatini.

The game of basketball has also become a notable sport in Argentina, following the influx of many North American athletes who were unable to play professional basketball in America or Europe. In 1995, the Argentine national team defeated the U.S. team for the gold medal in the Pan American Games in Mar del Plata.

Susan D. Rock

The best-known feature of popular culture in Argentina is tango music, a blending of cowboy ballads with melodies and harmonies similar to those heard in Spain and Italy.

17 ● RECREATION

The best-known and most striking feature of Argentine popular culture is the tango, both as music and dance. It first became popular in 1880, when it emerged from working-class districts. It was a blend of *gaucho* (cowboy) verse with Spanish and Italian music. Then came Carlos Gardel, the music's most famous performer, who created the *tango canción,* the "tango song." This lifted tango out of the poor streets and into the fashionable bars of Buenos Aires.

For many Argentines, the tango song sums up the fears and anxieties of life. It can carry themes as diverse as love, jeal-ousy, and betrayal to everyday subjects such as going to work or coping with one's neighbors. It is often full of nostalgia about a way of life that is fast disappearing.

Argentines are great movie-goers, although many theaters have shut down outside Buenos Aires due to the increasing popularity of at-home viewing of videos.

18 ● CRAFTS AND HOBBIES

In artisans' *ferias,* found throughout the country, the variety of handicrafts is extensive. *Maté* paraphernalia is widespread, and gourds and *bombilas* range from simple and inexpensive aluminum, which are often sold in street kiosks, to elaborate and expensive gold and silver found in jewelry stores. In the province of Salta, the distinctive *pon↓ chos de Guemes* are produced.

19 ● SOCIAL PROBLEMS

Runaway inflation seems to have been halted by the government under President Carlos Menem, elected in 1989. Menem, a former soccer player, has worked to cut government spending and state-owned enterprises. The trouble is that continuing privatization (the selling of government-owned businesses to investors) has led to high unemployment. The government justifies this as a necessary part of reform.

20 ● BIBLIOGRAPHY

Bernhardson, Wayne. *Argentina, Uruguay and Paraguay: A Lonely Planet Travel Survival Kit.* 2nd ed. Hawthorn, Australia: Lonely Planet Publications, 1996.

Caistor, Nick. *Argentina.* Austin, Tex.: Steck-Vaughn Library, 1991.

Fox, Geoffrey. *The Land and People of Argentina.* New York: Lippincott, 1990.

Gofen, Ethel. *Argentina.* New York: Marshall Cavendish, 1991.

Jacobsen, Karen. *Argentina.* Chicago: Childrens' Press, 1990.

Liebowitz, Sol. *Argentina.* New York: Chelsea House Publishers, 1990.

Peterson, Marge. *Argentina: A Wild West Heritage.* 2nd ed. Parsippany, N.J.: Dillon Press, 1997.

Sarvis, Shirley. *Woman's Day Home Cooking Around the World.* New York: Simon and Schuster, 1978.

WEBSITE

Interknowledge Corp. [Online] Available http://www.interknowledge.com/argentina/, 1998.

Latin American Alliance. Argentina. [Online] http://www.latinsynergy.org/argentina.html, 1998.

Armenia

Ethnic Armenians make up 93 percent of the population of Armenia. About 3 percent of the population are Azerbaijanis, and Kurds and Russians represent about 2 percent each. For more information on these groups, see the chapter on Azerbaijan in this volume; the article on the Kurds in the chapter on Turkey in Volume 9; and the chapter on Russia in Volume 7.

Armenians

PRONUNCIATON: ahr-MEE-nee-uhns
ALTERNATE NAMES: Hay
LOCATION: Armenia (in the southwest of the former Soviet Union)
POPULATION: 5–7 million
LANGUAGE: Armenian
RELIGION: Armenian Apostolic Church; some American Christian sects

1 ● INTRODUCTION

The exact origins of the Armenian people have been debated by historians. Some believe that Armenians are native to the Anatolian Highlands and the Ararat Valley of west-central Asia. Others believe they migrated there. Their presence, however, was documented before the fifth century BC. Armenia's location, on a major trade route between Europe and Asia, has made it subject to foreign invasion and domination. Throughout its history, the Armenian people have been ruled by many empires, including the Roman, Persian, Byzantine, Russian, and Ottoman.

In the twentieth century, the Armenian people struggled to create an independent homeland. During World War I (1914–18), they were treated as possible enemies when Turkey joined the Central Powers against Russia. In 1915, many Armenians were rounded up and sent to concentration camps in the Syrian desert where as many as one and one-half million were killed. This has come to be known as "the Armenian genocide" and it still deeply affects the character and mind-set of the Armenian people.

In 1936, Armenia became a republic within the Soviet Union. Armenians voted for independence from the Soviet Union in 1991, just months before its collapse in December of that year. The capital, Yerevan, is in the center of country.

Armenians live in the Republic of Armenia. A large Armenian diaspora (a community of people living as refugees) exists in many countries of the world.

Ethnic Armenians make up more than 90 percent of the total population of the Republic of Armenia. Large communities of Azerbaijani Turks and Kurds lived in Armenia until 1988. They left as conflict grew between Armenians and Azeris in the neighboring republic of Azerbaijan. Other minority populations in Armenia include Russians, Greeks, and Jews.

3 ● LANGUAGE

The Armenian language was written for the first time in the early fifth century. Its alphabet was invented by a scribe named Mesrop Mashtots, so that Christian liturgy and scriptures could be translated and written for the Armenian people.

The Armenian language has many dialects, some of which cannot be understood by speakers of other dialects. Two standard printed dialects exist: Western and Eastern. Western Armenian was the dialect of Armenians in the Ottoman Empire and is used by the Armenian diaspora. Eastern Armenian was the dialect of Armenians in the Russian Empire and Iran; it is the official language of the Republic of Armenia. Armenians everywhere think that being able to speak the language is an important part of being Armenian.

4 ● FOLKLORE

Armenian folklore is deeply historical. It draws on centuries of national heroes. Mesrop Mashtots, for example, has often been shown in works of art and in educational

2 ● LOCATION

The Republic of Armenia is located in the southwestern part of the former Soviet Union, and shares borders with Iran to the south, Turkey to the west, Georgia to the north, and Azerbaijan to the east. The country is landlocked, extremely dry, and has very few natural resources. Although the Republic of Armenia's area is only 11,620 square miles (30,100 square kilometers), Armenians have historically occupied a much larger territory. Their culture once spread throughout north- and west-central Asia.

Estimates of the worldwide Armenian population range between five and seven million. About three and one-half million

Common Phrases

English	Pronunciation of Armenian
Good day.	BAH-rev
Hi.	VOKH-tschwin
Yes	AI-yo
No	VOAWCH
Thank you.	schor-ra-KAH-lem
How are you?	EENSCH PAY-sus
Good bye.	hah-DZO-oo-tyoon [or] ste-SEE-oo-tyoon
What's your name?	EENSCH-ay AH-new-nut

and historical writings. Other folk heroes include a mythical King Ara and the fifth-century warrior Vartan Mamikonian, who was martyred defending Armenians against the Persians.

Another body of Armenian folklore is biblical in nature. For example, many people believe that Noah's Ark landed on Mount Ararat—a once-volcanic mountain that sits on the Turkish side of Armenia's western border. Gregory the Illuminator (Grigor Lusavorich) is the saint and popular national hero credited with bringing Christianity to Armenia by converting King Trdat III in AD 301, making him the first ruler to adopt Christianity as a state religion.

5 ● RELIGION

Some people believe that Christianity was introduced in Armenia by the apostles Thaddeus and Bartholomew. But it was not until King Trdat III's conversion that Christianity became the state religion. By the late twentieth century, the Armenian liturgy had not changed much since the Middle Ages.

Not all Armenians are members of the Armenian Apostolic Church, partly due to the pressures of communism in Soviet Armenia. Nevertheless, the Armenian Church has played an important role in preserving the history and culture of its people.

6 ● MAJOR HOLIDAYS

Armenians celebrate major Christian holy days such as Easter and Christmas (which they observe on January 6 followinng the calendar of the Orthodox Church). As elsewhere in the Orthodox world, Christmas is a religious holiday rather than an occasion for elaborate gift-giving as it is in the United States.

Like other people of Europe and North America, Armenians celebrate the New Year on January 1, by going from house to house visiting friends and relatives. Birthdays are celebrated with parties for friends and extended family members. It's customary for the birthday person to give classmates or co-workers a special treat such as chocolate.

Many other happy occasions are celebrated. For example, if someone enjoys very good luck, such as a good grade on an exam or a new job or a new home, it is customary to treat friends and co-workers to a celebration *(magharich)*. On Vardavar, a pre-Christian spring holiday, young boys and teenage men splash water on people passing by in the street. Some people think this is playful fun; others see it as a nuisance.

Each year on April 24, Armenians the world over sadly commemorate the Armenian genocide. On December 7, the anniversary of an earthquake that devastated northern Armenia in 1988, many Armenians visit cemeteries in mourning.

7 ● RITES OF PASSAGE

Major rites of passage in Armenian society include birth, marriage, and death. Birth is celebrated by family and friends, as is a baby's first tooth. This is celebrated by a playful ritual in which the baby is given a number of gifts, such as a pencil and a pair of scissors. The gift that the baby chooses is thought to predict its future career. For example, choosing the pencil might mean that a baby will become a writer or a teacher.

Today, marriages are performed both in church and in state registry offices. The groom's parents give the couple a big party at their home. When the bride and groom enter their home for the first time as a married couple, Armenian flat bread *(lavash)* is placed over their shoulders. For good luck, they then break a small plate by stepping on it. In traditional families, a new bride's parents visit her in her new home on the fortieth day after the marriage and give her a trousseau *(ozhit)*.

Funerals are usually held on the third day after death. The funeral procession includes traditional music. Families commemorate the seventh and fortieth days after death by visiting the cemetery.

8 ● RELATIONSHIPS

Family and friends are very close in Armenia. It is considered polite to visit without an invitation, unlike the custom in the United States where it is considered impolite to visit someone's home unannounced.

As a sign of affection and respect, most social gatherings include toasting (with alcoholic drinks) each other's families, health, and good luck.

Armenians greet one another with handshakes or with kisses on the cheek. Women and men alike show physical affection with friends of the same sex. It is as common to see two men walking down the street arm-in-arm as it is to see two women doing so. Teenage boys and girls date one another, usually going to the movies or talking together in coffeehouses.

9 ● LIVING CONDITIONS

More than one-third of the population lives in Yerevan, the capital. Another third lives in other industrial and urban areas. The remaining third lives in villages of varying sizes across the country.

In urban Armenia, most families live in apartment buildings ranging from four to fifteen stories high. By American standards, apartments are small. They consist of a kitchen, living room, separate bathroom, one or two bedrooms, and perhaps a balcony. Children and grandparents rarely have their own bedrooms. They sleep together on beds or sofas in the living room or balcony. Parents sleep together in the bedroom, sometimes with one or more children.

In villages, many Armenians have private houses, ranging in size from two rooms with a kitchen to very large houses with many rooms. Village homes may have small farming plots and small barns where cows, pigs, chickens, goats, and sheep are kept.

© Corel Corporation

Street scene in the capital city of Yerevan. Urban Armenians dress much like people in other European cities.

Compared with other republics of the former Soviet Union, Armenians enjoy a wide variety of goods and services, such as public transportation, telephones, indoor running water, and electricity.

10 ● FAMILY LIFE

In cities, towns, and villages alike, adults live with their parents even after marriage. A new bride will move into her husband's parents' home. Children care for their parents in old age, and grandparents play a large role in raising their grandchildren. Siblings and cousins play together as children, and usually remain close throughout adulthood.

In villages and towns, marriages are sometimes arranged by older relatives and friends. Divorce and remarriage is far less common in Armenia than in the United States. Armenians have large families, although the birthrate has declined recently.

11 ● CLOTHING

For more than one hundred years, urban Armenians have dressed like other urban peoples of Europe. Jeans are popular with young people.

Traditional costumes for both men and women include baggy pants worn under long shifts or overcoats. These costumes are worn for special cultural celebrations and

© Corel Corporation

Produce market in Yerevan, the capital of Armenia.

dances. Distinctive regional accessories include sheepskin hats, engraved metal belts, and jewelry, sometimes made of coins. Women traditionally wear their hair in two long braids.

12 ● FOOD

Armenians eat many of the same foods as other former Soviet peoples, including beet soup *(borscht)*; roasted meat *(khorovadz* or *shashlik)*; potatoes; and stews. Other Armenian delicacies are fresh trout from Lake Sevan; grapevine leaves stuffed with rice, ground meat, and herbs *(dolma)*; flat bread *(lavash)*; chicken porridge *(harissa)*; and yogurt *(madzun)*.

13 ● EDUCATION

Armenia has its own state education system. School begins with kindergarten and lasts through the equivalent of American high school, with a total of thirteen grades. Armenia has a large number of technical and vocational training schools and an American University with English-language graduate programs in business, engineering, political science, and health. There are seven colleges, including the historic Yere-

Recipe

Lahmajoun
(Armenian Pizza)

Ingredients

8 lavash (Armenia flat breads), or 4 pita breads, split to separate into two flat circles
6 Tablespoons tomato paste
1 eight-ounce can of chopped tomatoes
½ pound ground beef
½ pound ground lamb
1 onion, chopped
2 cloves garlic, chopped
1 two-ounce jar chopped pimentos

Directions

1. Preheat oven to 375°F.
2. Place lavash rounds (or split pita rounds) on cookie sheet. Try not to overlap.
3. Using a wooden spoon, mix all the other ingredients together in a mixing bowl.
4. Spread mixture over the lavash.
5. Bake in oven for 20 minutes, or until the edges of the lavash begin to brown and the meat is cooked through.
6. Cut each pizza into wedges and serve while warm.

Adapted from Webb, Lois Sinaiko. *Holidays of the World Cookbook for Students.* Phoenix, Ariz.: Oryx Press, 1995.

van State University, and the State Engineering Univeristy of Armenia.

14 ● CULTURAL HERITAGE

Armenia has rich traditions of church music and folk music. Choral arrangements by the Armenian composer Komitas (1869–1935) were inspired by both folksongs and liturgical music and are still extremely popular today. Folk music performed on traditional instruments and twentieth-century Armenian pop music (called *Rabiz*) are also popular.

Since the language was first written in the fourth century, an enormous amount of literature exists, including religious texts, histories, epics, poetry, drama, political writings, and modern novels. Armenia also has opera, ballet, folk dance, and cinema. Armenians of all ages take great interest in their musical, literary, and artistic traditions, which are important influences in popular culture today.

Armenians have contributed to international cultural traditions in literature, painting, architecture, music, politics, and science. Novelist William Saroyan, tennis player Andre Agassi, physicist Victor Hambartsumian, and composer Aram Khachaturian are a few examples of Armenians who have made valuable contributions in their fields.

15 ● EMPLOYMENT

Work in Armenia is much like work in other industrialized countries. Clothing manufacturing, shoemaking, and computer technology are among Armenia's light industries. Chemical industries include the production of neoprene rubber.

Women make up a large proportion of the work force as teachers, doctors, musicians, physicists, researchers, factory workers, and governmental and nongovernmental administrators.

In rural Armenia, farmers work the land and care for livestock. Rural women do domestic work. Even the smallest towns and villages have schools, regional government representation, shops, and other kinds of non-agricultural employment.

16 ● SPORTS

In the late twentieth century, Armenians received Olympic gold medals in wrestling, weight-lifting, and boxing. Skiing and tennis are also popular sports, but soccer is perhaps the most popular. The Armenian soccer team, Ararat, was the champion of the Soviet Union in 1973.

17 ● RECREATION

Armenian entertainment includes movies, music, and traditional and modern dance. The Armenian symphony in Yerevan gives weekly performances that draw large crowds of all ages to the Opera House, which also hosts national operas and ballets. Armenian men like to play backgammon and chess at home and in city parks when the weather is nice. Armenians of all ages enjoy walks and visits to outdoor cafes. In the summer, the most popular forms of relaxation are trips to the beach at Lake Sevan and picnics in the countryside, where they roast meat and vegetables over open fires.

18 ● CRAFTS AND HOBBIES

Popular Armenian folk art includes woodworking, stone-carving, metalworking and jewelry, painting, embroidery, and rug-weaving. Even the modern production of small salt dishes (*aghamanner*) may incorporate ancient symbols. There are several museums that feature folk arts and crafts, and an art fair known as *Vernissage* is held in Yerevan every weekend. Vernissage appeals not only to tourists, but also to local artists and the general public.

19 ● SOCIAL PROBLEMS

The main social problem in Armenia is its tense relationship with its neighbor Azerbaijan. There is a large Armenian section of Azerbaijan in which Armenians form a majority of the population but where they are treated as second-class citizens. Complicating the situation is the fact that Armenians are largely Christians and the people of Azerbaijan are mostly Muslim. There was a short but violent war fought in the early 1990s, followed by several years of uneasy peace.

20 ● BIBLIOGRAPHY

Bakalian, Anny. *Armenian-Americans: From Being to Feeling Armenian.* New Brunswick, N.J.: Transaction Books, 1993.

Bournoutian, George. *A History of the Armenian People.* Vol. I. Costa Mesa, Calif.: Mazda Publishers, 1993.

Bournoutian, George. *A History of the Armenian People.* Vol. II. Costa Mesa, Calif.: Mazda Publishers, 1994.

Lang, David Marshall. *The Armenians.* London: Unwin Paperbacks, 1988.

Walker, Christopher. *Armenia.* New York: St. Martin's Press, 1990.

WEBSITES

Embassy of Armenia, Washington, D.C. [Online] Available http://www.armeniaemb.org/, 1998.

World Travel Guide. Armenia. [Online] Available http://www.wtgoline.com/country/am/gen.html, 1998.

Australia

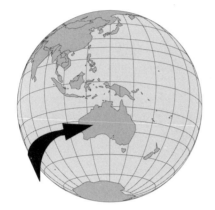

Most Australians (94 percent) are of British or Irish ancestry. About 5 percent of the population is of Asian descent. Approximately 1 percent of the population is of native Australian, or aboriginal, origin. This chapter has articles on the Anglo-Australians (British or Irish origin), and on Austrialia's native population, the Aborigines.

Australians

PRONUNCIATION: aw-STRAY-lee-uhns
LOCATION: Australia
POPULATION: 18 million
LANGUAGE: English
RELIGION: Christianity (majority); Islam; Buddhism; Judaism

1 ● INTRODUCTION

Australia is relatively young as a country, but it is a very ancient land. For over 40,000 years Aboriginal people lived in harmony there with their environment. When England first settled Australia in 1788, however, and made it a penal colony for its overcrowded prison population, all that was to change.

Today, Australia is considered a "settler colony," a term used to describe countries like Australia, New Zealand, Canada, and the United States: countries originally colonized by the British and where the indigenous (native) peoples were almost completely wiped out.

2 ● LOCATION

Australia is both a continent and an island, situated in the southern hemisphere between the Pacific and Indian oceans. It measures about the same in area as the United States (excluding Alaska), yet it has a population of only 18 million people. Of those 18 million people, 80 percent live in just ten cities, all by the sea. By far the largest of these cities are Sydney and Melbourne.

Because the country was first settled by England in 1788, most Australians are of English origin. Until the end of World War II (1939–45), some 90 percent of Australians were born there, and about 9 percent were immigrants from Britain. However, after the war ended, the country took in

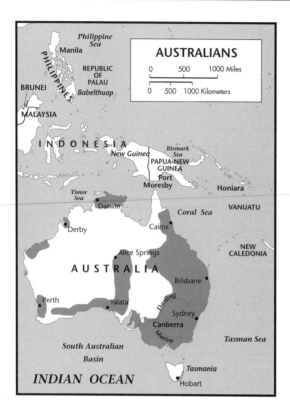

their high standard of living, they are part of the industrialized world.

Australians describe themselves as hearty and self-reliant. This feeling comes from having conquered a sometimes brutal landscape. They also see themselves as distinct because of their history of being founded as a penal colony. This means that the first settlers were prisoners from English jails. This creates a feeling of rebelliousness. Australians have almost a sense of being the "black sheep" of the English-speaking world.

5 ● RELIGION

Australia is a predominantly Christian country. In the 1990s, most people were Anglican, and the second-largest number were Catholic.

6 ● MAJOR HOLIDAYS

Apart from those holidays celebrated throughout the Western world, such as Christmas and Easter, Australia celebrates some of its own. Anzac Day on April 25 honors Australians who died in all wars. ("Anzac" stands for the Australian and New Zealand Army Corps.) Australia Day is celebrated on January 26. This was the day in 1788 when the English soldiers raised their flag and declared Australia a new colony. Today, it is celebrated with street fairs, parties, picnics, and fireworks. It coincides with the last days of the long summer vacation from school and is a fun time for families.

Boxing Day (December 26) is also a public holiday in Australia. It is known as a traditional day to spend at the beach. In practical terms it makes for a longer Christ-

more than 5 million immigrants from Europe. In the 1970s and 1980s, Australia was a major recipient of refugees from the wars in Vietnam and Cambodia. Aboriginal Australians (native people) make up about one percent of the total Australian population.

3 ● LANGUAGE

The language of Australia is English, brought by the first English settlers.

4 ● FOLKLORE

The folklore of the Australians is essentially the same as the folklore of British colonialists everywhere. Australians see themselves as part of European culture and, because of

mas break. Its name comes from the old English custom of giving boxed gifts to employees.

7 ● RITES OF PASSAGE

Many of the rites of passage among Australians center around schooling. When students are in the twelfth grade they attend a senior school dance called the formal. This is like the American tradition of prom night. Students hire limousines to attend a formal function sponsored by their school, usually held at a somewhat glamorous location.

The eighteenth birthday party is a large, peer-group party celebrating entry into the adult world. At age eighteen, the young adult is given all legal rights. The twenty-first birthday celebration, a much more traditional family-and-friend celebration party, is often held in a hotel or restaurant. Gifts are traditionally given, and this celebration often marks the time the young person leaves home to live independently.

8 ● RELATIONSHIPS

Men shake hands when introduced to each other or to a woman. Women often greet other women with a kiss on the cheek.

Pub life—the sharing of drinks with friends at a bar—plays a large role in most Australians' social lives. When invited to dinner, guests are usually asked to come at "7:30 for 8:30." This means guests should arrive somewhere between 7:30 and 8:30 PM for pre-dinner drinks, with dinner to be served at 8:30.

Young people in Australia usually begin dating around age fourteen or fifteen. They

Cory Langley
Children in Australia begin kindergarten at age five.

make their own choices of friends and partners in life. They tend to marry in their mid-twenties.

9 ● LIVING CONDITIONS

Australia has one of the highest levels of home ownership in the world. The most popular home is the freestanding brick house with a red tiled roof, a front lawn, and a back garden. Australia does not have the extremes of wealth and poverty that the United States does. There are few extravagant mansions or slums. Instead, homes tend to be more like those found in a typical American middle-class suburb. Young people in cities live in flats (apartments) or townhouses close to the inner city, where there is a great deal of nightlife.

Cory Langley

Australian boy feeding wallabies in a nature preserve. Australian wildlife includes many unique birds and animals.

Australia has a national health service called Medicare, under which medical and hospital treatments are free to all.

10 ● FAMILY LIFE

Family life in Australia is changing. The nuclear family unit of two parents and two children, with the father in the workforce and the mother at home, is becoming a thing of the past. Today, more than half of the adult female population works outside the home, though many work part-time. The divorce rate is also on the rise. There are more single-parent families today than in the past. Relationships within the family are relaxed, with everyone helping with chores.

However, most of the household responsibilities still fall upon the woman.

11 ● CLOTHING

Australia's temperatures are generally far warmer that those found in the United States. Australians favor easy-to-wear, light clothing in the summer. To stay cool, many Australians wear long socks and long tailored shorts instead of slacks. This is acceptable apparel even in the workplace. Clothing styles are a mixture of European and American fashions. People tend to dress stylishly in the city and at the office but wear jeans and sneakers on the weekends.

All school children wear uniforms. School caps are now standard. These are usually "legionnaire"-style cloth caps with a flap covering the back of the neck for protection from the sun.

12 ● FOOD

Good seafood is abundant along Australia's coastline and is very popular. Australians also eat a lot of meat, especially beef or lamb roasts. The influx of European and Asian immigrants over the past twenty to thirty years has led Australians to enjoy foods from all cultures. Australian families now incorporate Chinese, Thai, or Indian foods into their weekly meal planning. European foods, particularly Greek and Italian, have always been favorites.

One food remains an Australian tradition—a black spread called Vegemite. This is made from yeast extract and salt, and is spread on toast with butter for breakfast or is eaten in sandwiches for lunch. All children are brought up eating Vegemite from infancy. The other famous Australian food is meat pie. Approximately 260 million meat pies are eaten by Australians every year.

Favorite desserts include the Australian Pavlova—a cake-sized, soft meringue filled with fruits and cream. Also popular are small treats called Lamingtons. These are sponge-cake cubes coated with chocolate and grated coconut.

13 ● EDUCATION

School children enter kindergarten at about age five. Primary school covers grades one to six. High school consists of middle school (grades seven to ten) and senior

Recipe

Pavlova

Ingredients

4 egg whites
1 cup white sugar
2 teaspoons cornstarch
2 teaspoons vinegar
3 to 4 cups sliced fruit: may include bananas, crushed pineapple, strawberries, kiwi
Whipped cream

Directions

1. Butter an 8-inch cake pan. Cut a circle of waxed paper to fit the bottom of the pan. Place it in the pan and butter it, too. Dust the waxed paper and the sides of the pan with a little cornstarch.

2. Beat the egg whites in a large mixing bowl until stiff. Gradually beat in the sugar until the mixture is glossy and stiff.

3. Combine the cornstarch and vinegar and mix carefully into the egg-white mixture, using a folding motion with a rubber spatula.

4. Spoon the meringue into the cake pan, smoothing it around the edges but leaving a well in the center to hold the fruit.

5. Preheat the oven to 300°F. Place the pan into the oven, and immediately turn the temperature down to 250°F. Bake for about one hour, turn the oven off, and allow the meringue to cool in the oven with the door ajar.

6. Carefully remove from the pan and peel off the waxed paper from the bottom of the meringue. Place on a serving tray.

7. Fill with fruit, top with generous amount of whipped cream, and serve.

school (grades eleven and twelve). School is mandatory through the tenth grade.

At the end of the twelfth grade, when students are about eighteen years old, they take a public exam called the Higher School Certificate. From this exam alone, the student is ranked amongst all others in the country. The results of this test determine which university, if any, the student may enter. The results also determine which course of study to follow.

If the student does not plan to enter a university, he or she needs the exam to enter any other higher education institution or to get a job. This is a very stressful exam for the student.

University entrance is extremely competitive. Fees are very low by U.S. standards. Until the 1980s all university courses were free.

14 ● CULTURAL HERITAGE

Australia has an important film industry. In the 1980s and 1990s it produced such hits as *Babe*, *Muriel's Wedding*, *Mad Max*, and *Crocodile Dundee*. Sydney's Opera House is world-famous, designed by the Danish architect Utzen to resemble sails on the ocean. It houses the Australian Opera Company, theaters, concert halls, and restaurants, and attracts hundreds of thousands of tourists each year.

The country has wonderful wildlife and many natural attractions. The Great Barrier Reef, an underwater coral ridge, is one of these. It is the longest and most complex living system in the world. Another natural attraction is the beautiful Kakadu National Park. This park has 275 bird species and many ancient examples of Aboriginal folk art. It is classified by the United Nations Educational, Scientific and Cultural Organization (UNESCO) as a world heritage area.

Also classified as a world heritage area is Ayers Rock—a giant, red rock sacred to the Aborigines. The rock stands majestically in the middle of the desert.

15 ● EMPLOYMENT

In the 1990s, the average working Australian earned $525 a week. Full-time workers usually receive four weeks' annual vacation. They belong to investment plans that will give them income when they retire.

The working week is Monday to Friday, 9:00 AM to 5:00 PM. Workers' rights are protected by numerous laws, and Australia has an active union system. As of the late 1990s, there is an unemployment rate of 10 percent, which is of great concern to the government.

16 ● SPORTS

Australians love sports—both playing and watching them on television. The all-time favorite is football (soccer). Australians follow three different types, depending on which part of the country they come from. Another sport played by many children and adults is cricket, brought to Australia in the 1800s by British settlers.

Other popular sports include swimming, tennis, surfing, and sailing. However, the fastest-growing new sport in Australia today is baseball. Some players make it into the American major leagues.

EPD Photos

Schoolboy practices his cricket skills.

17 ● RECREATION

In the cities, many forms of entertainment are offered. Theaters, movies, bars, and discos, plus every type of restaurant imaginable, are common. Australians enjoy a pub life similar to that found in England. But mostly they enjoy the ocean. On summer weekends the beaches are packed with surfers, and the harbors are full of boats of all types.

Sunday afternoon barbecues at home are very popular. Traditionally, friends arrive around 2:00 PM for a barbecue lunch. The host cooks steaks, sausages, or seafood on a grill; friends talk, eat, and drink into the evening. Entertainment in Australia is mostly relaxed and informal. Of course, there is television. Statistics for 1993 showed that most Australians spent twelve hours per week watching TV.

Many Australians enjoy gambling, especially on horse races. The final horse race of the year—the Melbourne Cup—takes place on the first Tuesday of each November, at exactly 3:00 PM. This event brings the country to a standstill. It is even broadcast live over loudspeakers in most offices. Almost everyone has a small bet on the outcome.

18 ● CRAFTS AND HOBBIES

Australian hobbies are very similar to those pursued by people in the United States, and are just as varied.

19 ● SOCIAL PROBLEMS

Australia has yet to deal fairly with its Aboriginal population, whose standard of living is far lower than that of the rest of the population, and whose infant death rate is very high. The Aborigines have been victims of neglect by the authorities, though efforts are finally being made to improve Aboriginal life.

As Australia moves toward the year 2000, the question of when and how to become a republic (an independent parliamentary democracy without a royal head of state) is constantly debated. Australia is still part of the British Commonwealth, but by popular demand it may eventually break all formal ties with England and become a republic.

Immigration is a further concern. Many people feel that Australia cannot support too many more people, because of the nature of the land. Others are concerned that the country is becoming multicultural too fast. It is an issue that divides the country.

20 ● BIBLIOGRAPHY

Coppell, Bill. *Australia in Fact and Fiction.* Sydney: Penguin Books, 1994.

Cue, Kerry. *Australia Unbuttoned.* Sydney: Penguin Books, 1996.

Dale, David. *The 100 Things Everyone Needs to Know About Australia.* Sydney: Pan Macmillan, 1996.

Roberts, A., and C. P. Mountford. *Legends of the Dreamtime.* Sydney: International Limited Editions, 1975.

WEBSITES

Australian Tourist Commission. [Online] Available http://www.aussie.net.au, 1998.

Embassy of Australia, Washington, D.C. [Online] Available http://www.austemb.org/, 1998.

World Travel Guide. Australia. [Online] Available http://www.wtgonline.com/country/au/index.html, 1998.

Australian Aborigines

PRONUNCIATION: aw-STRAY-lee-uhn ab-or-RIDGE-in-eez
LOCATION: Australia; Tasmania
POPULATION: Approximately 265,000
LANGUAGE: Western Desert language; English; Walpiri and other Aboriginal languages
RELIGION: traditional Aboriginal religion; Christianity

1 ● INTRODUCTION

The original inhabitants of the continent of Australia took up residence there at least 40,000 years before Europeans landed at Botany Bay in 1788. In 1788, the Aborigines were clearly the majority, numbering around 300,000. In the late 1990s, they were a minority struggling to claim rights to their traditional lands. They also seek money for lost lands and resources. Relations between Aboriginal and non-Aboriginal inhabitants of Australia have not been very good. There is a great deal of resentment on the part of many Aboriginal people for the treatment their ancestors received from the European colonists. Australian Aborigines face many of the same problems that Native Americans face in the United States.

2 ● LOCATION

Australian Aborigines traditionally lived throughout Australia and on the island of Tasmania. In the Central and Western Desert regions of Australia, Aboriginal groups were nomadic hunters and gatherers. They had no permanent place of residence, although they did have territories and ate whatever they could either catch, kill, or dig out of the ground. In the southern parts of the island continent, winter is cold and Aboriginal populations had to shelter themselves from the cold wind and driving rain.

3 ● LANGUAGE

There were approximately three hundred different Aboriginal languages spoken in 1788. Now, there are only about seventy-five remaining. Some of these, like Walpiri, spoken in and around Alice Springs in the center of the continent, are well established and in no danger of being lost. Walpiri is taught in schools, and a growing body of written literature is produced daily in the language. Other languages such as Dyribal are nearly extinct.

The largest language in terms of number of speakers is called the Western Desert language, spoken by several thousand Aboriginal people in the Western Desert region of the continent.

Most Aboriginal people speak English as their first or second language. In parts of Australia, distinctive kinds of English have developed within Aboriginal communities. In the Northern Territory there is a kind of English called Kriol that is spoken by Aboriginal people.

4 ● FOLKLORE

Over their long history, a complex and rich Aboriginal mythology has evolved. It has been passed down from generation to generation. This mythology is known as the Dreamtime (Alchera) Legends. The Dreamtime is the mystical time during which the Aborigines' ancestors established their world. These myths from ancient times are accepted as a record of absolute truth. They dominate the cultural life of the people.

There are many myths of the Dreamtime. One tells how the sun was made:

Long ago in Dreamtime there was no sun, and the people had to search for food in the dim light of the moon. One day, an emu and a crane started quarreling. In a rage, the crane ran to the emu's nest and snatched one of its huge eggs. She flung the egg high into the sky, where it shattered and the yolk burst into flames. This caused such a huge fire that its light revealed for the first time the beauty of the world below.

When the spirits up in the sky saw this great beauty, they decided that the inhabit-

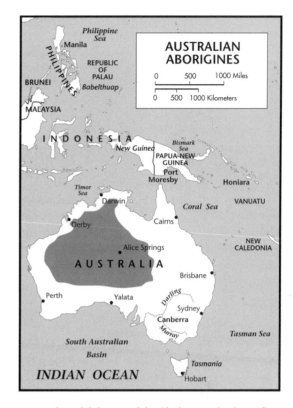

ants should have this light each day. So, every night, the sky-people collected a pile of dry wood, ready to be set afire as soon as the morning star appeared. But a problem arose. If the day was cloudy, the star could not be seen and no one lit the fire. So the sky people asked the Kookaburra, who had a loud, braying laugh, to call them every morning. When the bird's laugh was first heard, the fire in the sky was lit but threw out little heat or light. By noon, when all the wood was burning, the heat was more intense. Later, the fire slowly died down until the sun had set.

It is a strict rule of the Aboriginal tribes that nobody may imitate the Kookaburra's call, because that could offend the bird and it could remain silent. Then darkness would

The religious world of the Aboriginal Australians is inhabited by ghosts of the dead, as well as a variety of spirits who control certain aspects of the natural world, such as the Rainbow Serpent, who brings rain. Rituals are performed to placate these spirits and also to increase the fertility of certain species of animals that are important to the Aborigines.

Since the colonization of Australia, many Aboriginal people have converted to Christianity, either by choice or through the influence of education in mission schools. For generations, European colonists would remove children from Aboriginal families and send them to Christian schools. This practice was thought to be in the best interests of the Aborigines. Resentment over these kidnappings is still strong.

Cynthia Bassett

Australian Aboriginal woman seated in front of a mural.

again descend upon the earth and its inhabitants.

5 ● RELIGION

Traditional Aboriginal religion revolves around the Dreamtime. Totems are also an important part of Aboriginal religious identity. Totems are symbols from the natural world that serve to identify people and their relationships with one another in the social world. For instance, a family or clan may be associated with a certain bird. That bird's nature, whether it is ferocious or peaceful, a bird of prey or a songbird, is associated with the family or clan that uses it as its totem.

6 ● MAJOR HOLIDAYS

As part of the larger Australian society, Australian Aborigines can participate in major holidays. Australia Day, January 26, is the equivalent of Independence Day in the United States. This holiday is often the occasion of public protests on the part of Aboriginal people. Many Aboriginal people participated in major protests during the Australian Bicentennial in 1988. Traditional Aboriginal society, however, has no such holidays.

7 ● RITES OF PASSAGE

In some Aboriginal societies, there were both male and female rituals that marked the passage from childhood to adulthood.

Death in Aboriginal Australian societies was accompanied by complex rituals. Among the Walpiri of central Australia, a wife would have to isolate herself from the rest of the community upon the death of her husband. She would live in a "widows' camp" for a period of one to two years. During that time she would communicate through a system of sign language. She was not permitted to speak during this period. If a woman chose not to follow these traditions, her husband's ghost could steal her soul, which would lead to her death.

8 ● RELATIONSHIPS

Behavior and interpersonal relations among Australian Aboriginals are defined by family roles. In many Aboriginal societies, certain kinfolk stand in what are called "avoidance relationships" with each other. For instance, in some groups a son-in-law must avoid his mother-in-law completely. Individuals will often change course entirely and go out of their way to avoid meeting a prohibited in-law. In other types of relationships, a son-in-law can only speak to his mother-in-law by way of a special language, called "mother-in-law language." The opposite of avoidance relationships are "joking relationships." These are relationships between potential spouses that typically involve joking about sexual topics.

Aboriginal people find it odd that non-Aboriginal people say "thank you" all the time. Aboriginal social organization is based on a set of obligations between individuals who are related by blood or marriage. Such obligations do not require any thanks. For example, if a family asks to share a relative's food, the relative is obligated to share without any expectation of gratitude in response. Australians often see this Aboriginal behavior as rude.

9 ● LIVING CONDITIONS

Health care is a major problem for most Aboriginal people. For rural groups, access to health care may be extremely limited. In precolonial times, they would have relied on traditional health practices to cure illness and limit disease. However, through European influence, many rural societies have lost knowledge of traditional medicine and have come to rely on Western medicine, which is not always available to them.

Housing varies between urban and rural Aboriginal people. The national, state, and local governments have encouraged nomadic groups to settle in houses in the European manner. They have built houses for some groups that live in the desert regions of central and western Australia. Aboriginal people have adapted these structures to their own design. They use them for storage, but usually regard them as too small and too hot for eating, sleeping, or entertaining.

10 ● FAMILY LIFE

Marriage in traditional Aboriginal societies is complicated. Its customs have interested and puzzled anthropologists for centuries. In many societies, first marriages were arranged. Husbands were often much older than their wives.

Among the Tiwi of the Melville and Bathurst islands off the northern coast of Australia, females were betrothed at birth. Females in this society were always married. This practice was related to the Tiwi belief that females became impregnated by spirits. Human males were not understood to be a part of reproduction. However, Tiwi society also required that every individual have a "social father." Social fathers were husbands of children's mothers. They were necessary because the spirits that impregnated the women could not help raise the children.

11 ● CLOTHING

Australian Aborigines were one of the only groups of people in the world not to wear any type of clothing. Both men and women went naked. Today, of course, things have changed considerably and Aboriginals dress the same as Australians.

12 ● FOOD

Since many Aboriginal groups were nomadic hunters and gatherers, they did little in the area of food preparation. Meals were simple, as was their preparation.

13 ● EDUCATION

Most urban Aboriginal children have the opportunity to attend public school. They often encounter discrimination in the classroom, however. Some communities have developed their own programs to help Aboriginal children succeed in the educational system.

At Yuendumu in central Australia, the Walpiri have a very well developed educational system. It provides both European-style education and education in the areas of traditional language and culture. As is the case for Australians, school is mandatory through the tenth grade. Grades eleven and twelve are optional.

EPD Photos

This student, not an Australian Aboriginal, tries to produce the low tone of the Aboriginal dijeridoo by pursing his lips and blowing through the end. The instrument features carving along its entire length.

14 ● CULTURAL HERITAGE

Traditional Aboriginal societies were nomadic. Because of this, they did not value material objects. They also did not develop many musical instruments.

One that is well-known is the *dijeridoo*, a long tube made from a piece of wood that has been hollowed out by termites. These long trumpets produce a drone that accompanies ritual dancing. Dijeridoos have become popular instruments in modern world music. A few Aboriginal people teach dijeridoo to non-Aboriginal people who want to learn to play it.

In many Aboriginal societies men used a "bullroarer" to frighten women and uninitiated males at ceremonial events. The bullroarer is a decorated and shaped piece of flat wood. It is attached to a line and swung around above a person's head to produce a whirring sound. The sound is usually said to be the voice of important spirits of the land. Unlike their Oceanic neighbors, Australian Aborigines did not use drums.

Dance is an extremely important part of Aboriginal ceremonial life. Many dances mimic the movements and behaviors of animals such as the brolga crane of the northern wetlands. There are several performance troupes in Australia that travel to urban centers to perform both traditional and new dances.

15 ● EMPLOYMENT

In traditional Aboriginal societies, labor was divided according to age and sex. Women and children were responsible for gathering vegetables, fruit, and small game such as *goannas* (a large lizard). Men were responsible for obtaining meat by hunting both large and small game. Men in Aranda society hunted with a variety of implements including spears, spear throwers, and nonreturning boomerangs.

Aboriginal people in urban areas are employed in a variety of jobs. However, gaining employment is often difficult due to discrimination.

16 ● SPORTS

Rugby, Australian-rules football (soccer), and cricket are important spectator and participant sports in Australia. Basketball is a fast-growing sport. Aboriginal people play for some of the semiprofessional rugby teams.

17 ● RECREATION

In some parts of Australia, Aboriginal people have established their own broadcasting stations for radio and television. These have been most successful in the central region of Australia, in and around Alice Springs.

In these communities, elders have realized that if they do not provide programming for their youth, the youth will turn away from the traditional ways of life. Aboriginal bands also produce music videos for these programs, as well as for distribution to the larger Australian society.

18 ● CRAFTS AND HOBBIES

Australian Aboriginal art has been extremely popular on the world art market for some time now. The paintings of "dreamings" from the Central Desert region bring a high price, especially if the artist is one of the well-known Aboriginal artists. In the Walpiri community of Yuendumu, the elders decided to paint the doors of the classrooms of the school with various "dreamings." Boomerangs, decorated with stylistic Aboriginal symbols, are popular with tourists. According to Aboriginal legend, the boomerang was created by the snake, Bobbi-bobbi. According to this tale, Bobbi-bobbi sent flying foxes (perhaps like bats) for men to eat, but they flew too high to be caught. Bobbi-bobbi gave one of his ribs to be used as a weapon. Because of its shape, it always returned to the person who threw it. Using the boomerang as a weapon, men were able to cause the flying foxes to fall to earth. But the men became overconfident in their use of the boomerang, and threw it so hard that it crashed through the sky, creating a large hole. Bobbi-bobbi was angry when he learned of this, and he took back his rib when it fell back to earth.

19 ● SOCIAL PROBLEMS

Keeping the right to pursue traditional ways of life is one of the biggest social problems facing Aboriginal people. To pursue traditional lifestyles, Aboriginal language and folklore must be maintained. Many Aboriginal communities have hired teachers to help in the efforts to preserve the traditional language for future generations. There are more languages in need of preservation, however, than there are teachers willing to help preserve them.

Life in urban areas, where the standard of living is very low, has bred a high level of domestic violence and alcoholism among Aborigines. In an attempt to reverse this trend, some older males have "kidnapped" young men and taken them off to traditional lands. Once removed from the city, they are enrolled in a kind of "scared straight" rehabilitation program. There have been mixed reactions to this kind of behavior, both within Aboriginal society and in the larger Australian society.

20 ● BIBLIOGRAPHY

Bell, Diane. *Daughters of the Dreaming*. Minneapolis: University of Minnesota Press, 1993.

Berndt, R. M., and C. H. Berndt. *The World of the First Australians*. Sydney: Ure Smith, 1964.

Contested Ground: Australian Aborigines Under the British Crown. St. Leonards, Australia: Allen & Unwin, 1995.

Hiatt, Lester R. *Arguments About Aborigines: Australia and the Evolution of Social Anthropology*. New York: Cambridge University Press, 1996.

Holmes, Sandra Le Brun. *The Goddess and the Moon Man: The Sacred Art of the Tiwi Aborigines*. Roseville East, Australia: Craftsman House, 1995.

In the Age of Mabo: History, Aborigines, and Australia. St. Leonards, Australia: Allen & Unwin, 1996.

Kohen, James L. *Aboriginal Environmental Impacts*. Sydney, Australia: University of New South Wales Press, 1995.

WEBSITES

Australian Tourist Commission. [Online] Available http://www.aussie.net.au, 1998.

Embassy of Australia, Washington, D.C. [Online] Available http://www.austemb.org/, 1998.

Wood, Shana. Austalian History. [Online] Available http://www.iinet.net.au/~adan/shana, 1996.

World Travel Guide. Australia. [Online] Available http://www.wtgonline.com/country/au/index.html, 1998.

Austria

The people of Austria are called Austrians. Austrians are of mixed European origin.

Austrians

PRONUNCIATION: AH-stree-uhns
LOCATION: Austria
POPULATION: 7.5 million
LANGUAGE: German; Italian, Slovene, Croatian, Hungarian, and Czech in the border provinces; English
RELIGION: Roman Catholicism; Protestantism

1 ● INTRODUCTION

Located in the center of Europe, Austria has exercised great military and economic power for much of its history. The Celts (Western Europeans) settled in Austria in the middle of the first millennium BC. They called the area *Ostarrichi*—the empire in the East. The Celts were followed by Romans and Germanic and Slavic tribes. Around AD 1000 the Babenburger dynasty helped establish Christianity throughout the area. In 1278, Austria's most well-known period of history began when the Hapsburg monarchy came into power. With its capital city in Vienna, the Hapsburg Empire ruled over much of Europe for more than six hundred years and expanded both through war and marriage.

The Hapsburgs were defeated in World War I (1914–18) and their empire was taken apart. Once occupying an area as large as Texas, the newly created Republic of Austria had shrunk to approximately the size of Maine. In 1938, Austria was invaded by Nazi Germany under Adolf Hitler. Following Germany's defeat in World War II (1939–45), Austria was governed by the Allied powers (the nations that fought against Germany in World War II, including the United States) until 1955. It then returned to independence. In 1994 Austria was officially approved for membership in the European Community (EC).

2 ● LOCATION

A landlocked country, three-fourths of Austria is mountainous. The Alps, divided into three mountain ranges, are located mostly in western and central Austria. Passes through the mountains make Austria an important crossroads between different parts of

AUSTRIANS

| 0 | 100 | 200 | 300 Miles |
| 0 | 100 | 200 | 300 Kilometers |

3 ● LANGUAGE

Nearly ninety-nine percent of Austrians speak German, although at least four different dialects are in use. In the border provinces, Italian, Slovene, Croatian, Hungarian, and Czech are also spoken. Many people in large cities and resort areas speak English. Although Austrians speak German, certain Austrian words used in cooking differ from those used in Germany, reflecting Austria's diverse ethnic past. These include *Zwetschken* (plums) from the Bohemian *svestka, Palatschinken* (pancakes) from the Hungarian *palacsinta,* and *kafetier,* from the French term for a coffee-house owner. Some common terms as they are spoken in Austria appear below:

ENGLISH	GERMAN	PRONUNCIATION
Good day	Grüss Gott!	grOOS gott
yes	ja	yAH
no	na	nAH
thank you	danke	DAHN-kah
Bye!	Servus!	SAIR-voos
potato	Erdäpfel	AYRD-ahb-fell
chimney	Rauchfank	ROWKH-fahnk

4 ● FOLKLORE

The great German epic, *Das Niebelungenlied,* was written in Austria around AD 1250. It combined mythical warrior gods and goddesses of Teutonic (ancient northern European) times with real stories of court life in the Middle Ages. Vienna's Museum für Volkskunde houses exhibits on Austrian folklore.

5 ● RELIGION

Austria's capital city of Vienna was also the capital of the Holy Roman Empire. Roman Catholicism is still the dominant religion in Austria, practiced by 89 percent of Austri-

Europe. The remainder of Austria has varied terrain consisting of foothills, lowlands, plains, plateaus, and the fertile Danube River Valley.

Austria's population is now seven and one-half million, mostly German-speaking Catholic people. The only significant ethnic minorities are Slovenes, Croats, and small numbers of Czechs and Hungarians. World War II destroyed most of Austria's Jewish population, formerly a significant ethnic group in Austria.

About half of the Austrians live in cities and towns of more than ten thousand people. One-fifth of Austrians live in Vienna. The main population trends in recent times have been a shift from country to city areas and a migration from east to west.

ans. Catholic churches, shrines, monasteries, and cathedrals can be seen throughout the country. Other signs of religious faith that can be seen are roofed crosses and covered posts decorated with religious scenes. In the countryside, religious festivals, processions, and pageants take place throughout the year. In city areas, religious observance is often more casual and usually limited to holidays and major events such as births, weddings, and funerals. About 6 percent of Austrians are Protestant (Baptist or Methodist) or members of sects unique to Austria.

6 ● MAJOR HOLIDAYS

Austria's holidays are primarily the religious ones on the Christian calendar such as Easter and Christmas. Christmas festivities begin on December 6, when children receive presents from St. Nicholas. Many houses and churches display wooden cribs at this time of year. In rural areas, children celebrate the eve of the Epiphany by singing a song in honor of the Three Kings that asks for blessings in the new year. Epiphany, January 6, is also the beginning of a carnival season that is celebrated until Ash Wednesday, the beginning of Lent. Labor Day is celebrated May 1. There is also a National Holiday on October 26.

Rural Austrians also observe some traditional celebrations. One is the feast of St. Leonard, the patron saint of livestock, who is honored each November with festive horse-and-cart parades. Many villages still burn the "demon" of winter during Lent. In Vorarlberg, a figure of a witch that is stuffed with explosives is blown up on top of a water tower. It is believed that the weather

for the coming year will come from the direction in which the figure's head flies. In the Tyrol, *Schemenlaufen* (procession of ghosts) is celebrated every four years with a parade in which men wearing masks sound bells to ring out the winter.

7 ● RITES OF PASSAGE

Because the Roman Catholic faith is so widespread in Austria, almost all newborns are baptized. Godparents, chosen by the baby's parents, hold the baby during the baptism, and are expected to visit on birthdays, to give presents on important occasions, and to care for him if the parents die. Childhood firsts are celebrated, such as the first tooth and the first school holiday spent away from home. There are no special rites to mark puberty, but graduation from the teenagers' last school is marked with a party and gifts. People tend to marry young, and church weddings are common. Women generally establish their own careers before having a first child. Most relations between parents and adult children are close. Both generations play an active role in raising children. Many times adult children call their parents the same nicknames that the grandchildren use.

8 ● RELATIONSHIPS

In public, Austrians are both courteous and formal. This is a legacy from the days of the Austro-Hungarian Empire, when social position was determined by aristocratic or civil service hierarchy. A doctor or other professional is usually addressed as *Herr Doktor, Magister,* or *Professor.* Civil servants have titles of honor or respect consisting of various prefixes and the suffix *-rat* (councilor). Examples include *Hofrat* (privy councilor) and *Gehiemrat* (town councilor). Women are commonly addressed as *Gnädige Frau* (madam). The greeting *Grüss Gott* (God bless you) is often used instead of *Guten Tag* (good day). People shake hands when they meet and part. Doors are normally opened for women, and a woman may be kissed on the hand when being formally introduced.

9 ● LIVING CONDITIONS

After World War I (1914–18), the population shifted somewhat from the country to larger towns and cities. As a result, housing in rural or country areas remained plentiful and cheap. Most city-dwellers live in one- or two-room flats (apartments) with a separate kitchen. Fewer than one-fourth of these city people live in homes with four or more rooms. Housing costs are relatively low; Austrians spend less on housing than on recreation. Austrians enjoy excellent health care, all of it covered by a national health insurance program. There are also modern and efficient railroad, highway, and expressway (*Autobahn*) systems.

10 ● FAMILY LIFE

The most important Austrian family unit is the nuclear family (*Familie*). Soon after marriage, a bride and groom customarily establish their own household near one partner's (usually the wife's) family. They may eventually be joined by a widowed grandparent or unmarried aunt or uncle. Regular visits are exchanged with the extended family (*Grossfamilie*), consisting of grandparents, aunts, uncles, and first cousins. A wider network of relations (*Verwandschaft*) comes together for major events such as weddings. Children maintain a special relationship with godparents until adulthood.

Male and female roles in the family are not equal. For much of the twentieth century, Austria has had a high proportion of women in the labor force. Women are eligible for two years of paid maternity leave after the birth of a child, and many times grandparents take care of children so that a woman may return to work. Regardless of women's significant financial contribution to the household, Austrian men continue to look at domestic tasks and child-rearing as essentially women's jobs.

11 ● CLOTHING

Modern Austrians dress like people in the northeastern United States. Traditional peasant costumes are mostly saved for holidays and festivals. Then women wear embroidered blouses, lace aprons, and full, dirndl skirts. Men wear *lederhosen* (short leather pants) with wide suspenders, short jackets without collars or lapels, and green-brimmed hats decorated with feathers. A traditional costume worn on more formal occasions is the *Stierer Anzug:* gray or brown breeches (pants that buckle just below the knee) embroidered in green, a colorful cummerbund, bright vest, a long, flared coat with ornamental buttons, and high top hat.

12 ● FOOD

Austrians are known for their love of food and drink. Perhaps the most characteristic Austrian dish is the *Wienerschnitzel,* a veal or pork cutlet that is breaded and fried. Soups and stews with dumplings are very popular, and hot sausages are often served

Recipe

Schokoladen-Brezeln
(Chocolate Cookies)

Ingredients

For the cookies

2¼ cups all purpose flour
½ cup unsweetened cocoa powder
½ teaspoon baking powder
⅓ cup butter, softened
⅓ cup sugar
3 Tablespoons light corn syrup
2 eggs
1 teaspoon vanilla extract
½ cup finely ground walnuts
2 ounces semisweet chocolate, grated

For the glaze

1 cup powdered sugar
⅓ cup coffee or water
1 teaspoon shortening
1 teaspoon light corn syrup

Directions for cookies

1. Measure butter into a bowl and beat with an electric mixer until fluffy.

2. Add sugar and corn syrup and beat well.

3. Add eggs and vanilla and continue beating.

4. Add about half the flour with the cocoa powder and the baking powder, and beat well.

5. Beat in the ground walnuts and grated chocolate.

6. Switch to a wooden spoon for mixing, and add the rest of the flour.

7. Divide dough in half and shape each half into a six-inch log. Wrap in plastic wrap, and refrigerate about one hour.

8. Preheat the oven to 350°F. Lightly grease three cookie sheets.

9. Mark and cut each log into twelve sections, each one-half inch thick.

10. Knead the dough portions to soften, and then roll to make a rope about ten inches long and about as thick as a crayon.

11. Place the rope on the greased baking sheet, twisting it into a pretzel shape.

12. Repeat until all twelve sections are ready, leaving about one inch between pretzels.

13. Bake for nine to eleven minutes.

14. Leave on cookie sheet for about two minutes before transferring to a cooling rack.

Directions for glaze

1. Sift powdered sugar into a saucepan, and add coffee (or water), shortening, and corn syrup.

2. Heat gently to boiling, stirring constantly.

3. Remove from heat, add chocolate, and stir until chocolate melts.

4. Using tongs, dip pretzels into chocolate glaze to coat all over.

as snacks with beer. Austrian pastry chefs are famous for creating such delicacies as apple strudel, *Milchrahmstrudel* (a cheese crepe in vanilla custard sauce), *Sachertorte* (a rich chocolate cake with apricot jam and whipped cream), and *Dobostorte* (layers of

Austrian National Tourist Office

Austrian musicians in traditional costume playing folk music in a mountain setting. Three-fourths of Austria is mountainous.

sponge cake and chocolate butter cream glazed with caramel). Wine is an important part of Austrian meals. The area around Vienna produces very good white wines. Many Austrians have a late-afternoon snack called *Jause* (YOWS-seh), which is pastry and coffee, because they eat dinner very late in the evening. Chocolate pretzels (*Schokoladen-Brezeln*) might be served for Jause.

13 ● EDUCATION

Children attend primary school from age six through age ten. Then they are tested and placed into a continuing elementary school, a basic high school, or a college preparatory school. Formal secondary education continues through age fourteen. It is followed by either vocational school, teacher-training college, an apprenticeship in a trade, or more college-preparatory classes. Some form of secondary training is required through age fifteen. Austria has had free and mandatory education for two hundred years. As a result, nearly everyone is literate (able to read and write).

14 ● CULTURAL HERITAGE

For centuries, Vienna has been famous as a center for the arts, particularly music. The renowned Vienna Boys' Choir was founded in 1498. The six-year-old Wolfgang Amadeus Mozart first played for the Empress Maria Theresa in 1762. Vienna was either the birthplace or adopted home of many of the greatest classical composers, including Franz Josef Haydn, Ludwig van Beethoven, Franz Schubert, Johannes Brahms, Gustav Mahler, and, in the twentieth century, Arnold Schönberg. Austria's two great centers for classical music are Vienna—with its world-famous Boys' Choir, Vienna Philharmonic, and Vienna State Opera—and Salzburg, the birthplace of Mozart and site of a festival that draws thousands from around the world every summer. Vienna is also the home of the waltz.

In the late nineteenth and early twentieth centuries, Austria—and Vienna in particular—was known as a center for innovations in medicine. Sigmund Freud invented psychoanalysis there and his former home is now a museum.

15 ● EMPLOYMENT

Three major economic groups—labor, management, and farmers—are each represented by their own organization: trade unions, a management association, and the farmers' federation. Roughly 85 percent of Austrians work for hourly wages, 10 percent are self-employed in agriculture, and 5 percent are professionals who are paid fees for their services. White-collar workers, those who work in offices or are professionals, account for more than 50 percent of all wage earners. People usually start working at the age of fifteen and retire at age sixty. Retirees enjoy generous pensions and high social status. Paid vacation time is long, even for the youngest and most inexperienced workers. Workers receive an extra month's salary in December at the start of the Christmas season and in July before the August vacation season begins. This means that workers are paid for fourteen months rather than twelve months every year. Austrians also receive free medical care.

16 ● SPORTS

The natural beauty and variety of Austria's scenery are perfect for outdoor activities of all kinds. Skiing is Austria's leading winter sport, followed by ice skating and tobogganing. Popular summer sports include bicycling, mountain climbing, sailing, hiking, canoeing, and swimming. Many Austrians, like other Europeans, are avid fans and players of soccer, which they call *football*.

17 ● RECREATION

Austrians—especially the Viennese—are known for their cheerful spirit and enjoyment of life. According to a famous saying, "In Berlin, the situation is serious but not hopeless; in Vienna, the situation is hopeless, but not serious." Austrians are enthusiastic supporters of the arts and participants in all kinds of outdoor activities. They meet at coffeehouses and *Konditoreien* (pastry shops) to relax and enjoy fine food and conversation. Austrians spend many hours reading, socializing, or just relaxing and sipping a *brauner* (coffee with milk), a *konsul* (black coffee with cream), or a more elaborate coffee drink, such as *kaisermelange* (black coffee with an egg yolk and brandy).

18 ● CRAFTS AND HOBBIES

Crafts produced by Austrian folk artists include wood carvings, ceramics, jewelry, glassware, wax figures, leather products, and embroidery, as well as items made of wrought iron and pewter. A *Heimatwerk* (local crafts organization) in each province runs shops that sell the products of area craftspeople.

19 ● SOCIAL PROBLEMS

For an industrial nation, Austria has a relatively low rate of violent crime. It has, however, a high rate of property crime and white-collar crime (crime committed by business or professional people while at work), such as embezzlement and fraud. Alcoholism, suicide, and absenteeism from work are also serious problems. Domestic abuse is also a growing problem. People from Greece, the former Yugoslavia, Turkey, the Middle East, and Africa who settle in Austria are sometimes subjected to discrimination in employment and housing, and to open racial hostility, which is expressed verbally and through graffiti. Anti-Semitic (anti-Jewish) and anti-Gypsy sentiments are common as well. Austria has an illegal underground right-wing extremist movement that recruits young people (skinheads) who agitate against foreigners and commit acts of random violence.

20 ● BIBLIOGRAPHY

Eyewitness Travel Guide (Vienna). London: Dorling Kindersley Publishing, 1994.

Gall, Timothy, and Susan Gall, eds. Junior Worldmark Encyclopedia of the Nations. Detroit: U•X•L, 1996.

Moss, Joyce, and George Wilson. *Peoples of the World: Western Europeans.* Detroit: Gale Research, 1993.

WEBSITES

Austrian National Tourist Office. [Online] Available http://www.anto.com/, 1998.

Austrian Press and Information Service, Washington, D.C. [Online] Available http://www.austria.org/, 1998.

World Travel Guide. Austria. [Online] Available http://www.wtgonline.com/country/at/gen.html, 1998.

Azerbaijan

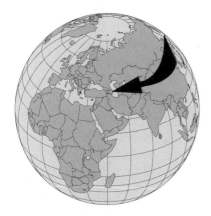

The people of Azerbaijan are called Azerbaijanis. About 83 percent of the population trace their origin to Azerbaijan. About 6 percent are Russians, and another 6 percent are Armenians. See the chapters on Russia in Volume 7, and on Armenia in this volume for more information on these two groups.

Azerbaijanis

PRONUNCIATION: ah-zer-bye-JAHN-eez
LOCATION: Azerbaijan; Iran
POPULATION: 35–40 million worldwide:
 Republic of Azerbaijan, 7.5 million; Iran, 20-25 million (estimate)
LANGUAGE: Azeri (also called Azerbaijani); Russian; English
RELIGION: Islam (majority); Christianity (Orthodox and Evangelical); Judaism

1 ● INTRODUCTION

Azerbaijan is located at the crossroads of Europe and Central Asia. Its territory lies in the region once called the Silk Route, a famous network of roads between China and Europe. Over the centuries, many kingdoms and empires have fought to gain control over the region.

By the beginning of the nineteenth century, the region was under Russian control. In 1918 Azerbaijan gained its independence and became known as the Democratic Republic of Azerbaijan. But freedom was very short-lived. In 1920, army troops from what was then the Soviet Union invaded and occupied the capital city, Baku. Azerbaijan then lived under the domination of the Soviet Union until 1991. That year, the Soviet Union collapsed and Azerbaijan was able to regain its independence as the Republic of Azerbaijan. Since 1988, Armenians have been fighting with the people of Azerbaijan, the Azerbaijanis. As of 1997, Armenians occupied 20 percent of Azerbaijan's territory.

2 ● LOCATION

The Republic of Azerbaijan covers 33,430 square miles (86,600 square kilometers), about the size of the state of Maine. It is a land of many contrasts, from coastal lowlands along the Caspian Sea to the high mountain ranges of the Caucasus. The mountain regions are extremely cold, but other parts of Azerbaijan are nearly as hot as the tropics.

The population of the Republic of Azerbaijan is approximately 7.5 million people.

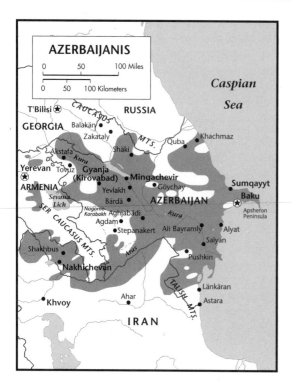

AZERBAIJANIS

0   50   100 Miles

0   50   100 Kilometers

Caspian Sea

However, three times as many Azerbaijanis (an estimated 20 to 25 million) live to the south in Iran.

3 ● LANGUAGE

Azerbaijanis speak Azeri (sometimes called Azerbaijani). It is a Turkic language belonging to the Altaic-Turkic language group. For centuries, Azerbaijanis wrote their language using the Arabic alphabet. However, a Latin-based alphabet (the alphabet used to write English) was adopted in 1928. In 1939, Soviet dictator Josef Stalin (1879–1953) ordered the Azerbaijanis to use the Cyrillic alphabet, which is used for the Russian language. Stalin wanted all the people under Soviet rule to use the same alphabet. All business communication and teaching was done in the Russian language.

When Azerbaijan gained its independence in 1991, its parliament adopted a Latin-based alphabet. In the 1990s, it faced the enormous task of rewriting everything from street signs to computer keyboards, as well as teaching in a new alphabet. The Azerbaijanis are motivated to accomplish this task, however, because the adoption of the Latin-based alphabet represents their new, independent country. It also reflects their desire to develop friendships with people in the West who use similar Latin alphabets.

Common Phrases

English	Azerbaijani	Pronunciation
Greetings! (or Hi!)	Salam.	sa-LAHM
Good morning.	Saharim kheyir.	sa-hah-REEM khay-YEAR
Good afternoon.	Junortan kheyir.	ju-nore-TAHN khay-YEAR
Good evening.	Akhshamim kheyir.	akh-shah-MOHM khay-YEAR
Thank you	Sag ol	SAHG OAL
Yes	Bali	BAH-lee
No	Kheyr	KHAYRHH

4 ● FOLKLORE

A rich tradition of oral folklore has developed in Azerbaijan. Songs, stories, proverbs, and sayings have been passed down over thousands of years.

One of the most famous Azerbaijani legends is about an ancient tower, called Maiden's Tower. This structure, which still stands today, is the most famous landmark in Baku. According to one version of the legend, a young girl ordered the tower to be built. When her father wanted her to marry against her wishes, she locked herself in the tower. In another version, she threw herself from its heights into the sea below.

Azerbaijanis have many proverbs, such as: "Wish your neighbor two cows so that you may have one for yourself" (wish good fortune for others so that you also may benefit); and "Even the ground has ears" (there is no such thing as a secret).

Like other people of the region, Azerbaijanis love the humor and wisdom of "Molla Nasreddin" stories, which deal with social issues and basic human nature.

5 ● RELIGION

During the period when Azerbaijan was controlled by the former Soviet Union (1920–91), religious worship was discouraged. Most Islamic mosques and Christian churches were destroyed. Today Azerbaijan enjoys freedom of religion. Muslims (those who practice Islam), Jews, and Christians can all worship openly and freely. The state has no official religion, though most people are traditionally Muslim.

6 ● MAJOR HOLIDAYS

The most anticipated and joyful holiday of the year is *Nawruz* (meaning "New Year"). Celebrated on March 21, it marks the coming of spring. This holiday is celebrated not only by Azerbaijanis, but by other peoples throughout Central Asia.

One of the most vivid symbols of Nawruz is a plate of green wheat seedlings tied up with a red ribbon. On the Wednesday before Nawruz, young boys build bonfires in their yards and in the streets. They dare each other to jump over the flames without getting burned. Women make cookies and sweets, and friends and relatives visit each other at home. Shops and government offices are closed, as are schools.

January 1 is celebrated as New Year's Day in Azerbaijan. Since 1992, the Azerbaijan Republic has celebrated Independence Day on May 28. The occasion marks the short period of Azerbaijan independence from 1918 to 1920. Azerbaijanis also commemorate the day they declared independence from the Soviet Union on October 18, 1991. The saddest public holiday of the year for Azerbaijanis is January 20. It commemorates "Black January" when Soviet troops attacked Baku in 1990.

7 ● RITES OF PASSAGE

The most significant Azerbaijani rites of passage are connected with birthdays, marriage, and death.

Weddings are important celebrations. In rural areas, weddings can continue for three days.

Thursdays are days for visiting cemeteries. Mourners place an even number of red flowers, usually carnations, on the grave. When a person dies, the funeral is usually held the next day. Friends also gather again one week later, forty days later, and then annually on the date of the death. When a person who has never married dies, a broken mirror wrapped with a red ribbon is often placed near the grave.

AP/Wide World

Azerbaijanis enjoy music informally at home and in concert halls.

8 ● RELATIONSHIPS

Azerbaijanis generally express their emotions openly. People feel very comfortable holding hands and touching. When people of the same sex meet, they generally kiss each other on the cheeks. Young girls often walk down the street holding hands. Parents often hold the hands of their children, even older ones.

9 ● LIVING CONDITIONS

The average life expectancy in Azerbaijan is lower than that in the industrialized nations of the West. However, Azerbaijanis living in the Caucasus mountains and certain other regions are famous for their longevity. Many live to be over one hundred years old. Their diet usually consists of yogurt and vegetables that they grow themselves. Most say they have spent much of their lives involved in hard physical work.

The war with Armenia over the Nagorno-Karabakh territory in Azerbaijan has resulted in more than 25,000 deaths and many permanent injuries to people who stepped on land mines.

Much of the water supply in Azerbaijan is unsafe due to high levels of chemical and biological pollution. In Baku, for example, it is essential to boil any water intended for drinking.

10 ● FAMILY LIFE

Extended kinship and the bonds between generations keep the elderly from feeling unneeded or alone. Older people are greatly respected in Azerbaijan and play a prominent role in the family and the community. Children are greatly revered among the Azerbaijanis as well.

11 ● CLOTHING

Clothing is very similar to Western styles. Azerbaijani women stopped wearing the traditional Muslim veil (chador) in 1928. This event is actually commemorated by various statues in Baku.

12 ● FOOD

The Azerbaijani diet consists primarily of bread, grains, fruits, and vegetables. As a light meal or snack, Azerbaijanis enjoy dipping pieces of fresh fruit into plain yogurt.

The staples are supplemented by meats such as lamb, chicken, and fish. In Iran, Azerbaijanis eat rice nearly every day. In Azerbaijan, the cuisine reflects a Russian influence, with greater emphasis on bread, potatoes, and cabbage. The traditional beverage is black tea with sugar cubes.

Azerbaijanis are excellent hosts and love to invite people to their homes to share meals. Dinners often last three or more hours.

Recipe

Yogurt and Fruit

Ingredients

3 Golden Delicious apples
3 Granny Smith apples
3 bananas
2 oranges
2 peaches, pears, or plums
bunch of red grapes
bunch of green grapes
2 eight-ounce containers of plain yogurt

Directions

1. Wash the fruit (except bananas and oranges which should be peeled). It is not necessary to peel the washed fruit.
2. Cut the fruit into serving-sized pieces for dipping into the yogurt. (For example, cut the apples into wedges, the bananas into ¾-inch slices. Arrange the fruit on a serving plate.
3. Put the yogurt into a shallow bowl. Serve with the sliced fruit.

13 ● EDUCATION

The Soviet period (1920–91) placed great emphasis on education. Azerbaijanis have a high level of literacy, estimated at about 99 percent. In recent years, the educational system has suffered due to the country's serious economic problems.

Until 1991, Russian was the predominant language taught in Azerbaijan. Today, young people have the greatest chances of getting the best jobs if they speak three languages: Azeri, Russian, and English. Great emphasis is being placed on learning

English. Popular music in English is played on local radio stations.

14 ● CULTURAL HERITAGE

Since ancient times, Azerbaijanis have held their poets and literary figures in the highest esteem. The city of Baku has many statues devoted to Azerbaijani poets and literary figures.

Azerbaijanis are famous for their music. The majority of Azerbaijanis receive training either in Western music or on traditional Eastern instruments. These include stringed instruments such as the *tar* or *kamancha,* and wind instruments such as the *zurna* and *balaban.* It is common to enjoy music with guests after dinner in the evenings. Azerbaijani classical music combines eastern melodies, rhythms, and modes with Western forms like symphonies, ballets, and opera. Prominent Azerbaijani composer, Uzeyir Hajibeyov, is honored as the founder of classical music in Azerbaijan.

15 ● EMPLOYMENT

The major sources of employment are the oil industry and agriculture. Enormous reserves of oil have been discovered in the Azerbaijan sector of the Caspian Sea.

16 ● SPORTS

Azerbaijanis excel at sports, especially wrestling. They are famous for chess, as well. World chess champion Garry Kasparov grew up playing chess in Baku.

17 ● RECREATION

It is a rare Azerbaijani home that does not have a television. Only homes in remote mountain villages do not have TVs. In Baku, satellite dishes can be seen on many of the narrow balconies above the streets. Western television programs are well liked among the Azerbaijanis, as are Russian and Turkish programs. Other electronic conveniences, such as VCRs, CD players, and personal computers, are still rare.

18 ● CRAFTS AND HOBBIES

In Azerbaijan more emphasis is placed on music than on crafts or hobbies. However, during the Soviet period (1920–91), many people enjoyed collecting postcards, stamps, and other souvenirs that made them feel more connected to the world.

19 ● SOCIAL PROBLEMS

Since the mid-1980s, Armenians and Azerbaijanis have been fighting over the territory of Nagorno-Karabakh within the borders of Azerbaijan. The Armenians of this region want it to separate from Azerbaijan and unite with Armenia. The fighting has caused a tragic loss of life (an estimated 25,000 people), and many more have been permanently injured.

20 ● BIBLIOGRAPHY

Azerbaijan, Then and Now. Minneapolis: Lerner Publications, 1993.

Roberts, Elizabeth. *Georgia, Armenia, and Azerbaijan.* Brookfield, Conn.: Millbrook Press, 1992.

Swietochowski, Tadeusz. *Russia and Azerbaijan: A Borderland in Transition.* New York: Columbia University Press, 1995.

WEBSITES

Office of President of the Republic of Azerbaijan. [Online] Available http://www.president.az/, 1998.

World Travel Guide. Azerbaijan. [Online] Available http://www.wtgonline.com/country/az/gen.html, 1998.

Bahamas

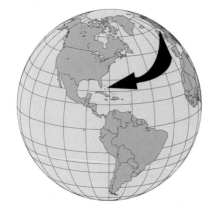

The people of Bahamas are called Bahamians. Descendants of slaves brought to the Western Hemisphere from Africa make up about 86 percent of the population. About 8 percent of the population is of mixed origin. The remainder is white, mostly of British descent.

Bahamians

PRONUNCIATION: bah-HAY-mee-uhns
LOCATION: Bahamas
POPULATION: 272,000
LANGUAGE: English; Bahamian dialect
RELIGION: Christianity

1 ● INTRODUCTION

The Bahamas were the first islands to be sighted by Christopher Columbus in 1492. Instead of settling the islands, the Spanish forced the native population there into slavery on neighboring islands. Within a quarter of a century, the Bahamas had been stripped of all their inhabitants. However, in the seventeenth century, British colonists began to arrive and settle there, bringing African slaves with them. By the end of the eighteenth century, there were twice as many Africans as Europeans on the islands.

The Bahamas remained economically backward throughout the nineteenth century and into the twentieth. With the growth of commercial aviation, however, the islands' tourism industry began. By the late 1940s, tourism had become the main source of income. Today the country welcomes over three million tourists a year, most of them from the United States. In the 1960s, the Bahamas began to develop as a center for international banking as well.

The Bahamas attained full national independence in 1973.

2 ● LOCATION

The Bahamas are located in the Atlantic Ocean off Florida's southeastern coast. They form an archipelago (a group or chain of islands) consisting of approximately 700 islands, of which about thirty are inhabited. Their total land area is 5,380 square miles (13,934 square kilometers). This is slightly more than the combined areas of New Jersey and Connecticut.

The two main islands of the Bahamas are New Providence, where the capital city of Nassau is located, and Grand Bahama. The

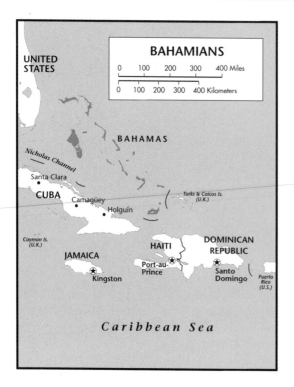

4 ● FOLKLORE

The Bahamas are rich in myths and legends. There are two different legends about a woman named Pretty Molly Bay, who is said to haunt Little Exuma Island. In one, she is a drowned slave who roams the beaches at night; in the other, she is a young white woman turned into a mermaid. There are stories about creatures called "chickcharnies." These are three-toed sprites with red eyes. It is said that they hang upside down from trees on the island of Andros and can turn a person's head around to face backward.

5 ● RELIGION

Most Bahamians are Christian. Baptists account for about 33 percent of the population, and Roman Catholics and Anglicans account for about 20 percent each. It is not unusual for Bahamians to attend services at their own church and other churches also. On some of the islands, Christian beliefs are combined with ancient African superstitions.

6 ● MAJOR HOLIDAYS

Public holidays in the Bahamas include the major holy days of the Christian calendar. Secular holidays include Labor Day (the first Friday in June), Independence Day (July 10), Emancipation Day (the first Monday in August), and Discovery Day (October 12).

The best-known celebration on the islands is Junkanoo, held on both Christmas and New Year's. It is similar to the Carnival festivities in countries like Trinidad and Tobago. Crowds of merrymakers parade through the streets to the sounds of whistles

remaining islands are generally called either the "Family Islands" or the "out islands."

The Bahamas has an estimated population of about 272,000 people.

3 ● LANGUAGE

Standard English is the official language of the Bahamas. However, most of the population speaks an English-based dialect. An example of the Bahamian dialect can be found in the following verse from the poem "Islan' Life" by poet and playwright Susan J. Wallace:

> Islan' life ain' no fun less ya treat errybody
> like ya brudder, ya sister, or ya frien'
> Love ya neighbour, play ya part, jes'
> remember das de art,
> For when ocean fen' ya in, all is kin.

Cory Langley

Until the 1960s, black Bahamians were prohibited from holding many jobs. Since then, government policies have improved opportunities for education and jobs, and many black Bahamian families have migrated to the cities seeking education for their children and employment for the parents.

and goatskin drums called *goombays*. Costumed groups compete for prizes.

7 ● RITES OF PASSAGE

Christian ceremonies such as baptism and confirmation mark the major passages from one stage of life to another.

8 ● RELATIONSHIPS

Race relations in the Bahamas have changed since the 1950s and 1960s. Until then, economic opportunities for blacks were severely limited. Black Bahamians were barred from many theaters, hotels, shops, and other public places. Since then, govern-ment policies have improved educational and job opportunities. The situation of black Bahamians has improved, and a new, black middle class has been created on New Providence and Grand Bahama.

9 ● LIVING CONDITIONS

Urban living conditions on the main islands of New Providence and Grand Bahama differ from those on the smaller Family Islands. Inhabitants of the Family Islands have little contact with tourists and live a simple, traditional life. Most live in villages near the shore. Their houses are simple wooden structures, some without plumbing or electricity. Two out of three households in the Family Islands did not have running water in 1986.

Migration to the cities for better jobs has produced an urban housing shortage, especially in low-income areas.

10 ● FAMILY LIFE

Adult migration to the cities of Nassau and Freeport has left many families in the Family Islands headed by grandparents. There are also households headed by single parents. A child's primary caretaker is also the person in charge of discipline in the family. Adult children often give their mothers gifts or financial assistance. It is unusual for unmarried couples to live together.

11 ● CLOTHING

Bahamians wear modern Western-style clothing. Colorful costumes of all kinds can be seen at the annual Junkanoo festivals in Nassau and other locations.

12 ● FOOD

Seafood is the most important part of the Bahamian diet. The conch shellfish is a national favorite used in many dishes. Peas with rice, a dietary staple, consists of dried pigeon peas and rice prepared with thyme and other spices. *Souses* (dishes containing lightly pickled meats) also figure prominently in Bahamian cuisine. Served with cooked grits and johnny cake (a type of bread), they are a popular breakfast food.

13 ● EDUCATION

The educational system of the Bahamas is modeled on that of Great Britain. Grade levels in secondary education are called

Recipe

Chicken Souse

Ingredients

2 chickens
2 cups chicken broth
2 cups chopped celery
10 allspice berries
4 potatoes, chopped
1 bay leaf
2 onions, chopped
1 teaspoon dried thyme
2 Scotch Bonnet peppers
½ cup lime juice

Directions

1. Put both chickens in a large pot with enough water to cover, and bring the water to a boil. Boil for 2 minutes.
2. Carefully drain off the boiling water. Add fresh water to cover the chickens, return to stove and bring the water to boiling.
3. Add the vegetables and all other remaining ingredients except the lime juice.
4. Reduce heat and simmer for 10 minutes.
5. Add the lime juice and simmer for 10 more minutes.
6. Skim the fat from the pot with a spoon.
7. Remove the chicken and vegetables and serve. (May also be served cold after refrigeration.)

"forms," and exams are required in order to attend college. Students must also take exams at the end of every school year in order to pass to the next grade. Education is mandatory between the ages of five and fourteen. However, most students continue their schooling until at least the age of sixteen.

The government-run College of the Bahamas opened in 1974. The Bahamas have also been home to a branch of the University of the West Indies since the 1960s.

14 ● CULTURAL HERITAGE

Susan Wallace is the nation's best-known poet. She has also edited *Back Home,* an anthology of Bahamian literature. Playwright Winston Saunders is the director of the Dundas Theatre, which stages plays by Bahamian and other authors.

Well-known artist Alton Lowe captures many aspects of Bahamian life in his realistic paintings.

The Royal Bahamas Police Force Band performs at all major public events. Folk dance in the Bahamas ranges from European dances to the African-derived jump dance and the West Indian limbo.

15 ● EMPLOYMENT

Tourism and related fields provide jobs for 50 percent or more of the labor force. Agriculture and industry are much smaller contributors to the nation's economy and employ far fewer people. Farming and fishing are the traditional occupations on the Family Islands. Their residents also earn money producing crafts or through seasonal employment in resort areas. There is a shortage of salaried jobs in these areas, and many residents move to Nassau or Freeport to seek employment.

Cory Langley

A Bahamian child's mother or grandmother is usually the primary caregiver and family disciplinarian.

16 ● SPORTS

Softball is the most popular sport in the Bahamas. Other favorite sports include basketball, volleyball, and track and field. Water sports, including sailing, windsurfing, and fishing, are popular with Bahamians and tourists alike. Many islanders race in the Family Islands regatta, held every April.

17 ● RECREATION

In addition to the native Bahamian *goombay* (goatskin drum) music, calypso, soca, and reggae are also popular. Gospel music is performed in concert halls and on outdoor stages as well as in churches.

There is approximately one television for every four persons in the Bahamas. Programming includes American situation comedies, professional sports, and educational broadcasting.

18 ● CRAFTS AND HOBBIES

Crafts include woodcarving, quilting, basketry, and shellwork. The straw handicrafts produced on the Family Islands are especially distinctive. Using palm fronds braided into long strips that are then sewn together, the island women make hats, baskets, purses, and other items, often decorating them with raffia paper and seashells.

19 ● SOCIAL PROBLEMS

The Bahamas have not traditionally had a violent society. In the past, serious crimes such as homicide were rare. However, in the 1990s, drug trafficking caused a major increase in crime. In New Providence the use of crack cocaine has led to frequent armed robberies.

20 ● BIBLIOGRAPHY

Boultbee, Paul G. *The Bahamas.* Santa Barbara, CA: Clio Press, 1989.

Craton, Michael, and Gail Saunders. *Islanders in the Stream: A History of the Bahamian People.* Athens, GA: University of Georgia Press, 1992.

McCulla, Patricia. *Bahamas.* New York: Chelsea House, 1988.

WEBSITES

Bahamas On-Line. The Bahamas. [Online] Available http://flamingo.bahamas.net.bs/, 1997.

Islands of the Bahamas. [Online] Available http://www.interknowledge.com/bahamas/, 1997.

World Travel Guide, Bahamas. [Online] Available http://www.wtgonline.com/country/bs/gen.html, 1998.

Bahrain

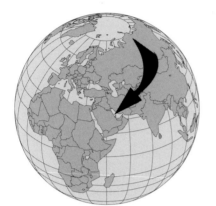

The people of Bahrain are called Bahrainis. About two-thirds of the population consists of native Bahrainis. Iranians are estimated to be about 20 percent, with other Arabs making up the rest of the population. To learn more about Iranians, consult the chapter on Iran in Volume 4.

Bahrainis

PRONUNCIATION: bah-RAIN-eez
LOCATION: Bahrain
POPULATION: 518,000 (1992 estimate)
LANGUAGE: Arabic (official); English; Farsi (Persian); Hindi; Urdu
RELIGION: Islam (Shi'ite, 70 percent; Sunni, 24 percent); Christianity; Hinduism; Judaism; Baha'iism

1 ● INTRODUCTION

Because of its climate, Bahrain (meaning "two seas") has been the only safe port on the Persian Gulf throughout history. Thus this tiny island nation has played an important role in the Gulf region since civilization began there. Despite this, it has had a relatively peaceful history.

At different points in history, Persia (now Iran) has laid claim to Bahrain. The Portuguese took control in 1521 but were forced out by 1602. In 1782, the Arab al-Khalifa family took over the islands and has ruled them ever since. In 1820, Bahrain agreed to become a British-protected state. Britain would protect Bahrain's sovereignty in return for safe sailing up the Gulf for Britain's ships. This agreement lasted until Britain terminated it in 1968. (British soldiers still supervise Bahrain's army and security forces.)

On August 15, 1971, Bahrain proclaimed independence. The constitution of 1972 provided for a parliament, or National Assembly. Elections were held in 1973. Two years later, however, the king disbanded the Assembly, accusing some of its members of subversive activities.

Oil was discovered in 1931, giving Bahrain the first oil well, and then the first oil refinery, on the Arab side of the Persian Gulf. Although production has always been much smaller than that of other Arab states, oil has given Bahrain an important source of income.

2 ● LOCATION

Bahrain is an archipelago (chain of islands) in the Persian Gulf. The six major islands

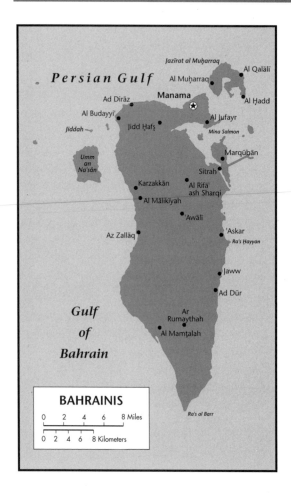

Persian Gulf

Jazīrat al Muḥarraq
Al Qalālī
Al Muḥarraq
Manama
Ad Dirāz
Al Ḥadd
Al Budayyi'
Al Jufayr
Jiddah
Jidd Ḥafṣ
Mina Salmon
Umm
an
Na'sān
Marqūbān
Sitrah
Karzakkān
Al Rifā'
ash Sharqi
Al Mālikīyah
'Awālī
Az Zallāq
'Askar
Ra's Ḥayyan
Jaww
Ad Dūr
Gulf
of
Bahrain
Ar
Rumaythah
Al Mamṭalah
Ra's al Barr

BAHRAINIS

0   2   4   6   8 Miles

0   2   4   6   8 Kilometers

In 1992, the Bahraini population was estimated at about 518,000 people.

3 ● LANGUAGE

The official language of Bahrain is Arabic. English is also spoken by many Bahrainis. Farsi (Persian) is spoken by the Iranians in Bahrain. The Indian population speaks Hindi, and the Pakistanis speak Urdu.

Throughout the world, Arabic dialects differ from one country to another. Even within Bahrain, city dwellers find the dialect of the rural population "uncultured." Arabic is written from right to left in a unique alphabet that has no distinction between capital and lower-case letters. It is not necessary for the letters to be written on a straight line, as English letters must be. Punctuation is also quite different from that of English.

"Hello" in Arabic is *marhaba* or *ahlan*, to which one replies, *marhabtayn* or *ahlayn*. Other common greetings are *as-salam alaykum* (Peace be with you), with the reply of *walaykum as-salam* (and to you peace). *Ma'assalama* means "goodbye." "Thank you" is *shukran,* and "you're welcome" is *afwan*; "yes" is *na'am,* and "no" is *la'a*. The numbers one to ten in Arabic are: *wahad, itnin, talata, arba'a, khamsa, sitta, saba'a, tamania, tisa'a,* and *ashara.*

Arabs have very long names, consisting of their first (given) name, their father's name, their paternal grandfather's name, and finally their family name (surname).

4 ● FOLKLORE

A popular Bahraini legend explains the origin of the freshwater springs that bubble up

are Bahrain (also known as as-Awal), Muharraq, Sitrah, Umm al-Nassan, Jidda (used as the Bahraini prison), and Nabi Salih. The twenty-seven minor islands include the Muhammadiyah and Hawar groups. The capital city, Manama, is located on the north coast of Bahrain island.

In spite of freshwater springs offshore, Bahrain is essentially a desert surrounded by water. In recorded history there has never been any rain during the months of June through September.

offshore from beneath the sea. According to the story, they were caused by falling stars that knocked holes in the ground.

Pearls have also inspired much folklore. Bahraini parents like to tell their children that pearls are created when a mermaid's tears fall into an open oyster shell. In addition, certain pearls are believed to have supernatural powers. It is thought that they can help locate lost objects or win someone's love.

5 ● RELIGION

At least 94 percent of the Bahraini population is Muslim. About 70 percent are Shi'ite, and 24 percent are Sunni. The royal family of Bahrain and the majority of its wealthy merchant class are Sunnis. This has created many conflicts between the majority Shi'ites and the ruling Sunnis.

Islam is a simple, straightforward faith with clear rules for correct living. Muslims pray five times a day; give alms, or *zakat,* to the poor; and fast during the month of Ramadan. All prayers are said facing Mecca. Each Muslim is expected to make a pilgrimage there (called a *hajj*) at least once in their lifetime.

First names usually indicate an Arab's religious affiliation. Muslims use names with Islamic religious significance, such as Muhammad and Fatima, whereas Christians often use Western names.

6 ● MAJOR HOLIDAYS

Secular holidays include New Year's Day on January 1, and National Day on December 16. Because of Bahrain's large Muslim majority, Muslim holy days are treated as official holidays. Among the most important is *Ramadan*, which is celebrated by complete fasting from dawn until dusk each day for an entire month. *Eid al-Fitr* is a three-day festival at the end of Ramadan. *Eid al-Adha* is a three-day feast of sacrifice that marks the end of the *hajj*, a month-long pilgrimage to Mecca. (Families who can afford it slaughter a lamb and share the meat with poorer Muslims.) Friday is the Islamic day of rest. Most businesses and services are closed on this day. All government offices, private businesses, and schools are also closed during Eid al-Fitr and Eid al-Adha.

7 ● RITES OF PASSAGE

Bahrainis observe the rites of passage common to all Islamic societies. Births, baby-namings, male circumcisions, and weddings are all occasions for celebration.

8 ● RELATIONSHIPS

Arab hospitality reigns in Bahrain. As in other Muslim societies, food and drink are always taken with the right hand. The left hand is reserved for "unclean" uses such as personal hygiene.

Arabs are spirited talkers. They speak loudly and use many gestures, repeating themselves often and interrupting each other constantly. When socializing, Arabs touch each other more often and stand closer together than Westerners do. People of the same sex will often hold hands while talking, even if they barely know each other. Members of the opposite sex, however, even married couples, never touch in public.

It is considered rude to ask personal questions.

9 ● LIVING CONDITIONS

Bahrain has one of the highest standards of living in the Arabian (or Persian) Gulf area.

Traditionally, Bahraini homes were made from palm fronds, or *barasti*. Modern homes are made of cement and lime brick. Rooms are built around an inner courtyard, and houses are built vertically (rather than horizontally, like ranch houses) to catch the breezes that blow higher in the air. "Wind towers" on the upper floors of many houses and other buildings catch these breezes and funnel the air down to the lower floors through air shafts.

Television sets, air conditioning, and refrigerators are common in modern Bahraini homes. The most prized furnishings in Bahraini households are handwoven rugs, either imported from Iran or locally crafted.

10 ● FAMILY LIFE

The family is the center of life for Bahrainis. Children live with their parents until they are married, and sometimes after marriage as well. Polygyny (up to four wives at a time) is legal, but few men practice it. Divorce is fairly simple, for both men and women, but it rarely occurs.

Bahraini women are more publicly active than are women in most other Arab countries. Traditional women's roles are beginning to change. Fewer marriages are arranged by the couple's parents as more couples choose their own partners. The dowry, or "bride-price," paid by the groom to the bride's family, is disappearing. However, these changes are taking place mostly among the wealthier classes. They are the ones who can afford to provide their daughters with higher education, and hire domestic help so women can work outside the home. The lower and lower-middle classes of Bahrain remain much more traditional.

Following Islamic tradition, women do not take their husband's name when they marry but rather keep their father's family name

11 ● CLOTHING

Bahraini women were never as strict as other Arabs about covering themselves up in public, and many no longer veil their faces at all. (Most do still wear some sort of head covering and long sleeves.) Bahraini men wear a *thobe*. This is a long outer robe reaching from neck to ankles. Made of white cotton, it keeps them cool in the hot sun. They also wear a *ghutra*, a large rectangular piece of material draped over the head. It is held in place with an *agal*, a thick, black woven band. This headscarf protects them from the sun as well as from sandstorms. (The scarf can quickly be drawn across the face.)

Western-style clothing is beginning to become more popular in the larger cities of Bahrain.

12 ● FOOD

Meals are taken very seriously by Bahrainis. All talking is done for the hour or so before sitting down to eat; there is no conversation during dinner. After the meal, coffee is served, and then any guests leave. Coffee is also always served as a way of welcoming guests when they first arrive. It is most often drunk unsweetened and flavored with cardamom. Fresh vegetables, lamb, fish, chicken, and beef are common foods. (Pork is forbid-

Recipe

Date Bars

Ingredients

1 cup rolled oats, plain or instant
½ cup all-purpose flour
½ teaspoon baking powder
½ cup dark brown sugar
½ teaspoon salt
1 teaspoon cinnamon
1 cup melted butter or margarine
2 eggs, well beaten
1 cup finely chopped pitted dates
1 cup chopped nuts (walnuts, peanuts, or pecans)
½ cup confectioner's sugar for garnish

Directions

1. Preheat oven to 350°F. Grease 8-inch-square baking pan.
2. Put oats, flour, baking powder, brown sugar, salt, and cinnamon in large mixing bowl and mix well.
3. Add butter or margarine, eggs, dates, and nuts, and mix well using clean hands.
4. Put mixture into greased baking pan and bake in oven for about 35 minutes, until firm.
5. Remove from oven and cut while still warm into 1½-inch squares. Sprinkle with confectioner's sugar. Makes 16 date bars.

Adapted from Albyn, C. L., and L. S. Webb. *The Multicultural Cookbook for Students.* Phoenix, Ariz.: Oryx Press, 1993.

bread) that is glazed with water or egg and then sprinkled with salt, sesame, or caraway seeds. One of the most popular dishes is *ghouzi*. A chicken stuffed with rice, nuts, onions, spices, and shelled hard-boiled eggs is placed inside a whole, slaughtered lamb. The lamb is then sewn up, trussed, and cooked on a spit.

Bahrainis love desserts, and they love dates. The accompanying recipe combines both.

13 ● EDUCATION

Bahrain has had the highest literacy rate in the Arab world for decades. More than 90 percent of Bahrainis are literate (able to read and write). Boys and girls are taught separately but receive a similar level of education. Primary education runs from age six to age eleven. Secondary education lasts from age twelve to age seventeen. The University of Bahrain graduated its first class in 1989.

14 ● CULTURAL HERITAGE

Bahrain has a well-established artistic community. It includes some of the most respected writers in the Persian Gulf region. Ibrahim al-'Urayyid and Ahmad Muhammad al Khalifah write poetry about heroes and romance in the classical Arab style. Younger poets have developed a more Westernized style, writing about personal and political subjects. Qasim Haddad (1948–) is the best-known present-day Bahraini poet. Hamdah Khamis (1946–) is a journalist and poet.

Popular stringed instruments include the *oud*, which is related to the European lute, and the *rebaba*, which has only one string.

den by Islam, as is alcohol.) Meals always include a dish made with basmati rice. *Khoubz* is the name of the local flatbread, and *samouli* is a white bread (like French

A traditional Arab dance is the *ardha*, or men's sword dance. Men carrying swords stand shoulder to shoulder. From among them a poet sings verses while drummers beat out a rhythm.

Islam forbids the depiction of the human form, so Bahraini art focuses on geometric and abstract shapes. Calligraphy (elaborate lettering) is a sacred art. The Koran (the Muslim holy book) serves as the primary subject matter. Muslim art finds its greatest expression in mosques.

15 ● EMPLOYMENT

Since 1931, the oil and natural gas industry has been a major employer in Bahrain. Unfortunately, Bahrain's oil and natural gas reserves are expected to run out soon after the year 2010. Therefore, the government has begun to develop other industries, including plastics and aluminum.

Shipbuilding has long been a respected trade in Bahrain. Some of the shipbuilders of today can trace their lineage back through many generations, with skills passed down from father to son. Due to the desert climate, there is not much farming in Bahrain, but fishing is a fair-sized industry.

16 ● SPORTS

Soccer is the national sport of Bahrain. Other popular modern sports include tennis, water sports, and dune-buggy racing. The ancient pastimes of horse racing and horse breeding are still greatly enjoyed. Falconry (hunting with falcons) is a sport for the rich. A well-trained falcon can cost up to $15,000.

17 ● RECREATION

Camping is perhaps the favorite Bahraini family recreation. Men spend a great deal of time in coffeehouses, drinking tea and chatting.

18 ● CRAFTS AND HOBBIES

Bahrain is known for its elaborate and uniquely designed coffee servers.

19 ● SOCIAL PROBLEMS

Bahrain's rapidly increasing population has put a tremendous strain on the country's water supply. Freshwater sources are beginning to dry up, and desalination plants (to purify salt water) cannot keep up with demand. The increase in population has also driven up the cost of housing. Many Bahrainis are forced to live in overcrowded, substandard conditions.

20 ● BIBLIOGRAPHY

Albyn, Carole Lisa, and Lois Sinaiko Webb. *The Multicultural Cookbook for Students*. Phoenix, Ariz.: Oryx Press, 1993.

Fox, Mary Virginia. *Enchantment of the World: Bahrain*. Chicago: Children's Press, 1992.

Slugged, Peter, and Marion Freak-Slugged. *Tuttle Guide to the Middle East*. Boston: Charles E. Tuttle Co., 1992 (originally published London: Times Books, 1991).

WEBSITES

ArabNet. Bahrain. [Online] Available http://www.arab.net/bahrain/bahrain_contents.html, 1996.

World Travel Guide, Bahrain. [Online] Available http://www.wtgonline.com/data/bhr/bhr.asp, 1998.

Bangladesh

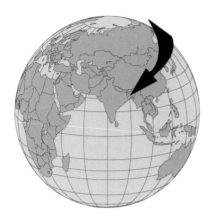

The people of Bangladesh are called Bangladeshis. Some 98 percent of the people are Bengalis (or Banglas). The Chakmas are the largest of the tribes inhabiting the Chittagong Hill Tracts.

Bangladeshis

PRONUNCIATION: ban-gla-DESH-eez
LOCATION: Bangladesh
POPULATION: 120 million
LANGUAGE: Bengali (Bangla)
RELIGION: Islam (majority Sunni Muslim)

1 ● INTRODUCTION

Modern Bangladesh is thought to have been settled around 1000 BC by people known as the "Bang." This ancient name is seen in modern words such as the country name, Bangladesh. A region of India, Bengal (where Calcutta is located), also takes its name from the Bang. In the thirteenth century AD, Bangladeshis began converting from Hinduism to Islam. Bangladeshi Muslims (followers of Islam) spoke the Bengali language and displayed a deep commitment to Bengali culture.

Britain was a colonial power in India until 1947. It granted independence to its empire that year and created two countries: India and Pakistan. India was predominantly Hindu and Pakistan was predominantly Muslim. The two areas of land designated as the new country of Pakistan were separated by about 1000 miles (1600 kilometers). These areas were East Pakistan and West Pakistan. Most people in both areas were Muslim, but their language and customs were different from each other. The people of East Pakistan fought for independence from West Pakistan for years. In 1971, after a short, brutal war, they won it, creating the country of Bangladesh.

2 ● LOCATION

Bangladesh lies in the eastern part of India at the head of the Bay of Bengal. It is roughly the size of the state of Iowa. In the late 1990s, it ranked as the eighth most populous country in the world. Except for its

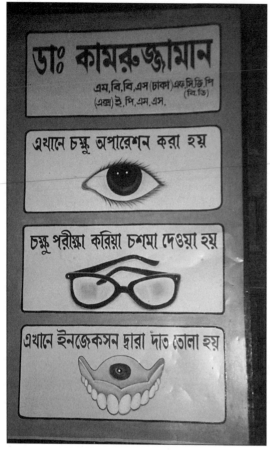

Cory Langley

A sign in Bangladesh for a shop providing eye exams and dentures.

winds of more than 100 miles (160 kilometers) per hour and waves of 18 feet (5.5 meters), struck Bangladesh (where there were no warning systems). About 250,000 people died.

Over 98 percent of the population of Bangladesh are Bengalis. They speak the Bengali language and identify with Bengali cultural traditions. Biharis, representing a little more than 1 percent of the population, speak Urdu. Most Biharis are Muslim refugees from Bihar and other parts of northern India. Tribal people make up less than 1 percent of Bangladesh's population. The largest of these groups are the Chakmas who, along with the Marmas, occupy the highland valleys of the Chittagong Hills.

3 ● LANGUAGE

Bengali, or Bangla, is the country's official language. An example of the Bangla script can be seen in the accompanying photo. The pronunciations of some common Bangla words appear below:

ENGLISH	PRONUNCIATION IN BANGLA
Hello	ah-sah-lAHm-oo ah-LIE-koom
yes	hAH
no	nAA
please	dAH-yah kAH-ray
thank you	dOYNg-no bAHd

4 ● FOLKLORE

Most Bangladeshis follow the folk traditions of the Bengali culture. They believe in the powers of *fakirs* (Muslim holy men who are viewed as exorcists and faith healers), *ojhas* (shamans with magical healing powers), and *bauls* (religious beggars and wandering musicians). Sufism, a Muslim system of beliefs based on meditation and experiences that seem magical, is strongly

southern coastline, Bangladesh is virtually surrounded on all sides by India. It shares a short border with Myanmar (Burma).

Roughly 80 percent of Bangladesh is located on a huge river delta. There are about seven hundred rivers in Bangladesh. Bangladesh has a subtropical monsoon climate. During the late monsoon season, tropical cyclones (hurricanes) sweep in from the Bay of Bengal, often with disastrous consequences. A cyclone in November 1970, with

entrenched in Bangladesh. Shah Jalal and Khan Jahan Ali are the most celebrated Sufi saints.

Bangladesh's national heroes are those who won the fight for independence. Sheikh Mujibur Rahman, their leader, and the fighters are known as the Mukti Bahini.

5 ● RELIGION

At its creation, Bangladesh was a secular (nonreligious) state. However, a series of constitutional amendments in 1977 and 1978 led to the adoption of Islam as the state religion. Most Bangladeshis are Muslims, with almost 90 percent of the population claiming Islam as their religion. Hindus account for about 10 percent of the population. Buddhists, Christians, and other groups form other religious minorities, each with less than 1 percent of the total population.

6 ● MAJOR HOLIDAYS

Bangladesh officially celebrates the Muslim festivals of *Eid al-Fitr, Bakr-Id, Muharram,* and other Muslim festivals as public holidays. In addition, several Hindu festivals (for example, *Janamashtami, Durga Puja*), Christian holy days (Good Friday, Easter Monday, and Christmas), and Buddhist celebrations (*Buddha Purnima*) are recognized as holidays.

Secular holidays include *Shaheed Dibosh* (National Mourning Day or National Matyrs Day) on February 21. This holiday remembers the four people who were killed while marching in a procession, demonstrating their support for the establishment of Bengali as a national language (Bangladesh was still part of Pakistan at the

Cory Langley

Bangladeshis are friendly and hospitable. More than half of the population has no formal schooling.

time). Independence Day, March 6, commemorates the day when Bangladesh won its independence from Pakistan. National Revolution (or Solidarity) Day on November 7 and *Bijoy Dibosh* (Victory Day) on December 16 are also national holidays.

7 ● RITES OF PASSAGE

The rites of passage of Bangladeshis follow normal Muslim patterns. Births are occasions for rejoicing, with male babies preferred over females. Muslim prayers are whispered into the baby's ears. The naming ceremony is accompanied by the sacrifice of a sheep or goat. Male children undergo the *Sunnat,* or circumcision. It is becoming fashionable, especially in urban communities, to celebrate children's birthdays.

Death rituals are performed according to Muslim rules. The corpse is washed, shrouded, and carried to the cemetery where it is interred while prayers are said for the departed soul. The next forty days are marked by various rituals.

8 ● RELATIONSHIPS

Bangladeshis are friendly and helpful. Home visitors, even casual ones, are expected to stay for refreshments. Even the poorest host will provide a visitor with a glass of water and a spoonful of molasses, a piece of betel nut (areca nut), or offer a *hukka* (a pipe used for smoking tobacco).

When people meet, one person says, *Salaam aleykum* (Peace be unto you). The other replies, *Wa aleykum as-salaam* (Unto you also peace).

9 ● LIVING CONDITIONS

Bangladesh is desperately poor. Its living conditions reflect this fact. Life expectancy in 1995 was fifty-seven years—almost twenty years less than in the United States. Bangladesh's infant mortality rate is the highest in South Asia. More than one of every ten babies die during birth.

Bangladeshis are a rural people. About 80 percent of the population live in villages. Rural houses and construction materials depend on local conditions. Reeds are used in the delta. Houses further inland are made

of mud, bamboo, and brush wood. Roofs are thatched with palm leaves, though the more prosperous now use corrugated iron. People in the eastern hills build their houses on raised platforms.

Villages may also contain the more substantial houses of former landowners and Hindu moneylenders. Per capita income is among the lowest in South Asia at $220 per year. However, the middle classes in cities such as Dhaka (the capital) live like other urban elites throughout South Asia.

10 ● FAMILY LIFE

The basic social unit in rural Bangladesh is the family. This consists of an extended family living in a household (*chula*) residing in a homestead (*bari*). Individual nuclear families known as *ghar* are often found within the extended family. Beyond the circle of immediate relatives is an institution known as "the society" *(samaj)*. The samaj deals with issues such as the maintenance of the local mosque, support of a mullah (priest), and settling village disputes.

Women remain subordinate to men in Bangladeshi society. *Purdah,* the separation of women from men after puberty, is practiced to varying degrees. Some modern groups have rejected purdah, but the custom of separating men and women is still the norm. At public performances or lectures, for instance, it is common for men and women to sit in separate parts of the hall. Purdah also limits the ability of women to work.

Cory Langley

Construction materials for houses depend on local conditions. Reeds, mud, bamboo, and brush wood are all used for the walls of houses. Roofs may be thatched with palm leaves or made with tar paper or corrugated metal.

11 ● CLOTHING

In rural areas, Bangladeshi men wear the *lungi* and a vest or a shirt. The lungi is a piece of cotton cloth, usually checkered, that is wrapped around the waist. The better-educated wear a collarless, tunic-length shirt known as a *punjabi* and *pyjamas* (loose cotton trousers).

On formal occasions, the *sherwani* (long jacket), tight trousers known as *churidar,* and a turban are worn. Women typically wear a sari (long cloth that forms a skirt on one end and a head or shoulder covering on the other end) and blouse, although girls and young women prefer the *salwar-kamiz* tunic and pants combination. Western-style shirts, pants, and jackets are commonly worn by men in urban areas.

12 ● FOOD

Rice, vegetables, pulses (beans), fish, and meat are the staples of the Bangladeshi diet. The tastes and preferences of Muslims and other groups, however, differ. Beef is popular with Muslims, though it is taboo (forbidden) for Hindus. All communities eat with their hands rather than with utensils.

Recipe

Sandesh

Ingredients

1 gallon whole milk (do not use fat-free, 1 percent, or 2 percent milk)
6 Tablespoons lemon juice
½ cup sugar
1 Tablespoon butter (Bangladeshis use ghi, or clarified butter)
10 pistachios, finely crushed
2 teaspoons cardamom (or more)
cheesecloth and string or twine

Directions

1. In a large, heavy saucepan, slowly heat the milk to boiling.

2. Add lemon juice and stir until milk curdles. Remove from heat and allow to cool for 5 minutes.

3. Pour curdled milk into a bowl lined with a clean piece of cheesecloth.

4. Gather up the ends of the cheesecloth to make a tight bundle of curds. Tie with a piece of string or twine.

5. Squeeze the cheesecloth bag to remove moisture. Curds should be dry, like dry-curd cottage cheese.

6. Turn the curds onto a clean flat surface, and sprinkle with the sugar. Knead the curds, thoroughly combining them with the sugar. The sweetened curds will become a smooth, soft cheese.

7. Melt the butter over low heat in a large frying pan. Add the cheese and cook over low heat for 7 minutes, stirring constantly to prevent sticking.

8. Add crushed pistachios and cardamom. Remove from heat.

9. Press the cheese firmly with a spoon onto a cookie sheet. Cut into bite-sized portions and serve warm. Sandesh may also be chilled, and served cold. In Bangladesh, the cheese is pressed into a fancy mold.

At feasts or formal dinners, Muslims often serve pilaf and *biriyani* (rice dishes containing meat and vegetables), *kebabs* (barbecued cubes of meat), and *kormas* (meat served in various kinds of sauces). *Ghi* (clarified butter) is commonly served at such meals.

Milk forms an important element in the diet. Bangladesh is known for its milk-based sweets, such as *sandesh* (which means good news), a sweet cheese dessert served on happy occasions and during festivals.

13 ● EDUCATION

Nearly 59 percent of Bangladeshis five years of age and over have no formal schooling. Only about 15 percent have completed their secondary education. This is reflected in literacy rates that are among the lowest in South Asia, with only 35 percent of the population over fifteen years old able to read and write. This figure drops to 24 percent for females.

14 ● CULTURAL HERITAGE

Bangladeshis are proud of their Bengali culture, with its traditions of music, dance, and literature. The country shares in the classical and devotional traditions of Hindu and Muslim music. It has also developed its own regional forms of popular music. These include *bhatiali* songs about boatmen and life on the river, and *baul,* mystical verse sung by a group of religious musicians called Bauls. Indigenous dance forms include the *dhali, baul, manipuri,* and snake dances.

The Bengali literary tradition is one of the oldest in South Asia. Its greatest figure was the poet Rabindranath Tagore (1861–1941), who was part of the nineteenth-century revival of Bengali culture. Kazi Azrul Islam is a modern poet and playwright known as the "voice of Bengali nationalism and independence." A distinctive regional style of architecture may be seen in mosques and other monuments built by Muslims beginning in the early fifteenth century.

15 ● EMPLOYMENNT

Bangladesh is primarily an agricultural country. About 65 percent of the people work in agriculture. Rice is the dominant food crop. Jute is the country's major cash crop and an important export item.

The manufacturing sector of the economy is small. Since 1965, it has been illegal for children under the age of fifteen to work in factories. Since the 1970s, however, Bangladesh has become a major producer of ready-made clothes for export to the West (particularly the United States). Based on cheap Bangladeshi labor (mostly women), this now accounts for over 60 percent of export revenues. The export of frozen shrimp and fish has also increased in importance over the last two decades.

Large numbers of Bangladeshis are working in other countries. Money sent home from these people is an important source of income for the country.

16 ● SPORTS

Children in rural areas play games such as hide-and-seek, flying kites, and spinning tops. *Ha-do-do* is a traditional child's variation on the sport of *kabaddi.* Teams are formed, and each team establishes a territory. Teams then take turns sending one member into the opponent's territory to tag as many people as possible while holding his or her breath. The tagged players are eliminated. The first team to tag all of the opponent's members wins.

Kabaddi is a popular sport in Bangladesh. Two teams of six players each defend a territory. Each team attempts to tag and capture opponents who enter their territory. Soccer (known as football) is the most popular modern sport, while cricket, field hockey, badminton, and table tennis are also played. Wrestling is a favorite pastime for young men.

17 ● RECREATION

In villages, festivals and fairs are occasions for entertainment and relaxation. Dance, music, and song are popular, as are the *jatras* (village operas based on local myths).

In urban centers and those villages that have cinema houses, movies are by far the most popular form of entertainment. Chess was becoming more popular as a pastime in the 1990s. Radio and television broadcasts are available, but these are controlled by the government. The press is relatively free, but because of the low literacy rates, newspapers have low circulations.

18 ● CRAFTS AND HOBBIES

Among the arts and crafts for which Bangladesh is known are *kathas* (finely embroidered quilt-work); handprinted textiles; terra-cotta dolls, toys, and idols; and *sikhars* (elaborate rope hangings for pots, bottles, etc.).

Alpana drawings are designs made on floors and courtyards out of rice-paste. They are prepared by Hindu women in connection with certain religious festivals and rites. Copper and brass metalwork, basketry, and mat-weaving are also traditional crafts among Bangladeshi artisans. The region also has an important boat-building industry. The decoration of boats is a thriving folk art in Bangladesh.

19 ● SOCIAL PROBLEMS

When Bangladesh became independent in 1971, it suffered from overpopulation, extreme poverty, malnutrition, and lack of resources. By the late 1990s, little had changed.

Yet the country's very survival is an achievement. Slowly, with generous foreign aid, the economy is struggling upward. Food production has increased and a nationwide birth control program has lowered population growth. Flood control projects help limit the incidence of flooding. Economic reform has increased the value of the country's exports.

Ethnic unrest by Chakmas and other groups in the Chittagong Hill Tracts has resulted in violent conflict. Groups living in the Chittagong Hill Tracts want to be independent, but the Bangladeshi Army keeps troops in the area to discourage violence. The way the army has treated civilians has caused many Chakmas to flee to India.

20 ● BIBLIOGRAPHY

Bailey, Donna, and Anna Sproule. *Bangladesh.* Austin, Tex.: Steck-Vaughn, 1991.
Brace, Steve. *Bangladesh.* New York: Thomson Learning, 1995.
Heitzman, James, and Robert L. Worden, eds. *Bangladesh, A Country Study.* 2nd ed. Washington, D.C.: Federal Research Division, Library of Congress, 1988.
Lauri, Jason. *Bangladesh.* Chicago: Children's Press, 1992.
McClure, Vimala Schneider. *Bangladesh: Rivers in a Crowded Land.* Minneapolis, Minn.: Dillon Press, 1989.
Nugent, Nicholas. *Pakistan and Bangladesh.* Austin, Tex.: Raintree/Steck-Vaughn, 1992.

WEBSITES
Bangladesh Web Ring. [Online] Available http://www.bangla.org, 1997.
Virtual Bangladesh. [Online] Available http://www.virtualbangladesh.com, 1998.

Bengalis

PRONUNCIATION: ben-GAWL-eez
ALTERNATE NAMES: Bangalis
LOCATION: Bangladesh (Bengal region); India (state of West Bengal and other northeastern states)
POPULATION: 205 million (estimate, including expatriates)
LANGUAGE: Bengali
RELIGION: Islam; Hinduism

1 ● INTRODUCTION

Bengalis live in the northeastern part of the South Asian subcontinent. Historically, the area was known as Banga, after local peoples (the Bang) who settled in the region over one thousand years ago. This ancient term survives in many modern names. These include the region of Bengal, the Bengali (or Bangla) language, and the country of Bangladesh (literally, "the land of the Bengali people").

Bengal has been ruled by many political empires. It was ruled by the Buddhist Pala dynasty from the eighth to the twelfth centuries AD. By the late sixteenth century it was part of the Moghal Empire. In the mid-eighteenth century the British established a colonial base there. Bengal remained under British rule for nearly two hundred years. It was from here that the British expanded to take over the rest of India.

The British were driven out of the area in 1947. They divided the subcontinent into two countries, India and Pakistan. The eastern part of Bengal, where Muslims were most numerous, became part of Pakistan. East Pakistan, as it was known, became the

Cory Langley
Bengali women wear the sari and blouse, with rings and bangle bracelets. Most rural women go barefoot.

independent nation of Bangladesh in 1971, following a bloody civil war between Bengalis and West Pakistanis.

2 ● LOCATION

There are just over 174 million Bengalis. Most live in Bangladesh (106 million). The remainder live in the Indian state of West Bengal (68 million). Large communities of Bengali-speaking peoples, totaling perhaps ten million or more, are distributed throughout other states in northeastern India. Bengalis have also emigrated in large numbers to the United Kingdom, Canada, and the United States. The worldwide population of Bengalis, including the nonresident communities, is estimated to be around 205 million.

The lower plains and vast delta of the Ganges and Brahmaputra rivers lie at the heart of the Bengal region. The many rivers that cross the landscape provide an important means of transportation. They also hinder land travel. Frequent floods in the region cause extensive damage and loss of life. In the extreme north, a narrow strip of West Bengal State reaches into the foothills of the Himalayas.

3 ●LANGUAGE

The language of the region is Bengali. Dialects spoken in the western region are quite different from those in the east. Bengali is written in its own alphabet, which contains fifty-seven letter symbols. See the article on Bangladeshis in this chapter.

4 ●FOLKLORE

Bengali folklore is rich and varied. One popular folk tale, known all over the region and even forming the basis for a film, is "Seven Champa Brothers and One Sister Parul." The Champa and Parul are local trees.

There once was a king, so the story goes, who was married to seven queens. When the favorite youngest queen gave birth to seven sons and a daughter, the barren elder queens were jealous. They killed the babies, buried them in a garbage heap, and substituted puppies and kittens instead. Fearing witchcraft, the king banished the youngest queen. Seven Champa trees and one Parul tree grew out of the garbage heap where the babies were buried.

When the evil queens, and even the king, tried to pluck the flowers from the trees, the flowers moved away. They asked for the banished queen to be brought to them. She plucked the flowers, and a boy emerged from each Champa flower and a girl from the Parul flower. They were reunited with their mother and their father, the king. When the king learned the truth, he had the jealous queens killed and lived happily ever after with his remaining wife and children. The main theme of this tale is that jealousy leads to wrongdoing, and that this will eventually be found out and punished.

5 ●RELIGION

Over 60 percent of Bengalis are Muslim. Even in the mostly Hindu country of India, more than 20 percent of West Bengal's population is Muslim. Most Muslim Bengalis belong to the Sunni sect.

Bengalis in India are mainly Hindu. Among the mainstream Hindus, there are some unusual sects. Vaishnavas are followers of the Hindu god Vishnu. But Bengali Vaishnavas believe that Krishna is the supreme god, rather than an incarnation of Vishnu.

Shaktism is a religion based on the worship of female energy (sakti, literally "energy"). The Bengal form of Shaktism involves the worship of the goddess Kali. Kalighat in Calcutta, where animal sacrifices are carried out in the name of the goddess, is one of the major Shakti centers in the region.

6 ● MAJOR HOLIDAYS

Bengalis celebrate the major holidays of the Muslim and Hindu faiths. For Muslims, these include *Eid al-Fitr, Eid al-Adha (Bakr-Eid),* and *Muharram.* Bengali Hindus observe *Holi, Divali,* and other important religious festivals. *Durga Puja* is of particular importance to them. Dedicated to the goddess Durga, who is a manifestation of Shakti, the festivities last for nine days. Months before the festival, special images are made of Durga. These show her mounted on a lion and killing the evil demon Mahishasura. These images are lavishly painted and decorated. They are worshiped on each day of the festival.

On the tenth day, the image is decorated with flowers and carried through the streets. The parade makes it way to a river or the ocean, where the image of Durga is thrown into the water to be carried away by the current or tide.

7 ● RITES OF PASSAGE

Rites of passage for Bengalis are similar to those followed by other Muslims and Hindus. But, they have a distinctly Bengali flavor to them.

For example, Muslims follow the custom of saying the Call to Prayer *(azan)* to the newborn. The umbilical cord, however, is cut by the midwife who is usually a Hindu. Hindus observe the naming ceremony, the initiation ritual known as the "first feeding of rice" *(annaprasana),* and the sacred thread ceremony *(upanayana).* Muslim boys undergo the all-important circumcision rite *(sunnat).*

As with other Hindus, Bengalis cremate the dead. The funeral pyre is usually lit on the banks of a river or stream. The necessary rites are performed by the deceased's eldest son. Death is followed by a period of mourning (which varies in length), purification rites, and the *sraddha* or death feast held at the end of the mourning period.

8 ● RELATIONSHIPS

Hindu Bengalis greet each other by saying *Namaskar,* placing the hands together in front of the body with the palms touching. This form of greeting is widespread throughout India. Sometimes the phrase *Kamen asso* (How are you?) is added. Muslim Bengalis greet each other with *Salaam* or *Salaam alaikum.*

9 ● LIVING CONDITIONS

Rural living conditions in Bengal vary widely. House types and construction reflect local environmental conditions. In the interior, houses are made of mud, bamboo, and brush wood. Roofs are thatched. The more prosperous now use corrugated iron.

In Bangladesh, a typical village house consists of several huts around a compound. Facing the compound is the main house, with a porch in front that leads to the living quarters. These may consist of one or more bedrooms, a sitting room, and a kitchen. Other huts on the sides of the compound are used for storage and cattle sheds.

Such a lifestyle and standard of living are in marked contrast to those of the urban elites who enjoy all the modern conveniences of city living. Some of the wealthy industrialists and business owners of Cal-

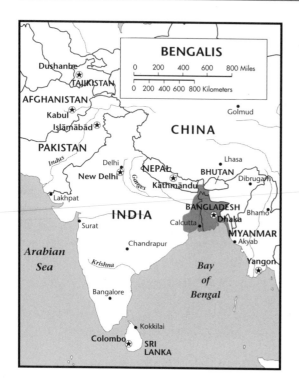

BENGALIS

0 200 400 600 800 Miles

0 200 400 600 800 Kilometers

social standing. Cousin marriage is common among Bengali Muslims.

11 ● CLOTHING

In rural areas, Muslim men wear the *lungi,* a piece of (often checkered) cloth that is wrapped around the waist. Hindus dress in the *dhoti,* the long piece of white cotton cloth that is wrapped around the waist, then drawn between the legs in the manner of a loincloth. Village men usually go shirtless but on occasion may put on a vest or a long shirt called a *punjabi* as an upper garment.

Women wear the *sari* (long cloth that forms a skirt on one end a head or shoulder covering on the other end) and blouse. Younger Muslim girls may favor the combination of *salwar* (loose trousers) and *kamiz* (tunic). Women in the countryside go barefoot. A variety of rings, bangles, and other ornaments are worn by women of all classes.

In cities, safari suits or Western-style business suits are common. Younger urban women may also dress in Western fashions, although the sari is retained for formal occasions.

12 ● FOOD

Boiled rice is the staple food in rural Bengal. It is eaten with vegetables such as onion, garlic, eggplant, and a variety of gourds according to the season. Fish and meat are favorite foods. Their cost places them beyond the reach of most villagers. Vegetables, fish, and meat are prepared as spicy curried dishes.

Beef and water-buffalo meat are popular with Muslims. Hindus view the cow as

cutta (India) have a style of living that compares favorably with that found among the wealthy in the United States.

10 ● FAMILY LIFE

Bengali Hindus, like all Hindus, belong to castes *(jati).* A caste is a social group into which people are born. It determines their place in society, who they can marry and, often, the kinds of education and employment opportunities they will have. Castes are unchangeable.

Marriages are arranged by the parents. Hindu marriages are governed by rules of caste. In contrast, Muslims have no caste restrictions, although marriage partners are usually chosen from families of similar

sacred. They do not eat beef. Most Bengali Hindus are not vegetarians, however, and will eat goats, ducks, chickens, and eggs, in addition to fish.

Cuisine among the upper classes includes pilaf and *biryani* (rice dishes containing meat and vegetables), *kebabs* (barbecued cubes of meat), and meat dishes known as *korma*. Milk forms an important element in the diet. Milk-based sweets are popular throughout the region.

13 ● EDUCATION

Bengalis living in Bangladesh, especially in rural areas, are likely to be poorly educated and illiterate. About 35 percent of Bangladeshis are literate (able to read and write). This is one of the lowest literacy rates in the region. By contrast, literacy in West Bengal (a part of India) is nearly 60 percent, slightly higher than the average for all of India (53 percent).

Education has long been a mark of higher social status. Vishva-Bharati University, founded by Bengali poet Rabindranath Tagore (1861–1941) in the city of Shantiniketan, is world-famous as a center for the study of Indian history and culture.

14 ● CULTURAL HERITAGE

Bengalis have one of the richest literary traditions in the region known as the Indian subcontinent. The earliest known works in Bengali are Buddhist books that date to the tenth and eleventh centuries AD. Islam also contributed to medieval Bengali literature.

Modern Bengalis have created literature recognized worldwide. Rabindranath Tagore (1861–1941), the Bengali poet and

Cory Langley

Bengalis living in rural areas are likely to be poorly educated. It is a mark of higher social status that these young people (except for the youngest one) attend school.

writer, was awarded the Nobel Prize for Literature in 1913. Bengalis have also achieved great success in the field of classical Indian music and dance.

Satyajit Ray (1921–92), the film director from India who won international fame was a Bengali.

15 ● EMPLOYMENT

Bengalis are predominantly rural and agricultural in nature. More than two-thirds of them are farmers. West Bengal, in India, is an industrial area. The cities and towns along the banks of the Hooghly River (an arm of the Ganges) make up one of India's most important manufacturing regions. It is here that Calcutta is located. Founded in 1690 as a British trading post, Calcutta is now one of the world's largest cities. Its population is just over twelve million people. Its industries include jute processing, engineering, textiles, and chemicals.

Calcutta is perhaps the most important intellectual and cultural center of India. Bengalis take great pride in this. The city is the birthplace of Indian nationalism, and of modern Indian literary and artistic thought.

16 ● SPORTS

Bengali children play games common to children all over the region of South Asia. These include tag, hide-and-seek, kite-flying, marbles, and spinning tops. Cricket, soccer, and field hockey are major spectator sports, and many children play these games at school as well. Tennis, golf, and horse-racing are popular among the urban middle classes who have adopted the sports and hobbies of Western countries.

17 ● RECREATION

Recreational activities among Bengalis vary widely. Villagers may derive their greatest pleasure from fairs and religious festivals. They also enjoy Bengali folk traditions such as *jatra* (traveling folk theater), the *bhatiali* (boater's songs), and the *baul* (mystical songs performed by wandering minstrels).

City dwellers have access to radio, television, theater, movies, films, museums, and other cultural activities.

18 ● CRAFTS AND HOBBIES

The folk arts and crafts of Bengal reflect the diversity of its people and the skills of its artisans. Among the items produced are handprinted textiles, embroidered quilt-work, terra-cotta dolls, toys, and religious idols.

Alpana drawings are religious designs prepared by Hindu women. They are made on walls, floors, and courtyards out of rice-paste. The decoration of boats is a thriving folk art in the delta region. Copper and brass metalwork, pottery, weaving, basketry, and carpentry are among the many activities pursued by the craftspeople in the region.

19 ● SOCIAL PROBLEMS

Problems among Bengalis vary considerably. Some problems, such as frequent flooding in Bengal, are caused by nature. Bangladesh is also one of the poorest nations in the world. It has experienced civil unrest, suspension of democratic rights, and repressive military governments.

20 ● BIBLIOGRAPHY

Bailey, Donna, and Anna Sproule. *Bangladesh.* Austin, Tex.: Steck-Vaughn, 1991.

Brace, Steve. *Bangladesh.* New York: Thomson Learning, 1995.

Heitzman, James, and Robert L. Worden, eds. *Bangladesh, A Country Study.* 2nd ed. Washington, D.C.: Federal Research Division, Library of Congress, 1988.

Lauri, Jason. *Bangladesh.* Chicago: Children's Press, 1992

McClure, Vimala Schneider. *Bangladesh: Rivers in a Crowded Land.* Minneapolis, Minn.: Dillon Press, 1989.

Nugent, Nicholas. *Pakistan and Bangladesh.* Austin, Tex.: Raintree/Steck-Vaughn, 1992.

Ray, Niharranjan. *History of the Bengali People.* Calcutta, India: Orient Longman, 1994.

WEBSITES

Bangladesh Web Ring. [Online] Available http://www.bangla.org, 1997.

Virtual Bangladesh. [Online] Available http://www.virtualbangladesh.com, 1998.

West Bengal Home Page. [Online] Available http://westbengal.com, 1998.

Chakmas

PRONUNCIATION: chahk-MAHZ
ALTERNATE NAMES: Changma; Sawngma
LOCATION: Bangladesh; India; Myanmar (Burma)
POPULATION: 550,000
LANGUAGE: Bengali dialect (Bangla)
RELIGION: Theravada (Southern) Buddhism

1 ● INTRODUCTION

Chakma is the name of the largest tribe found in the hilly area of eastern Bangladesh known as the Chittagong Hill Tracts. Their name was first used by British census-takers to describe certain hill people.

When the British were driven from India in 1947, the land was divided into two countries, Pakistan and India. The people who lived in the Chittagong Hill Tracts region expected to become part of India. Instead, the region was given to Pakistan. This caused resentment because the people, mostly Chakma, are primarily Buddhist. They saw themselves more culturally similar to the Hindu peoples of India than the Muslims of Pakistan.

Pakistan's two regions were known as East Pakistan (where the Chakma lived) and West Pakistan. In 1971, East Pakistan fought successfully to win independence from West Pakistan. East Pakistan then became the nation of Bangladesh. The Chakma felt just as alienated from the Bangladesh government as they had from Pakistan. In 1973, the *Shanti Bahini* (Peace Force) began to stage violent attacks against the government to try to win independence for the Chittagong Hill Tracts. Guerrillas attacked government forces and the Bangladeshi Army responded with attacks on civilian tribal peoples. As of the late 1990s, this conflict continued.

2 ● LOCATION

The Chakma population is estimated to be around 550,000. It is spread over three different countries. The majority (approximately 300,000 people) are located in the Chittagong Hill Tracts of Bangladesh. There are also about 80,000 Chakmas in Mizoram State in India, and 20,000 in Burma (Myanmar).

The Chakmas are a Mongoloid people related to people of southwestern Burma. The Chittagong Hills form part of the western fringe of the mountain regions of Burma and eastern India. The region has warm temperatures, monsoon rains, and high humidity.

3 ● LANGUAGE

The Chakmas speak a dialect of Bengali (Bangla) and use the standard Bengali alphabet. See the article on Bangladeshis in this chapter.

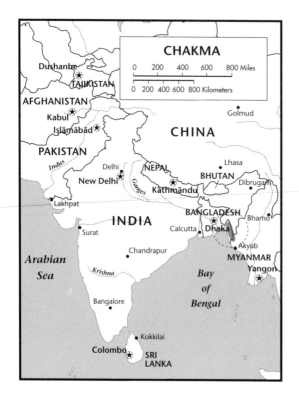

CHAKMA

0   200   400   600   800 Miles

0 200 400 600 800 Kilometers

4 ● FOLKLORE

The myth that describes the origin of the Chakma traces the tribe to the ancient kingdom of Champaknagar. One of the king's sons marched east with a large army in the hope of conquering new lands. He crossed the "sea" of the Meghna River and captured the kingdom of Arakan in Burma, where he settled. His people intermarried with the Burmese and gradually adopted the Buddhist religion.

The last king of this dynasty was a ruler named Sher Daulat. He was credited with supernatural powers and was supposed to purify himself from sin by bringing out his intestines to wash in the river. His wife, out of curiosity, hid herself and watched him do

this one day. Sher Daulat found her spying on him and, in a fit of rage, killed her and all his family. His eccentricities and tyranny grew so great that finally his people killed him. Fearing the consequences of this, the people left the Arakan kingdom, moving north into the area of the Chittagong Hills they occupy today.

5 ● RELIGION

The Chakmas are Buddhists. Chakmas officially follow the Southern, or Theravada, form of the Buddhism. But, their form of Buddhism has aspects of Hinduism and traditional religions as well.

Almost every Chakma village has a Buddhist temple (*kaang*). Buddhist priests or monks are called *Bhikhus*. They preside at religious festivals and ceremonies. The villagers support their monks with food, gifts, and offerings to Buddha.

The Chakmas also worship Hindu deities. Lakshmi, for example, is worshipped as the Goddess of the Harvest. Chakmas offer the sacrifice of goats, chickens, or ducks to calm the spirits that are believed to bring fevers and disease. Even though animal sacrifice is totally against Buddhist beliefs, the Chakma Buddhist priests ignore the practice.

6 ● MAJOR HOLIDAYS

Chakmas celebrate various Buddhist festivals. The most important is *Buddha Purnima*. This is the anniversary of three important events in Buddha's life—his birth, his attainment of enlightenment, and his death. It is observed on the full moon day of the month of Vaisakh (usually in May).

On this and other festival days, Chakmas put on their best clothes and visit the temple. There, they. offer flowers to the image of Buddha, light candles, and listen to sermons from the priests. Alms (offerings) are given to the poor, and feasts are held for the priests.

The three-day festival known as *Bishu*, which coincides with the Bengali New Year's Day, is celebrated with much enthusiasm. Houses are decorated with flowers, young children pay special attention to the elderly to win their blessings, and festive dishes are prepared for guests.

7 ● RITES OF PASSAGE

After the birth of a child, the father places some earth near the birth bed and lights a fire on it. This is kept burning for five days. Afterward, the earth is thrown away and the mother and child are bathed. A woman is considered unclean for a month after childbirth and is not allowed to cook food during this period. Children are breastfed for several years by their mothers.

Chakmas cremate their dead. The body is bathed, dressed, and laid out on a bamboo platform. Relatives and villagers visit the body. A drum used only at this time is beaten at intervals. Cremation usually occurs in the afternoon. The ritual is presided over by a priest.

Buddists believe in reincarnation. This means that they believe that the dead person's spirit will return to earth in another living form. The morning after the cremation, relatives visit the cremation ground to search for footprints. They believe that the departed will have left some mark of his or her new incarnation (living form). Some remains of bones are collected, put in an earthen pot, and placed in a nearby river.

The mourning period for the family lasts for seven days. No fish or animal flesh is eaten during this time. On the seventh day, the final ritual *(Satdinya)* is held. At this time the family offers food to their ancestors, Buddhist monks deliver religious discourses, offerings are made to the monks, and the entire village participates in a communal feast.

8 ● RELATIONSHIPS

Chakma hospitality is overflowing. Guests are given home-brewed liquor and the *hukka* (hooka) pipe. The hukka is a pipe used for smoking tobacco. It has a long flexible tube attached to a water bottle. The smoke is cooled by passing over the water before being inhaled by the smoker.

Chakmas greet each other with the traditional cry, *Hoya!* This exuberant shout is also used to express pleasure at victory in sports such as tug-of-war that accompany the numerous hill festivals held throughout the year. After living for so many years near Muslims, some Chakmas use the Muslim greeting, *Salaam.*

9 ● LIVING CONDITIONS

Chakmas build their houses on slopes near the banks of a river or a stream. A few related families may build on the same plot of land, creating a homestead *(bari)*. Baris cluster together to form hamlets *(para)* and a number of hamlets make up a village *(gram)*.

The traditional Chakma house is made of bamboo. It is constructed on a bamboo or wooden platform about two meters (six feet) above the ground. The house is built on the rear of the platform. Mat walls divide the house into separate compartments. A porch in the front of the house is divided in two by a mat partition. One area is used by men and boys and the other by women and girls. Small compartments may be built for storage of grain and other possessions. Household objects ranging from baskets to pipes for smoking tobacco are made out of bamboo.

10 ● FAMILY LIFE

Chakmas are divided into clans *(gojas),* which are further subdivided into subclans *(guttis).* Members of the same subclan are forbidden to marry each other. Parents arrange marriages, although the wishes of sons and daughters are taken into account. A bride price (goods given by groom's family to bride's family) is fixed when the two families negotiate the marriage.

The marriage ceremony is known as *Chumulong* and is performed by Buddhist priests. If young people elope, the marriage can be formalized on payment of fines. Polygyny (marriage to more than one wife) is acceptable but rare. Divorce is allowed, as is remarriage after the death of a spouse.

11 ● CLOTHING

Chakma men have given up their traditional clothes for Western-style shirts and trousers. It is the women who maintain the traditional Chakma style of dress, which consists of two pieces of cloth. One is worn as a skirt, wrapped around the lower part of the body and extending from waist to ankle. Its traditional color is black or blue, with a red border at top and bottom.

The second piece of cloth is a breastband, woven with colored designs, that is tightly wrapped around the upper body. This is worn with a variety of necklaces, bracelets, anklets, rings, and other ornaments. Chakma women are skilled weavers and make their own cloth.

12 ● FOOD

The staple food of the Chakmas is rice, supplemented by millet, corn (maize), vegetables, and mustard. Vegetables include yams, pumpkins, melons, and cucumbers. Vegetables and fruit gathered from the forest may be added to the diet. Fish, poultry, and meat (even pork) are eaten, despite the Buddhist taboo on consuming animal flesh.

Traditional diets have slowly been abandoned, as the Chakmas have been forced to flee their homeland. Some typical Chakma dishes include fish, vegetables, and spices stuffed into a length of bamboo and cooked in a low fire; foods wrapped in banana leaves and placed beside a fire; and eggs that are aged until they are rotten.

Chakmas do not like milk. They drink alcoholic beverages freely, and every household makes its own rice liquor. Alcohol is consumed at all festivals and social occasions.

13 ● EDUCATION

Chakmas live in isolated areas of Bangladesh. They are not part of the majority population and are quite poor by Western standards. They do not have access to Western-style education. Literacy (ability to read and write) among men of the hill tribes is about 15 percent. This figure drops to 7 percent for women.

14 ● CULTURAL HERITAGE

Buddhists books, translated into Chakma and written on palm leaves, are known as *Aghartara*. The *Tallik* is a detailed account of medicinal plants, methods of their preparation, and their use in the treatment of disease.

Folk music is a major aspect of Chakma tribal culture. It includes romantic love songs known as *Ubageet*. The *Genkhuli* ballads relate incidents from the past. There are also epic poems like *Radhamon and Dhanapati*.

Traditional musical instruments include a bugle made from buffalo horn, a circular piece of iron with a string stretched across it that vibrates to produce sound, and a drum. The bamboo flute is played by almost all Chakma youth. Unlike other tribal groups of the eastern hills, dancing is not an important part of Chakma life.

15 ● EMPLOYMENT

The Chakmas are farmers. There is no ownership of land, but Chakma custom holds that no one should interfere with fields that look like someone else is farming there. Land is cleared of trees and bushes, and any remaining vegetation is burned during the dry season in April. Crops are planted after the first heavy rains. Harvesting usually takes place in October and November.

Some Chakmas have given up their farming lifestyle and have entered the labor market. Those fortunate enough to have the necessary education have gone on to clerical and other white collar jobs. Many, however, work as laborers in the factories and industrial projects that have grown up along the valley of the Karnafuli River.

16 ● SPORTS

Ha-do-do is a game played throughout the region. Two teams stand on either side of a central line. They take turns sending a player into opposing territory to touch as many people as he or she can during the space of one breath, while at the same time saying "Ha-do-do." If the player runs out of breath or is caught by his or her opponents, he or she is out.

On the other hand, if the player successfully returns to his or her own territory, the players he or she has tagged must leave the game. Other pastimes include *Gila Khela,* a game similar to marbles except that small wooden disks are used instead of marbles; *Nadeng Khela,* played with a spinning top; and various wrestling games. Girls do not have dolls or play at being "mother" as they do in Western cultures.

17 ● RECREATION

Traditional forms of recreation include popular folk songs and music, and *jatra,* the village opera. Wrestling and other sports held at fairs are popular. In the past, hunting and fishing were favorite pastimes.

18 ● CRAFTS AND HOBBIES

The Chakma are skilled at making a variety of household goods from bamboo, often using nothing more than a simple knife. Women are expert weavers and dyers and make their own cloth called *Alam.* They are skilled in the art of making baskets from bamboo.

19 ● SOCIAL PROBLEMS

The Chakma people face difficult situations today. Their population is larger than that of over sixty independent nations. Yet the tribe is fragmented and scattered over three countries. In each country, Chakmas form a minority and many are refugees from their homeland, living in conditions of squalor.

The most serious problem faced by the Chakmas is in Bangladesh, where they are fighting for an independent homeland. Some Chakmas and other tribal peoples have resorted to armed warfare against the government. This, in turn, has led to reprisals by the police and Bangladeshi Army. Both Amnesty International (the human rights organization) and the United States have reported human rights violations against Chakma civilians.

20 ● BIBLIOGRAPHY

Brace, Steve. *Bangladesh.* New York: Thomson Learning, 1995.

Brown, Susan. *Pakistan and Bangladesh.* Englewood Cliffs, N.J.: Silver Burdett Press, 1989.

Chakma, Sugata. "Chakma Culture." *Folklore (The Journal of the Folklore Research Institute, Bangladesh)* 7 (January): 58–75, 1982.

McClure, Vimala Schneider. *Bangladesh: Rivers in a Crowded Land.* Minneapolis, Minn.: Dillon Press, 1989.

Talukdar, S. P. *Chakmas: An Embattled Tribe.* New Delhi: Uppal Publishing House, 1994.

WEBSITES

Bangladesh Web Ring. [Online] Available http://www.bangla.org, 1997.

Virtual Bangladesh. [Online] Available http://www.virtualbangladesh.com, 1998.

Barbados

About 90 percent of all Barbadians (sometimes called Bajans) are the descendants of former African slaves. Some 5 percent are mulattos (mixed descent) and another 5 percent are white.

Barbadians

PRONUNCIATION: bar-BAY-dee-uhns
ALTERNATE NAMES: Bajans
LOCATION: Barbados
POPULATION: 264,400
LANGUAGE: English with West African dialect influences
RELIGION: Christianity: Anglican church (majority); Roman Catholicism; Methodism; Rastafarianism; also Jehovah's Witness, Hinduism, Islam, Baha'ism , Judaism; Apostolic Spiritual Baptist is the island's only indigenous religion

1 ● INTRODUCTION

Barbados is the only Caribbean island that was governed by only one colonial power, Great Britain. Its influence has given the country the nickname "Little England." The Barbadians' name for themselves is "Bajans" (BAY-juns). It comes from "Bar-bajians," the way the British pronounced "Barbadians."

The British first landed on Barbados in 1625. They soon began growing sugar cane and brought in African slaves to work on plantations. Even after slavery was abolished in the British Empire in 1834, things changed very little. The black workers stayed on the plantations while a small group of white landowners held on to economic and political power.

The Barbados Progressive League was founded in 1937. It promoted social, economic, and political reform. Citizens won the right to vote (known as universal suffrage) in 1950. In 1966, Barbados became an independent nation within the British Commonwealth.

2 ● LOCATION

Barbados belongs to the group of islands known as the Lesser Antilles. Barbados is the easternmost Caribbean island. Its total area is 166 square miles (430 square kilometers). The pear-shaped island consists of lowlands and terraced limestone plains. Its total population was estimated at 264,400 in 1995. With this many people on an island about the size of San Antonio, Texas, Barbados is one of the world's most densely populated countries. It has five times the population density of India.

3 ● LANGUAGE

English is the official language of Barbados. The Barbadian dialect (variation on the language) has strong West African influences. Many words, such as *duppy,* meaning "ghost," come from African languages. Another African feature is duplicate words (sow-pig, bull-cows, gate-doors).

Some expressions in Barbadian English and their American English equivalents are:

BARBADIAN ENGLISH	STANDARD ENGLISH
again	now
all two	both
black lead	pencil
cool out	relax
duppy umbrella	mushroom
fingersmith	thief
jump up	dance
nyam (or yam)	eat
sand side	beach
t'ink	think
yuh	you
break fives	shake hands
tie-goat	married person
hag	bother

4 ● FOLKLORE

The folklore of Barbados goes back to the people's African roots. Many folk beliefs involve methods for keeping ghosts, or *duppies,* from returning to haunt living people. These folk methods include sprinkling rum on the ground, walking into the house backward, and hanging herbs from the windows and doorways. Another figure from Barbadian folklore is the *heartman,* who kills children and offers their hearts to the devil. The *baccoo* is a tiny man who lives in a bottle and can decide a person's destiny.

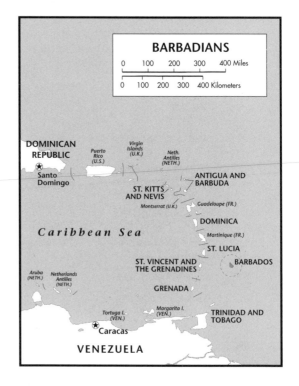

Some examples of Barbadian proverbs are:

"One-smart dead at two-smart door."
(No matter how smart you are, there's always someone who can outwit you.)

"Coconut don' grow upon pumpkin vine."
(Children turn out like their parents.)

5 ● RELIGION

The main religion is Christianity. The Anglican, or Episcopal, Church has the most members. Other Christian denominations include the Roman Catholic Church, Methodist Church, and the Jehovah's Witnesses. Altogether, there are more than 140 different sects and denominations. Other

Cory Langley

Houses in Barbados are usually symmetrical, with a door in the center and windows on either side. Galvanized iron has replaced wooden shingles for the roof. The metal roof makes the inside uncomfortably warm.

religious groups include the Hindus, Muslims, Jews, and Baha'is.

Religion is important in the lives of Barbadians. The school day usually begins with a prayer. A popular Sunday afternoon television program, *Time to Sing,* presents a different church choir every week. There are many religious programs on the radio.

The Apostolic Spiritual Baptists (also known as "Tie-heads") belong to a religion founded on Barbados in 1957. They combine Christian and African religious practices. Tie-heads, both men and women, wear turbans on their heads and colorful gowns. The colors symbolize specific qualities.

6 ● MAJOR HOLIDAYS

Barbadians celebrate the major holidays of the Christian calendar. Other holidays include New Year's Day (January 1), May Day (May 1), CARICOM Day (first Monday in August), Independence Day (November 30), and United Nations Day (first Monday in October. CARICOM day commemorates the founding in 1973 of the Caribbean Community and Common Market.

The island's biggest celebration is the Crop Over festival. It is held in July and early August, and is similar to Thanksgiving in the United States. Crop Over began as a festival celebrating the sugar cane harvest.

Events include the presentation of the Last Canes. The climax of the festival is the judging of costumed groups (called bands) on Kadooment Day (August 1).

7 • RITES OF PASSAGE

Most Barbadians mark major life events (birth, puberty, marriage, death) within the Christian tradition.

8 • RELATIONSHIPS

Barbadians are known for their politeness. This has been linked to the influence of the British. It may also reflect the island's high population density; living so close to others makes it important to prevent conflict.

9 • LIVING CONDITIONS

The standard of living on Barbados is one of the highest in the Caribbean. Nearly all Barbadian households have running water. Almost all have refrigerators and televisions, and most have telephones.

The traditional Barbadian wooden house, or chattel house, is still common on the island. A chattel house has one story and is built from a single layer of wooden planks. It has a unique feature: it can be taken apart easily and moved to another location. The shape of the house is usually symmetrical, with a door in the center and windows on either side. Traditionally, the roof was made of wooden shingles. As of the late 1990s, it is usually galvanized iron, which makes the inside uncomfortably warm.

The most popular type of house is the suburban wall house. It is built of cement blocks and stucco and has a small cement wall around it. It is often built in stages.

Many families can afford only a very small house at first. Later, they often add to it, one room at a time.

10 • FAMILY LIFE

Many Barbadian households consist of couples who are not legally married. This may reflect the island's history of slavery, which often separated men from women and from their children. There is also a shortage of men on the island because many have left for other places.

A woman's economic survival is closely connected to her children. When the children are young, the woman receives child support from their father. As the children grow older, they begin to help out with chores and begin to earn money. Children are a woman's main source of support when she is old. Grandmothers are important in raising the children. Often they take care of the children so that mothers can work.

11 • CLOTHING

Barbadians wear modern Western-style clothing. Colorful, inventive costumes can be seen at festivals, especially the Crop Over celebration. Members of the Apostolic Spiritual Baptist Church are known for their turbans and their colorful gowns.

12 • FOOD

Barbadian cooking draws on West African, English, Spanish, French, and other traditions. *Cou-cou* is one of the most popular dishes. It is a cornmeal and okra pudding. Usually it is served with gravy and salt cod. Salt cod is codfish preserved with salt. It is a staple, or important part, of the Barbadian diet.

Recipe

Coconut Bread

Ingredients

6 ounces brown sugar
6 ounces shortening
1 large egg, beaten
3 cups grated coconut
1 teaspoon powdered cinnamon
1 teaspoon powdered nutmeg
2 teaspoons almond extract
¼ pound raisins or mixed fruit
1 cup milk
1¼ pounds flour, sifted
½ teaspoon salt
1 Tablespoon baking powder

Directions

1. Preheat oven to 350°F.
2. Combine shortening and sugar.
3. Add the beaten egg, and mix thoroughly.
4. Mix in the spices, almond extract, fruit or raisins, grated coconut, and milk.
5. Add flour, salt, and baking powder and mix thoroughly.
6. Pour the batter into two greased loaf pans—a one-pound pan and a two-pound pan.
7. Bake loaves for one hour, or until browned. Cool on racks before serving.

Rice served with peas (including green, blackeye, cow, and gunga) is another staple. Pork is used in many different ways by Barbarians. They joke that the only part of a pig they can't use for food is its hair. A favorite dessert is coconut bread. If you would like to make coconut bread see the recipe above.

13 ● EDUCATION

Barbados has a literacy rate (the percentage of people who can read and write) of 95 to 100 percent. This is the highest in the Caribbean. Children five to sixteen years of age are required to attend school. All education is free, including college.

To emphasize Barbadians' African heritage, children learn about African folklore and music in school.

14 ● CULTURAL HERITAGE

The most famous Barbadian writer is poet and playwright Derek Walcott. He won the 1992 Nobel Prize in Literature. Other well-known writers include essayist John Wickham, novelist George Lamming, and poet Edward Kamau Braithwaite.

Barbados has an active community of artists. They produce paintings, murals, sculptures, and crafts. Many of their works reflect strong African influences.

15 ● EMPLOYMENT

About 40 percent of employment on Barbados is in service jobs. This includes about 20 percent in the government. The other main areas are business, manufacturing, and construction, making up 9 percent. Equal numbers of men and women work outside the home.

16 ● SPORTS

Cricket is the most popular sport on Barbados. Some people say it is like a national religion. Other popular sports include horse racing, soccer, hockey, rugby, volleyball, and softball. The local game of *road tennis* is a cross between ping-pong and lawn tennis. It is played with a homemade wooden paddle, and the "net" is a long piece of wood.

17 ● RECREATION

Barbadian men traditionally spend their leisure time in the rum shop. It combines the functions of grocery store, bar, and domino parlor. The island has one rum shop for every 150 adults. Women tend to prefer the local church as a social center. Dance, music, and theater are popular. As of the late 1990s, about 80 percent of Barbadian households had television sets.

18 ● CRAFTS AND HOBBIES

The Barbadian *tuk* band provides the music for all major celebrations on the island. With its pennywhistles, snare drums, and bass drums, it is like a British military band, but with an African flair. The calypso, reggae, and steel band music of Trinidad and Jamaica are also very popular.

Barbadian crafts include pottery, mahogany carvings, and jewelry.

19 ● SOCIAL PROBLEMS

The great number of tourists has contributed to water pollution. The island's coral reefs have also been damaged. Some people blame the growth of tourism for problems such as crime, drug use, and prostitution.

20 ● BIBLIOGRAPHY

Beckles, Hilary. *A History of Barbados: From Amerindian Settlement to Nation-State.* New York: Cambridge University Press, 1990.

Broberg, Merle. *Barbados.* New York: Chelsea House, 1989.

Meditz, Sandra W., and Dennis M. Hanratty. *Islands of the Caribbean Commonwealth: A Regional Study.* Washington, DC: US Government, 1989.

Pariser, Harry S. *The Adventure Guide to Barbados.* New York: Hunter, 1990.

Potter, Robert B. *Barbados.* Santa Barbara, Calif.: Clio Press, 1987.

WEBSITES

Barbados Tourism Authority. [Online] Available http://barbados.org/, 1998.

World Travel Guide, Barbados. [Online] Available http://www.wtgonline.com/country/bb/gen.html, 1998.

Belarus

■ BELARUSANS 139

The people of Belarus are called Belarusans (sometimes spelled Belarussians). Over three-fourths of the population are native Belarusans; Russians represent 13 percent; Poles, 4 percent; Ukrainians, 3 percent; and Jews, 1 percent. For more information, see the chapters on Russia and Poland (Volume 7) and Ukraine (Volume 9).

Belarusans

PRONUNCIATION: Byeh-lah-ROOS-ans
ALTERNATE NAMES: Byelorussians; "White Russians"
LOCATION: Belarus
POPULATION: 10.5 million
LANGUAGE: Belarusan
RELIGION: Christian (Russian Orthodox, Roman Catholic, Pentecostal, Baptist, other sects); minority of Muslim, Jewish, and other faiths

1 ● INTRODUCTION

Belaya Rus, the name for the Belarusan homeland, dates back to the twelfth century. Belarusans have stubbornly struggled for centuries to defend their independence, language, culture, and national way of life. In the last half of the eighteenth century, Russia took over Belarus. By the late nineteenth century, an independence movement was growing. In 1918, an independent Belarusan Democratic Republic was declared. However, Russia arranged to have it overthrown. It was replaced with the Belarussian Soviet Socialist Republic (BSSR), which formally joined the Soviet Union in 1922.

In August 1991, Belarus became the sixth republic to secede from the Soviet Union. That December, Minsk, the capital of Belarus, became the capital of the new Commonwealth of Independent States (CIS). The CIS is a loosely united group of former Soviet republics. It was formed to further their shared military and economic interests.

2 ● LOCATION

Belarus is a landlocked nation in Eastern Europe. Its capital is Minsk. Its area is 80,154 square miles (207,600 square kilometers), about the size of the state of Minnesota. The land of Belarus is mostly flat. Belarus has a temperate continental climate, with a mild and humid winter, a warm summer, and a wet autumn. As of 1994, Belarus had a population of ten and one-half million. Nearly four-fifths (or 8.4 million) were ethnic Belarusans.

3 ● LANGUAGE

The influence of political control by Poland and Russia is evident in the Belarusan language. Modern Belarusan is very close to older forms of the Slavic languages, and some words are borrowed from modern Polish and Russian. While part of the Soviet Union, Belarusans were pressured to use Russian as their main language.

Everyday terms in the Belarusan language include *dobraya zdarovya* (hello), *tak* (yes), *nye* (no), *kali laska* (please), *dzyakooi* (thank you), and *da pabachenya* (goodbye).

4 ● FOLKLORE

A historical event that is now part of Belarusan folklore is the sad story of princess Rahnieda.

The story begins with Prince Vladimir, who later brought Christianity to Russia. When he was a young man, Vladimir became angry when his father, Svyatoslav, made Yaropolk, Vladimir's brother, ruler of the city of Kiev. Vladimir decided to fight Yaropolk for Kiev and wanted to marry Princess Rahnieda and receive her father's help. But Rahnieda turned Vladimir down because she liked Yaropolk. Then Vladimir (helped by his uncle, Dobrinya), attacked and killed Rahnieda's family and forced her to marry him. Then Vladimir won Kiev by killing Yaropolk.

Rahnieda gave birth to a boy and named him Iziaslau. She continued to hate Vladimir and decided to kill him, but she failed. Vladimir wanted to punish Rahnieda by death, but Iziaslau made him change his

mind. Instead, Vladimir banished both Iziaslau and Rahnieda to a city built for them. It was named Iziaslau (today it is known as Zaslauje, and it is located near Minsk). According to legend, Rahnieda became a nun. She took the name Anastasia and lived in a monastery until she died around the year AD 1000.

Rahnieda's story has inspired many tales about a heartbroken princess. She wanders across her native land comforting grieving people, healing wounded soldiers, and helping other unfortunate people.

5 ● RELIGION

The Eastern Orthodox form of Christianity came to Belarus in about AD 1000. It was spread through the country by order of its ruler, Vladimir. Later, Belarus' ties with

Poland encouraged the spread of Roman Catholicism.

In the early years of the Soviet Union, many parishes were destroyed, and religious leaders were often sent away or killed. In the early 1990s, about 60 percent of Belarusans identified themselves as Orthodox.

6 ● MAJOR HOLIDAYS

Major holidays in Belarus include New Year's Day (January 1), Eastern Orthodox Christmas (January 7), Labor May (May 1), Victory Day (May 9), Independence Day (July 27), and Christmas (December 25).

The *Kolady* (Christmas) celebration starts with a solemn, special supper on *Kootia* (Christmas Eve). Twelve or more Lenten dishes are served in a specific order. A portion of each dish is set aside for the family's ancestors.

A beautiful Christmas tradition that has come back into practice is the *Batlejka* show. This puppet show depicting the Nativity of Jesus is performed with wooden puppets. Decorating Christmas trees is also very popular. Young people usually decorate the tree with handmade toys. The Christmas Tree Show, another favorite custom, includes songs and dramatic readings. After the show, presents are given out by Dzied Maroz (Father Frost) or Sviaty Mikola (St. Nicholas).

The celebration of Easter begins with Palm Sunday *(Verbnica)*. Each girl brings a bouquet of pussy willows, decorated with artificial flowers and evergreen twigs, to

Embassy of the Republic of Belarus
The woman's folk costume features elaborate embroidery on the blouse, kerchief, and woven sash.

church. After the service, there is a contest to select the girl with the prettiest bouquet.

After the service on Easter Sunday, Easter eggs are blessed and everyone goes to a brunch called *razhaveny,* held in the church hall. *Babkas* (Easter bread), *kaubasy* (sausage), and other traditional foods are served. The people then go home to take a brief nap because the Easter service began at midnight and has lasted several hours.

During the day, people play games, crack eggs, and have contests to select the most beautifully painted eggs. It is also traditional to visit friends, relatives, and neighbors on Easter Sunday.

7 ● RITES OF PASSAGE

Graduation from high school and from college are seen as important events that mark the beginning of adulthood. Entrance into military service has a similar significance.

8 ● RELATIONSHIPS

Belarusans typically shake hands when they greet each other. Family members and close friends often greet each other with a hug. Belarusan cooks welcome their guests with traditional greetings, such as "Guest into the house—God into the house."

Unlike members of some other cultures, Belarusans do not avoid eye contact with poor people on the street. They believe that "No one should walk the street hungry," and it is customary for them to help people in need.

9 ● LIVING CONDITIONS

About 75 percent of all the housing in Belarusan cities and villages was destroyed during World War II (1939–45). Housing shortages were even worse after 1986, when there was a very serious accident at the nuclear power station at Chernobyl in Ukraine. Thousands of people in Belarus had to move because their homes were contaminated with radiation.

Most Belarusans living in cities have small apartments in high-rise apartment buildings.

10 ● FAMILY LIFE

One traditional Belarusan wedding gift is a *rushnik*—a handcrafted towel. Wedding guests are traditionally greeted with round rye bread and salt on a rushnik.

11 ● CLOTHING

Most people in Belarus wear modern, Western-style clothing. Traditional ethnic costumes are also worn, especially in the southern part of the country. The man's folk costume includes an embroidered white linen shirt, a wide decorated belt or sash, white linen trousers, and black leather boots or sandals. The woman's folk costume is either a loose white dress or an embroidered blouse with a full skirt, embroidered apron, and kerchief. Modern clothes are often decorated with traditional embroidery.

12 ● FOOD

Belarusan cuisine includes dishes made with potatoes, beets, peas, plums, pears, and apples. The dishes are relatively simple and healthful, and they vary with the seasons. Potatoes are the most plentiful and popular food. Belarusans boast that they can prepare potatoes in more than a hundred different ways.

Some typical Belarusan dishes are potato pancakes with bacon, *vireshchaka* (pork ribs with gravy and pancakes), *varlley kuccia* (hot barley cereal with bacon and fried onion), *kvass* (a fermented drink), and *holodnik* (cold beet soup with cucumbers, dill, hard-boiled eggs, radishes, and sour cream).

Recipe

Potato Pancakes with Bacon

Ingredients

1 pound of bacon
4 large, firm white potatoes
3 eggs
1½ Tablespoons flour
1 teaspoon salt
1 Tablespoons finely chopped onion
Vegetable oil

Directions

1. Fry bacon until crisp. Drain on paper towels and set aside.
2. Grate potatoes using a grater or food processor with the coarse grater blade.
3. Wrap the grated potatoes in a clean dish towel and squeeze the towel to remove as much moisture as possible.
4. Mix in remaining ingredients.
5. Shape mixture into pancakes about 3-inches in diameter and about ¼-inch thick.
6. Heat oil in a large frying pan, and sauté for 2 to 3 minutes until the bottom begins to brown.
7. Turn the pancakes over and cook the other side until brown and crispy.
8. Serve with bacon.

13 ● EDUCATION

Required public education lasts about nine years. Students may then attend two or three years of secondary school. Many secondary schools prepare students for specific types of jobs. Colleges with the largest enrollment are the University of Minsk and the Academy of Sciences. Several religious colleges have also opened in recent years.

14 ● CULTURAL HERITAGE

Dr. Francishak Skaryna printed the first book in the Belarusan language—the Bible—in 1517. Belarusan literature developed most strongly in the nineteenth and twentieth centuries. Among the most famous Belarusan writers are Maksim Bagdanovich (1891–1917), Janka Kupala (1882–1942), Janka Bryl (1917–), Vasil Bykau (1924–), and Ryhor Baradulin (1935–).

Folk dancing reflects the feelings, work habits, and lifestyle of the Belarusan people. Dances such as the *Bulba, Lanok,* and *Ruchniki* represent kinds of work. The *Miacelica* and *Charot* demonstrate humanity's relationship to nature. The *Liavonicha, Mikita,* and *Yurachka* express feelings and illustrate folk tales. Belarusan dances are often accompanied by singing.

15 ● EMPLOYMENT

Although Belarus officially has a low unemployment rate, many workers are underemployed. Instead of laying off workers, factories and businesses often reduce the number of hours to be worked, reduce wages, or force employees to take unpaid leave. Because of generous benefits such as clinics, day care, and affordable housing, employees often hesitate to quit low-paying jobs.

16 ● SPORTS

Soccer and hockey are popular as both spectator and participant sports. International competitions such as the Olympics have helped bring together and encourage Belarusan athletes. Belarusan gymnasts are now known internationally for their skill.

Svetlana Belaia

Belarusan girls enjoy an outing in the country. They are wearing traditional clothing with embroidery.

17 ● RECREATION

Fishing in the rivers and streams of Belarus was once a popular activity. However, irrigation projects and pollution of rivers and streams during the Soviet era have greatly reduced sport fishing.

18 ● CRAFTS AND HOBBIES

Ceramics and pottery are traditional Belarusan crafts. The most famous type is *charnazadymlenaya*—a style of black, smoked pottery developed centuries ago.

Weaving and textiles are also important. Different types and colors of straw are woven together to make pictures. Traditional Slavic color motifs often are red (which stands for goodness and joy) and white (for purity). Red and white are also the national colors of Belarus, and they are used in patriotic artwork.

19 ● SOCIAL PROBLEMS

The change to independence from the former Soviet Union has been difficult for Belarusan society. There are serious economic problems, including high unemployment, inflation, and shortages of needed goods. There has been an increase in crime, especially muggings and murders. Organized crime activities have also increased. In addition, Belarus has become a major transfer point for illegal drugs headed for Western Europe. There is continuing corruption among public officials.

A serious problem for Belarusans today is the continuing economic and social cost of the 1986 accident at the Chernobyl nuclear power plant in Ukraine.

20 ● BIBLIOGRAPHY

Fedor, Helen, ed. *Belarus and Moldova: Country Studies.* Lanham, Md.: Federal Research Division, Library of Congress, 1995.

Gosnell, Kelvin. *Belarus, Ukraine, and Moldova.* Brookfield, Conn.: Millbrook Press, 1992.

Zaprudnik, Ian. *Belarus: At a Crossroads in History.* Boulder, Colo.: Westview Press, 1993.

WEBSITES

World Travel Guide, Belarus. [Online] Available http://www.wtgonline.com/country/by/gen.html, 1998.

WWW Belarus. [Online] Available http://www.belarus.net/, 1997.

Belgium

The people of Belgium are called Belgians. The ancestors of Belgium's present population are believed to have settled there during the fourth century AD. The Flemings, comprising about 60 percent of the population, are of Dutch descent. The Walloons, about 35 percent, are of French descent.

Belgians

PRONUNCIATION: BELL-juhns
LOCATION: Belgium
POPULATION: About 9 million
LANGUAGE: Dutch; Flemish; French; German
RELIGION: Roman Catholicism; smaller numbers of Muslims and Jews

1 ● INTRODUCTION

The history of the Belgian people has made them strong and resourceful. For centuries their land was invaded and occupied by different groups, including the Romans, French, Burgundians, Spanish, Austrian, and Germans. In 58 BC, the Roman leader Julius Caesar called the region's Belgae tribes the toughest opponents he had faced. Some of history's major battles were fought in this small country. They include the Battle of Waterloo that signaled the downfall of the French ruler Napoleon Bonaparte (1769–1821), and the Battle of the Bulge in World War II (1939–45). Although it was always recognized as a distinct region, Belgium did not become a nation until 1831. Today, Belgium's capital, Brussels, serves as headquarters for major international organizations, including the European Community (EC) and the North Atlantic Treaty Organization (NATO).

2 ● LOCATION

Located in northwestern Europe, Belgium is one of the "low countries" (much of its land is at or below sea level). This small country is about as large as the state of Maryland. Belgium's major geographic divisions are the coastal lowlands, the central plain, and the high plateau of the Ardennes.

Belgium's two major population groups are the Flemish and the Walloons. They live side by side but maintain sharply separate ethnic identities. The Walloons were long considered the dominant group. Their region had most of the nation's industries, and their French cultural roots were considered an advantage. However, since World War II (1939–45), the northern Flemish region (Flanders) has gained an economic advantage through the growth of commerce. The Flemish have also grown more numerous than the Walloons.

3 ● LANGUAGE

Belgium has three official languages: French, German, and Flemish, which is similar to Dutch. Highway signs indicate the names of cities in two languages (for example, Brussels/Bruxelles, Luik/Liège, Bergen/Mons). The Flemish and the French-speaking Walloons have had many conflicts over language-use in schools, courts, business, and government.

NUMBERS

English	Flemish
one	een
two	twee
three	drie
four	vier
five	vijf
six	zes
seven	zeven
eight	acht
nine	negen
ten	tien

DAYS OF THE WEEK

English	Flemish
Sunday	Zondag
Monday	Maandag
Tuesday	Dinsdag
Wednesday	Woensdag
Thursday	Donderdag
Friday	Vrijdag
Saturday	Zaterdag

4 ● FOLKLORE

Many of Belgium's colorful festivals are based on local myths. One is the famous Cat Festival of Ypres. According to legend, medieval Ypres was overrun by rats, and cats were brought in to kill them. But the cats multiplied too fast, and people took to throwing them off the tops of buildings. (Today this action is imitated during the festival with toy cats.) Folklore also surrounds Belgium's traditional puppet theater, whose marionettes are based on characters from the tales of their particular cities.

5 ● RELIGION

Belgium is a mostly Catholic country. In 1993 about 86 percent of the population was Roman Catholic. Belgian Catholics are usu-

Belgian men at a sidewalk cafe.

ally baptized and receive a religious education. However, many do not actively take part in other religious practices. Some only remain members of the church because of its link with many of the nation's social services. Beauraing and Banneaux in Wallonia are popular destinations for pilgrimages (religious journeys).

6 ● MAJOR HOLIDAYS

Belgium's legal holidays are New Year's Day (January 1), Easter Monday (March or April), Labor Day (May 1), Independence Day (July 21), All Saints' Day (November 1), and Christmas (December 25). Another important day is the Anniversary of the Battle of the Golden Spurs on July 11.

In addition to these official holidays, Belgians love festivals of all kinds. One of the most famous is the Shrove Tuesday Carnival in the town of Binche, with its "March of the Gilles." On this Tuesday before Ash Wednesday (the beginning of Lent), men dress in padded, brightly colored costumes and white hats adorned with enormous ostrich plumes. They dance down the street throwing oranges at the spectators, who are also pelted with bags filled with water. Anyone who throws oranges back at the marchers risks being beaten up by the other townspeople.

7 ● RITES OF PASSAGE

Rites of passage include major Catholic ceremonies such as baptism, first communion, marriage and funerals. Special gifts are given for baptisms, first communions, and marriages.

8 ● RELATIONSHIPS

When relatives greet each other, they shake hands, hug, or kiss each other on the cheek. Friends usually hug. Men and women or two female friends might exchange kisses on the cheek. American-style "high fives" (slapping each other's hands held high in the air) have become popular among Belgian youth.

The languages of both the Flemings and the Walloons have formal and informal modes of addressing another person. Both groups tend to use the informal forms (*jÿ* in Dutch, and *tu* in French) more often than do the Dutch in Holland or the French in France.

9 ● LIVING CONDITIONS

Belgium has no significant housing shortage and few slums. In many Belgian homes, part of the first floor is used for the family business. Common terms for this arrangement include *winkelshuis* (shop house) and *handelshuis* (business residence). Many houses have large kitchens in which closely knit Belgian families can gather.

10 ● FAMILY LIFE

Men and women usually marry in their teens and twenties and begin their families early. Most families have between two and four children. Married couples often work side by side in either business or farming.

Instead of divorcing, couples who are in business together may remain legally married in order to protect the business, maintaining separate households with new partners. Children generally live with their parents until they marry. The elderly are commonly cared for in homes run by religious or social organizations. Women make up roughly 40 percent of the work force.

11 ● CLOTHING

Belgians, especially those in the cities, wear modern Western-style clothes. Men who work in offices are expected to wear suit jackets to work. It is generally acceptable for women to wear slacks to work. The ethnic costumes of the Flemings and Walloons are seldom worn today. On some farms women still wear the traditional dark-colored clothing and white aprons, and men wear the old-fashioned caps.

12 ● FOOD

Belgium is known for its rich, tasty food—the Belgians' daily consumption of calories is among the world's highest. Two of the best-known dishes are *carbonades* of beef (stewed in beer), and a chicken or fish chowder called *waterzooi*. The North Sea and Atlantic Ocean supply many varieties of fish. The daily catch also includes eels, cockles, and mussels, all of which are considered delicacies. Other Belgian specialties include waffles, over 300 varieties of beer, and chocolate.

13 ● EDUCATION

Belgium has an unusually high literacy rate. Education is required between the ages of six and fifteen. (Nearly all children start

Cory Langley

People cruising on a canal. Belgium is one of the so-called "low countries" of Europe because much of its land is at or below sea level.

earlier with nursery school and kindergarten.) Depending on the region, classes may be taught in either French, Dutch, or German. Belgium has eight major universities, including institutions in Brussels, Ghent, Liège, and Antwerp.

14 ● CULTURAL HERITAGE

Belgium's cultural heritage includes the paintings of Pieter Breugel the Elder (c. 1515 or 1530–69), Jan van Eyck (1395–1441), and Peter Paul Rubens (1577–1640), and the music compositions of Orlando di Lasso (1532–94) and César Franck (1822–90). Modern Belgians writers include the Nobel Prize-winning dramatist Maurice

Maeterlinck (1862–1949), and the popular detective novelist Georges Simenon (1903–89), who was born in Liège. Prominent modern painters include expressionist James Ensor (1860–1949) and surrealist René Magritte (1898–1967).

15 ● EMPLOYMENT

Belgians put in long hours at work. A businessperson who arrives at the office at 9:00 AM is considered lazy. In recent years, industrial jobs have increased in the north (in the Flemish region). Jobs in service industries like tourism have also expanded. However, small family businesses are still common, and farmers grow vegetables, fruit, and grains. Commercial fishing and fish processing are important in cities near the North Sea.

16 ● SPORTS

The most popular participant sport in Belgium is bicycling. Belgians also participate in and watch soccer, and there are many regional teams. Other sports popular in Belgium include tennis, horseback riding, hiking, and skiing.

Belgians also enjoy the popular European sport of sand sailing. A sort of mini-car with sails called a "sand yacht" is driven along the coast, powered by the wind. Also popular, especially in Wallonia, is pigeon racing. As many as 100,000 pigeons may be entered in a single race.

17 ● RECREATION

Like many other Europeans, Belgians are avid soccer fans. There are over sixty teams in the national league. Concerts and theater are popular evening pastimes in the cities, and Brussels also has opera, ballet, and cafe cabarets (restaurants with musical entertainment such as singing and dancing).

18 ● CRAFTS AND HOBBIES

Traditional Belgian crafts include lacemaking (for which Brussels is especially famous), tapestry, glass, and pottery. Other folk arts include folk opera and street singing, as well as marionettes (small wooden figures operated with strings) and hand puppets. Popular hobbies include stamp collecting, model trains, and gardening.

19 ● SOCIAL PROBLEMS

Ethnic differences between Belgium's Flemings and Walloons have been sources of social conflict. Religious divisions have also caused tension within the country. Social problems include unemployment, high rates of immigration, gradually increasing crime, and the high taxes needed to support Belgium's generous system of social benefits.

20 ● BIBLIOGRAPHY

Egan, E. W. *Belgium in Pictures*. Minneapolis: Lerner, 1991.

Hargrove, Jim. *Belgium, Enchantment of the World*. Chicago: Children's Press, 1988.

Pateman, Robert. *Belgium*. New York: Marshall Cavendish, 1995.

WEBSITES

Belgian Tourist Office. [Online] Available http://www.visitbelgium.com/, 1998.

Embassy of Belgium. Washington, D.C. [Online] Available www.belgium-emb.org/usa/, 1998.

World Travel Guide. Belgium. [Online] Available http://www.wtgonline.com/country/be/gen.html, 1998.

Flemings

PRONUNCIATION: FLEH-mings
ALTERNATE NAME: Flemish
LOCATION: Belgium (northern region, called Flanders)
POPULATION: 5.5 million
LANGUAGE: Flemish
RELIGION: Roman Catholicism; Protestantism; small numbers of Jews and Muslims

1 ● INTRODUCTION

The Flemings (or Flemish) are Belgium's ethnic majority. They live in the northern part of Belgium, which is called Flanders, and speak the Flemish language, which is closely related to Dutch. Present-day Belgium was originally inhabited by Celtic tribes and was overrun by the Romans in the first century BC. In the fifth century AD the Franks, a Germanic people, invaded the region and ruled over it. They maintained a stronger presence in its northern portion, where early forms of the Dutch language eventually developed.

During the feudal period between the ninth and twelfth centuries AD, Belgium's Flemish and Walloon cultures continued developing along separate lines. Beginning in the fourteenth century, the merchants of cities such as Antwerp, Bruges, and Ghent became more powerful. Flemish cities began to play an important role in European trade, and a cultural golden age began, in both music and art. Beginning in the sixteenth century, both the Flemish and the French-speaking Walloons to their south came under the rule of a series of foreign powers. These included Spain, the Austrian Hapsburg monarchy, the French under Napoleon Bonaparte (1769–1821), and, finally, The Netherlands. Both the Flemings and Walloons revolted against Dutch rule, and the new Kingdom of Belgium was established in 1830 as a constitutional monarchy.

Throughout the nineteenth century, the Walloons had most of the political and economic power in Belgium. Flanders remained a primarily agricultural area. However, by the 1930s the Flemings had gained enough influence to make Flemish their official language. They legalized its use in education, the courts, and the government. In the 1960s, the Flemings and Walloons gained political, social, and cultural autonomy (self-rule) over their respective regions. Since then, Flanders has become a center for international trade, high-tech manufacturing, and tourism. In 1993, Belgium's constitution was amended, making Flanders and Wallonia autonomous regions within the Belgian kingdom.

2 ● LOCATION

The Flemings live in the northern part of Belgium, above an east-west line dividing the country's Flemish- and French-speaking regions. The Flemish-speaking provinces are East and West Flanders, Antwerp, Limburg, and part of Brabant. The land is mostly low, some of it below sea level. The Flemings account for 55 percent of Belgium's ten million people.

3 ● LANGUAGE

Flemish (Vlaams) is a variant of Dutch that has been spoken for about 1,000 years in the north of Belgium. Recognized as an official state language, it is different from the Dutch spoken in the neighboring Netherlands. Flemish does not have its own alphabet. It uses standard Dutch with some alterations.

NUMBERS

English	Flemish
one	een
two	twee
three	drie
four	vier
five	vijf
six	zes
seven	zeven
eight	acht
nine	negen
ten	tien

DAYS OF THE WEEK

English	Flemish
Sunday	Zondag
Monday	Maandag
Tuesday	Dinsdag
Wednesday	Woensdag
Thursday	Donderdag
Friday	Vrijdag
Saturday	Zaterdag

4 ● FOLKLORE

The name of Antwerp—the major city in the Flemish part of Belgium—is derived from the name of a Roman hero who is said to have killed an evil giant and cut off his hand. (The city's symbol is a red hand.) Some of the Flemings' colorful pageants and festivals are based on local folklore, such as the Cat Festival of Ypres. This celebration is based on a legend about the use of cats to get rid of rats in the city of Ypres in the Middle Ages. For a long time, it was the festival custom to throw live cats out of windows. Today, cloth cats are used instead.

5 ● RELIGION

The great majority of Flemish are Catholic. Although many are not observant on a daily basis, nearly all Flemings are baptized and receive a Catholic education.

6 ● MAJOR HOLIDAYS

The Flemish observe Belgium's ten public holidays: New Year's Day (January 1), Easter Monday (March or April), Labor Day (May 1), Independence Day (July 21), All Saints' Day (November 1), and Christmas (December 25). They also celebrate other dates on the Christian calendar, and folk holidays from olden times. Fancy masks and papier-mâché "giants" are often used at folk festivals and processions. The Flemings are especially well known for their high-spirited celebration of the pre-Lenten carnival season. They begin with the *bommelfeesten* in the East Flanders town of Ronse and continue for weeks.

7 ● RITES OF PASSAGE

Rites of passage include major Catholic ceremonies such as baptisms, first communion, marriage and funerals. Although most Flemish do not practice Catholicism, the important events in a person's life tend to be occasions of major family reunions and stress their religious heritage. Special gifts and wishes are given for baptisms, first communions, and marriages.

8 ● RELATIONSHIPS

Flemish manners are generally formal and polite. In conversation, Flemings frequently exchange compliments and shake hands repeatedly.

9 ● LIVING CONDITIONS

Most Flemish homes, like those in neighboring Wallonia, are built of red brick. Often the house will have a combined living room and dining area; large kitchens are also common. Many Flemings have a shop or other small business at the same site as the family home (an arrangement referred to as a *winkelshuis* or *handelshuis*).

10 ● FAMILY LIFE

The Flemish generally have larger families than their Walloon neighbors to the south. Nuclear rather than extended families are the norm. Many single young people live at home and save their earnings, which they spend on clothes, cars, and recreation. Since the 1970s it has become increasingly common for unmarried couples to live together. Married couples often run small businesses together. The divorce rate among the Flemish, as elsewhere in the West, has risen in recent decades. The elderly commonly live in retirement communities or homes for the aged.

11 ● CLOTHING

The Flemish, like all Belgians, wear modern Western-style clothing. However, in some rural areas, the traditional dark-colored farmer's clothing can still be seen.

12 ● FOOD

Flemish cuisine (style of cooking) shows the cultural influence of the Dutch, but it is still unique. Fish and shellfish are central to Flemish cooking. Mussels, herring, lobster, shrimp, and oysters are all popular. Rabbit cooked in brown beer with stewed prunes is a regional specialty. Another regional dish is *waterzooi,* a chowder made from vegetables and either chicken or fish. Dinner, the main meal of the day, is eaten at midday. The Flemings are great beer drinkers and brew some of the best beers in the world. Fruit is included in almost every meal. A recipe for *stoofperen* (stewed pears) follows.

13 ● EDUCATION

Education for all Belgians is required from age six through age fifteen. Many Flemish children go to Catholic private schools. At the high school level, students choose between trade-oriented, business, or college preparatory training. Some vocational schools operate work-study apprenticeship programs.

14 ● CULTURAL HERITAGE

In the fine arts, the Flemish are especially famous for their painting. The best-known Flemish painters are those of the Renais-

Recipe

Stoofperen (Stewed Pears)

Ingredients

6 firm, ripe pears, peeled
Juice of 2 lemons
2 cups water
½ cup sugar
1 teaspoon cinnamon
12 red or green maraschino cherries for garnish

Directions

1. Cut peeled pears in half and remove cores.
2. Sprinkle pears with juice from ½ lemon to prevent discoloration.
3. Pour juice from 1½ lemons into a medium saucepan. Add 1 cup water, sugar, and cinnamon. Heat to boiling.
4. Add pears and reduce heat. Simmer with the cover on the pan for about 20 minutes. Pears should be cooked but still holding their shape. Garnish with a maraschino cherry and serve.

Adapted from Webb, Lois Sinaiko. *Holidays of the World Cookbook for Students.* Phoenix, Ariz.: Oryx Press, 1995.

sance, often called the "Flemish masters." They include Jan van Eyck (1395–1441), Hieronymus Bosch (1450–1516), Pieter Bruegel the Elder (c. 1515 or 1530–69), Pieter Bruegel the Younger (1564–1638), Peter Paul Rubens (1577–1640), and Anthony van Dyck (1599–1641).

Flemish literature began in the Middle Ages. After suffering a decline during centuries of foreign rule, it was revived when independence was attained in 1830. Prominent nineteenth-century Flemish writers include Hendrik Conscience (1812–83), author of *The Lion of Flanders* (*De Leeaw van Vlaenderen*), and lyric poet Guido Gezelle (1830–99). Well-known modern Flemish authors include novelists Louis Paul Boon and Hugo Claus.

In the sixteenth century, the music compositions of Orlando di Lasso (1532–94) combined the musical traditions of The Netherlands and Italy.

15 ● EMPLOYMENT

The Flemish are hard workers. They spend long hours running family-owned businesses. Sometimes they hold more than one job. Major industries in Flanders include textiles, automobiles, and chemicals. Manufacturing in new areas such as electronics and computer technology is growing, while the traditional heavy industries, including steelmaking and shipbuilding, are on the decline.

The Flemish regions have benefited from the growth of tourism in such cities as Antwerp, Bruges, Ghent, and Brussels. Today, two out of three Belgians have service-oriented jobs.

16 ● SPORTS

The Flemish are enthusiastic players and fans of soccer, Belgium's national sport. Cycling is another favorite sport.

17 ● RECREATION

The Flemish people enjoy typical leisure activities such as watching television and reading. Like many Belgians, they are enthusiastic gardeners, and every home has a carefully tended garden. Other typical hobbies include stamp collecting and model trains. The Flemish also share the Belgian love of festivals.

18 ● CRAFTS AND HOBBIES

The Flemish are known for their lacemaking. Other crafts include glassblowing, tapestries, and pottery. There has also been a revival of folk arts including street singing, folk opera, and puppet and marionette theaters.

19 ● SOCIAL PROBLEMS

The incidence of public violent crime is comparatively low among the Flemish. However, domestic violence, including child abuse, remains a problem.

20 ● BIBLIOGRAPHY

Hargrove, Jim. *Belgium, Enchantment of the World.* Chicago: Children's Press, 1988.

Pateman, Robert. *Belgium.* New York: Marshall Cavendish, 1995.

Wickman, Stephen B. *Belgium: A Country Study.* Washington, D.C.: U.S. Government Printing Office, 1984.

WEBSITES

Belgian Tourist Office. [Online] Available http://www.visitbelgium.com/, 1998.

Embassy of Belgium. Washington, D.C. [Online] Available www.belgium-emb.org/usa/, 1998.

World Travel Guide. Belgium. [Online] Available http://www.wtgonline.com/country/be/gen.html, 1998.

Walloons

PRONUNCIATION: wah-LOONS
LOCATION: Belgium (southern region, called Wallonia)
POPULATION: 3.2 million
LANGUAGE: French
RELIGION: Roman Catholicism; Islam; Protestantism; Judaism; Russian Orthodox; Greek Orthodox

1 ● INTRODUCTION

The Walloons, who live in Belgium's southern provinces, are the country's French-speaking inhabitants. Their culture contrasts with that of the Flemings, who inhabit the northern part of the country and speak Flemish, a language similar to Dutch. The Walloons' closest cultural ties are to France and other countries in which Romance languages are spoken.

In the fifth century AD the Franks, a Germanic people, invaded the region that includes modern Belgium. They gained the most power in the northern area, where early forms of the Dutch language took hold. In the south, the Roman culture and Latin-based dialects continued to flourish. During the feudal period between the ninth and twelfth centuries AD, the Flemish and Walloon cultures continued developing along separate lines.

Beginning in the sixteenth century, both the Flemings and the Walloons came under the rule of a succession of foreign powers. These included Spain, the Austrian Hapsburg monarchy, the French under Napoleon Bonaparte (1769–1821), and, finally, The Netherlands. Both groups then joined together in a revolt against Dutch rule. The new Kingdom of Belgium was created in 1830 as a constitutional monarchy.

Throughout the nineteenth century, the Walloons held most of the political and economic power in Belgium. The rich natural resources of their region (known as Wallonia) brought the mines, mills, and factories of the Industrial Revolution to the region early. Their language, French, was the language of government, law, the Roman Catholic Church, and education. By comparison, the Dutch-based Flemish language was associated with rural poverty and lack of education. This language division was dramatized when French-speaking Belgian officers in World War I (1914–18) couldn't communicate with their Flemish-speaking troops.

Since World War II (1939–45), Wallonia's traditional heavy industries (especially steelmaking) have declined, and its coal mines have closed.

In the 1960s, the Flemings and Walloons were given increased control over their respective regions. In 1993 Belgium's constitution was amended, making Flanders and Wallonia autonomous (self-governing) regions within the Belgian Kingdom.

2 ● LOCATION

With an area of 6,600 square miles (17,094 square kilometers), Wallonia covers 55 percent of Belgium's territory and includes the provinces of southern Brabant, Hainautl, Namur, Liège, and Luxembourg. Wallonia is a densely populated area with 3.2 million inhabitants.

3 ● LANGUAGE

The language of Wallonia is French. There are also a number of regional dialects. These dialects, which are referred to collectively as "Walloon," are grouped into Eastern (Liège), Central (Namur), and Western (Charleroi, La Louvière, Nivelles).

4 ● FOLKLORE

Traditionally, the spirits of the departed were thought to return to earth on All Saints' Day (November 1). Families still visit cemeteries to clean the tombs of their deceased relatives on that date. Some rural villagers still believe in the powers of folk healers. Walloon folklore includes many tales involving the devil.

5 ● RELIGION

Catholicism is the traditional religion of Wallonia. The Walloons are generally less religious than the Flemings to their north. Even the elderly who keep statues of the Virgin Mary in their windows often are not regular churchgoers. Wallonia is the site of two popular pilgrimage shrines, at Beauraing and Banneaux. Lourdes in southwestern France has traditionally drawn many pilgrims from Walloon.

6 ● MAJOR HOLIDAYS

The Walloons observe Belgium's ten public holidays as well as many folk holidays. The town of Binche is famous for its carnival festivities in the weeks before Lent. The best-known part of the annual celebration is the Dance (or March) of the Gilles. Over 1,000 people dressed in brightly colored, padded costumes throw oranges at the spectators.

7 ● RITES OF PASSAGE

Most Walloon young people undergo religious rituals such as baptism and first communion. In addition, a student's progress through the educational system is marked with graduation parties in many families.

8 ● RELATIONSHIPS

Walloon manners are generally formal and polite. Conversations are marked by frequent exchanges of compliments and repeated handshaking. Relatives greet each other by shaking hands, hugging, or kissing each other on the cheek. A hug is a common greeting among friends. Men and women or two female friends may exchange kisses on the cheek.

9 ● LIVING CONDITIONS

The majority of Walloons are city dwellers. Most live in multistory brick row houses with large kitchens and gardens. Walloon houses, like those of other Belgians, often include an area used for a family business.

10 ● FAMILY LIFE

The modern nuclear family (parents and children only) is the norm in Wallonia. However, it is not unusual for an elderly grandparent to join the household. Couples generally marry in their mid- to late twenties. Wallonia's divorce rate is rising, and divorce and remarriage are considered socially acceptable.

11 ● CLOTHING

The Walloons, like all Belgians, wear modern Western-style clothing.

12 ● FOOD

Walloon cuisine is derived from that of France. However, it tends to be spicier and higher in calories than modern-day French food. The main meal of the day, which is eaten at noon, might consist of a pork dish, potatoes, and salad with mayonnaise. Both breakfast and supper are light meals that may include the popular regional cheese, *makèye,* served on slices of bread. Soup is a staple of the Walloon diet, often served as a first course for the midday and evening meals. Walloons drink a lot of coffee. It is common to take a 4 PM coffee break called a *goûter,* often consisting of coffee and a piece of pie. Walloons also like to drink and brew beer.

13 ● EDUCATION

Education for all Belgians is required from age six through age fifteen. At the secondary level, students choose between trade-oriented, business, or college-preparatory training.

14 ● CULTURAL HERITAGE

The Walloons are best known for their contributions to modern art, notably the work of painters René Magritte (1898–1967) and Paul Delvaux (1898–1994). The best-known Walloon author is mystery writer Georges Simenon (1903–89), creator of the character of the police commissioner Maigret. Wallonia's most famous music composer was César Franck (1822–90). The concert violinist Eugène Ysaye (1858-1931) founded the Queen Elisabeth of Belgium Music Competition. The saxophone was invented by a Belgian, Adolphe Sax (1814–94), who was born in Wallonia.

15 ● EMPLOYMENT

With its steel, glass, and textiles industries, Wallonia was a leading manufacturing center in the nineteenth century. Since World War II (1939–45), however, its coal mines have closed and its traditional heavy industries have fallen into decline. The Walloons were hit harder by Belgium's high unemployment of the late 1980s and early 1990s than were their neighbors to the north.

16 ● SPORTS

Walloons share Belgium's national passion for soccer. Another favorite national pastime that the Walloons share is bicycling. Pigeon racing, practiced throughout Belgium, is especially popular in Wallonia.

17 ● RECREATION

The Walloons enjoy typical leisure activities such as watching television and reading. Like other Belgians, they are avid gardeners and maintain well-tended gardens. Other typical hobbies include stamp collecting and model trains. Many Walloons enjoy gathering with friends in neighborhood cafes after work.

18 ● CRAFTS AND HOBBIES

The talents of traditional artists can be seen in the elaborate costumes and giant figures used in festivals and processions. Folk art can also be seen in puppet and marionette theaters.

19 ● SOCIAL PROBLEMS

Wallonia has suffered from high rates of unemployment in the 1990s. Some of its inhabitants have been forced to commute to jobs in Brussels or Flanders. The cultural, linguistic, and political divisions between the Walloons and the Flemings are a continuing source of conflict.

20 ● BIBLIOGRAPHY

Hargrove, Jim. *Belgium, Enchantment of the World.* Chicago: Children's Press, 1988.

Pateman, Robert. *Belgium.* New York: Marshall Cavendish, 1995.

Wickman, Stephen B. *Belgium: A Country Study.* Washington, D.C.: U.S. Government Printing Office, 1984.

WEBSITES

Belgian Tourist Office. [Online] Available http://www.visitbelgium.com/, 1998.

Embassy of Belgium. Washington, D.C. [Online] Available www.belgium-emb.org/usa/, 1998.

World Travel Guide. Belgium. [Online] Available http://www.wtgonline.com/country/be/gen.html, 1998.

Belize

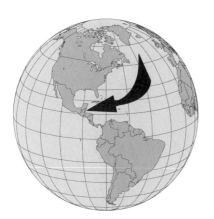

The people of Belize are called Belizeans. About one-third of the population is of African descent, while about 45 percent is mestizo (mixed race). Another 15 percent is Maya and 7 percent Garifuna (Carib Indian). There are small numbers of people of European, Chinese, Asian Indian, and Syrian-Lebanese ancestry. For more information on the Maya, see the chapter on Mexico in Volume 6.

Belizeans

PRONUNCIATION: buh-LEE-zhuns

LOCATION: Belize

POPULATION: Over 200,000

LANGUAGE: English; Spanish; local Creole

RELIGION: Roman Catholicism (62 percent); various Protestant denominations (30 percent); evangelical groups such as Pentecostals, Jehovah's Witnesses, and Seventh-Day Adventists; Mennonites; Mormons; Baha'is

1 ● INTRODUCTION

Mayan Indians built several major centers within what is now Belize. Probably at least four hundred thousand people lived in the Belize area around AD 900—twice as many as today. Mayan civilization had collapsed by the sixteenth century, when Spanish expeditions reached the area. Diseases like smallpox and yellow fever killed many.

The Spanish controlled the western part of present-day Belize. But English pirates used the eastern side, on the Caribbean Sea, as a base for their raids on ships. On land, they plundered *logwood,* a tree used to produce a dye used in the woolen industry. Mahogany later became the major export.

British settlers arrived in 1638 and brought in slaves from Africa to work the plantations. Slavery ended in 1838. The colony of British Honduras was established in 1862.

Other groups arrived and settled. Free Creoles were of mixed African and European descent. Garifuna, descendants of Africans and Carib Indians, also came to the colony. Mayan Indians began fleeing into the colony from a war in the Yucatán Peninsula and from forced labor in Guatemala. Even with all these additions to the population, British Honduras had only thirty-seven thousand inhabitants in 1901.

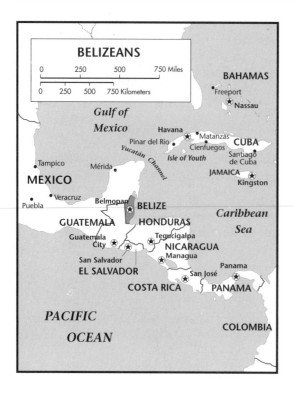

BELIZEANS

British Honduras became the independent Republic of Belize in 1981. But Mexico and Guatemala had held Spain's original claim to the land. Mexico had dropped its claim in 1893. Guatemala never officially gave up its claim, but it established full diplomatic relations with Belize in 1991.

2 ● LOCATION

Belize is a little larger than the state of Massachusetts. It is bordered on the north by Mexico, on the west and south by Guatemala, and on the east by the Caribbean Sea. It is flat and swampy along the southern coast and mostly level in the north. The southern part has mountains reaching a high point of 3,861 feet (1,177 meters). Belize's climate is warm and humid. There are seventeen rivers. The longest barrier reef in the Americas (about 180 miles, or 290 kilometers) runs parallel to its coastline.

Belize is more thinly settled than any other part of Central America. It had a population of just over 200,000 in the mid-1990s. Creoles had been the largest group, but the 1991 census showed that they accounted for only 30 percent of the population. Mestizos, of Indian and European descent, made up 44 percent. Another 15 percent were Mayan Indians. The Garifuna, or Black Caribs, made up 7 percent. There were also East Indians (descended from immigrants from present-day India), Arabs and Chinese. About 6,000 Mennonites, members of a Protestant religious denomination who had come from Mexico and Canada, also lived in Belize at that time.

As many as 65,000 Belizeans were living in the United States in the late 1980s. Most of them were Creole or Garifuna.

3 ● LANGUAGE

English is the only official language in Belize and the only teaching language in the public schools. The 1991 census found that at least 80 percent of the population could speak some English or some Belizean Creole, a dialect of English difficult for outsiders to understand. Spanish was spoken by about 60 percent of the people. It was the first language of 33 to 50 percent of the population. Smaller numbers spoke Mayan languages or Garifuna as their first language. Many of the people speak more than one language.

4 ● FOLKLORE

Belizean folklore is a combination of European, African, and Mayan beliefs. Creoles speak of a phantom pirate ship seen at night, lit by flickering lanterns. It is believed to lure sailors to death on the dangerous coral reef.

Many supernatural beings are part of the folklore. "Greasy Man" lives in abandoned houses, and "Ashi de Pompi" in the ashes of burned houses. They come out at night to frighten people. *Sisimito* or *Sisemite* are giant, hairy creatures that kidnap women. They are impossible to track because they can reverse the position of their feet. This makes it seem that they are walking in the opposite direction.

The Mayans contributed the belief in four-fingered "little people" of the jungle, the *duende*. Any person meeting one must give a four-fingered salute, hiding the thumb. The duende can cause disease, but placing gourds of food for them in a doorway will prevent an epidemic. They can capture people and drive them mad. But they can also grant wishes and make a person suddenly able to play a musical instrument. *Xtabay* is a lovely maiden who leads men astray in the forest. Also of Mayan origin is the belief that Saturdays and Mondays are lucky, while Tuesdays and Fridays are unlucky.

Many Creoles and Garifuna believe in *obeah,* or witchcraft. It is believed that if a person makes a doll from a black sock and then buries it under the victim's doorstep, great harm will come to that person. Shoes are frequently crossed at bedtime to keep evil spirits out of them during the night. A certain species of black butterfly is said to bring early death or at least bad luck to a person who sees it. To ward off the evil eye,

Cory Langley

Two boys in Belize return from the market.

the Garifuna paint an indigo cross on the forehead of an infant.

5 ● RELIGION

In 1993, 62 percent of the Belizean people were Roman Catholic, while 30 percent belonged to various Protestant denominations, including the Mennonites and Mormons. Other groups include the Baha'is.

6 ● MAJOR HOLIDAYS

St. George's Caye Day, on September 10, originally celebrated a British victory over Spain, but it now commemorates local heroes. It is marked by parades, patriotic speeches, and a pageant. Independence Day is September 21. Both of these days are occasions for street parades, floats, and block parties in Belize City. The birthday of Queen Elizabeth II, April 21, is also a national holiday, along with Commonwealth Day, May 24, and Columbus Day, October 12. Garifuna Settlement Day is November 19. It marks the day in 1832 on which a large number of Garifuna reached Belize from Honduras in dugout canoes. The Garifuna also hold a New Year's celebration, called *Yancanú,* from December 25 through January 6. It is named for a Jamaican folk hero, "John Canoe."

The town of San José Succotz has fiestas on March 19 and May 3. In the south there are other traditional fiestas, in San Antonio around January 17 and in San Pedro toward the end of June.

7 • RITES OF PASSAGE

Mestizo and Mayan customs are similar to those of the same groups in Guatemala and in Mexico's Yucatán Peninsula.

Garifuna infants are baptized as soon as possible. They will have already been bathed in a ritual on their ninth day, in water steeped with herbs and leaves. Godfathers are more important than godmothers. Children are sometimes sent to live with another family, usually of a higher economic and social position, so that they can get an education. Sometimes the Catholic Church takes care of such children.

A death in the Creole community is observed with an evening wake in the family's home. Guests bring gifts and take refreshments while praying, singing, dancing, and playing games. Burial is usually the next day. A second wake is held nine days later.

Although Catholic, the Garifuna also have a deep belief in the power of the *gudiba,* deceased ancestors, who are honored.

8 • RELATIONSHIPS

Greetings, gestures, body language, visiting customs, and dating among Mestizos and Mayans are similar to those of the same groups in Guatemala and the Yucatán.

Creoles carry European-style courtesy to the extreme of hesitating to say "no." So "maybe" or "possibly" usually means "no."

Young people often meet at public dances, but Creole or "Spanish" (Mestizo or Mayan) girls are rarely allowed to attend except on special occasions.

9 • LIVING CONDITIONS

In numbers of dollars, the national income per person in Belize is one of the highest in Central America. However, the cost of living is also high because so many goods must be imported.

In the early 1990s, about 60 percent of all children under three years of age suffered some form of malnutrition. Poor sanitation in rural areas helped cause a high percentage of people, especially children, to have intestinal parasites. Malaria remained the leading health problem. Dengue fever, which, like malaria, is also carried by mosquitoes, began to appear again in the 1980s. There were fewer than a hundred physicians in Belize in the late 1980s.

The 1980 census found that 70 percent of Belizean houses were made of wood, 12 percent of concrete, and 7 percent of adobe. Creoles generally live in white-painted wooden bungalows. These houses are often built on stilts and have corrugated-iron

Cory Langley

Creoles generally live in white-painted wooden bungalows. These houses are often built on stilts and have corrugated-iron roofs.

roofs. Outside the towns, most Garifuna live in two-room oblong wooden houses. These houses have palm thatch or iron roofs and have floors of leveled mud. The kitchen is a separate building. Yucatán Maya mostly live in huts of plastered limestone or tree trunks with steep thatched roofs. Kekchí Maya have houses of rough planks topped with palm thatch. In Belize City, families of high social and economic status live in wealthy neighborhoods along the coast.

10 ● FAMILY LIFE

For many ethnic groups, and for the lower social and economic groups, a formal marriage ceremony is not necessary. However, family ties beyond the immediate family are strong, including close links to grandparents, aunts and uncles, and nephews and nieces.

Marriage between members of different groups has been very common. Many poorer households in Belize City are headed by single parents, usually women.

11 ● CLOTHING

Business clothing for men is a short-sleeved cotton shirt and trousers of lightweight fabric. Ties are rarely worn. Women generally wear simple cotton dresses.

12 ● FOOD

In Belize, the main meal is eaten at midday. For Mestizos and Mayans, the diet is much like that of Guatemala. Corn tortillas and beans are the staple foods. In the interior of the country, dishes of wild game like roast armadillo and roast *paca* have a Yucatán flavor. (The paca is a large rodent.)

Creoles call dinner "tea." Among Creoles, rice and red kidney beans are the staples, often with fried bananas or plantains. (The plantain is somewhat like a banana.)

The Creoles and Garifuna eat a great deal of fish. They usually boil or stew it in coconut milk or fry it in coconut oil. The Garifuna also make fiery-hot cassava fritters from a paste of cooked cassava in coconut milk. Another Garifuna dish is *hudut,* a stew composed of crushed plantains, fish, and coconut milk.

Nanche is a sweet alcoholic drink made from *crabou* fruit. Many Belizeans drink the local rum mixed with condensed milk.

13 ● EDUCATION

By Central American standards, Belize has done a very good job of educating its citizens. More than 90 percent of all adults can read and write. Education is free and required between the ages of six and fourteen. In 1992, 96 percent of all primary-school-age children were in school. However, only 36 percent of high school-age children were. A joint partnership of government and churches manages the school system. The University College of Belize was established in the 1980s. Other colleges are Belize Teachers' College, Belize School of Nursing, and Belize College of Agriculture.

14 ● CULTURAL HERITAGE

Among Mestizos, marimba music is popular. A marimba group is made up of half a dozen musicians, two of them playing large, wooden marimbas, which resemble xylophones. Other musicians play a double bass and the drums. Belize's top marimba group in the early 1990s was Alma Belicena. Mexican-style mariachi music is also heard.

Brukdown is a kind of Creole music played on the guitar, banjo, accordion, and steel drums, with someone also playing the jawbone of a donkey. It is accompanied by words that often make fun of people or events. Calypso music is also sometimes heard but has mostly been replaced by reggae.

In the 1980s, Garifuna players made "punta rock" the most popular style of music in Belize. Its instruments include maracas, drums, and turtle shells. Salsa, punk, and rap music are also popular.

Among Belizean painters are Manuel Carrero and Manuel Villamer. Important sculptors include George Gabb and Frank Lizama. Writers include Zee Edgell, Zoila Ellis, Felicia Hernandez, Sharon Matola, Yasser Musa, Kiren Shoman, and Simone Waight.

15 ● EMPLOYMENT

Although there is a serious shortage of workers, the unemployment rate was about 15 percent in the early 1990s. For school dropouts, the rate was over 40 percent. Many Creoles seek higher-paying work outside the country and send money home to their families. Garifuna men often go outside their communities for seasonal work, then return to their villages off season. The labor shortage has been lessened by large numbers of migrant workers from other parts of Central America.

In 1994 the minimum wage was $1.12 an hour, but only 87 cents an hour for domestic workers. By law, the normal work week was no more than six days or forty-five hours.

The unemployment rate for women is two and one half times that of men. Jobs available to women usually have low status and low wages. Few women are in top management jobs. The law requires equal pay for equal work, but women often are paid less for doing work similar to men's.

16 ● SPORTS

Soccer is the most popular sport, closely followed by basketball. Belizeans also play baseball and softball. There are a number of horse-racing meets around New Year's Day, and bicycle races are also held. Other sports include polo and boxing.

17 ● RECREATION

Among Creoles, all national celebrations are accompanied by open-air dancing, called "jump-up." Almost all villages, particularly those along the Caribbean coast, have their own discos, playing Afro-Caribbean music.

There are few movie theaters, which mainly show films from the United States. Dish antennas now receive more than fifty television channels via satellite signals. Belizeans can watch CNN News from Atlanta, Georgia; Chicago Cubs baseball games; and Spanish-language *telenovelas* (soap operas) from Venezuela.

18 ● CRAFTS AND HOBBIES

Souvenirs such as straw baskets and carvings in wood, slate, and stone can be found at the National Handicrafts Center in Belize City. Jewelry is made from black coral.

19 ● SOCIAL PROBLEMS

The migration of "Spanish" people from other countries in Central America to Belize has caused social tension. Until recently, Belize had been a mostly English-speaking Creole society. A "brain-drain" of educated Creoles to the United States has made things worse.

Petty crime is very common in Belize City, and youth gangs have gotten a foothold there. Imported powdered and crack cocaine are in use, as is marijuana.

About half the rural population is without pure water. The barrier reef and its animal and plant life are threatened by water pollution, the removal of coral, and spearfishing.

20 ● BIBLIOGRAPHY

Setzekorn, William D. *Formerly British Honduras: A Profile of the New Nation of Belize*. Rev. ed. Athens, Ohio: Ohio University Press, 1981.

Whatmore, Mark, and Peter Eltringham. *Guatemala & Belize: The Rough Guide*. 2nd ed. London: Rough Guides, 1993.

WEBSITES

Belize Tourism Industry Association. [Online] Available http://www.belize.com/, 1998.

Green Arrow Advertising. Belize. [Online] Available http://www.greenarrow.com/belize/belize. htm, 1998.

World Travel Guide. [Online] Available http://www.wtgonline.com/country/bz/gen.html, 1998.

Garifuna

PRONUNCIATION: gar-ih-FOO-nah
LOCATION: Eastern coasts of Belize, Guatemala, Honduras, and Nicaragua; United States; Caribbean islands
POPULATION: 200,000–500,000
LANGUAGE: Spanish; English; Garifuna
RELIGION: Catholicism, incorporating aspects of the traditional religion

1 ● INTRODUCTION

The Garifuna live in Central America along the coast of the Caribbean sea. Their territory spreads across the borders of four different nations—Belize (formerly British Honduras), Guatemala, Honduras, and Nicaragua. They are descendants of the Caribs, a people of the island chain known as the Lesser Antilles. In the seventeenth and eighteenth centuries, Caribs on the island of St. Vincent intermarried with captured or escaped African slaves.

These people tried to prevent Great Britain from colonizing the island of St. Vincent, but they failed. The Garifuna were deported to the island of Roatan off the coast of Honduras in 1797. The deportees, about one-fourth of the total Garifuna population, survived and rebuilt their culture in this unfamiliar place. They eventually returned to Central America. They settled mainly in the coastal lowlands of the area that would become the four present nations.

Over the next two centuries, Garifuna population and territory increased greatly. Garifuna formed a major part of the work force on the Central American coast for over a hundred years. In 1823, additional Garifuna migrated to Belize, fleeing a civil war in Honduras. In spite of moving to new places and taking in other peoples, the Garifuna have preserved their cultural identity. They have kept their language and many of the customs, beliefs, and ceremonies of their island ancestors.

2 ● LOCATION

The Garifuna live in a chain of villages and towns along the eastern coast of Belize, Guatemala, Honduras, and Nicaragua. These Caribbean lowlands have a varied terrain. It includes mangrove swamps, tropical rain forests, river valleys, coastal plains, and grassy plains with some pines and palm trees. Many Garifuna have moved to large cities in Central America and the United States. Those in the United States live in communities in New York, Chicago, Los Angeles, and other major cities. There are also small groups of Garifuna on the Caribbean islands of Trinidad, Dominica, and St. Vincent.

Because of their migrations to other countries, it is impossible to arrive at exact population figures for the Garifuna. (In addition, only Belize counts them as a distinct ethnic group.) Their total numbers have been estimated between two hundred thousand and five hundred thousand. Some estimates figure the Garifuna in the United States alone at around one hundred thousand.

3 ● LANGUAGE

Spanish is the official language of most of the countries in which the Garifuna live. In Belize and the United States, the main language is, of course, English. The native lan-

Cory Langley

Four Garifuna girls on their way home from a visit to the village.

guage of the Garifuna (called *Garifuna* or *Garinagu*) comes from the Arawak and Carib languages of their island ancestors.

4 ● FOLKLORE

Although it has been illegal for a long time, *obeah,* the traditional witchcraft of the Caribbean, still exists. Some Garifuna still practice it secretly. Its rituals involve dances, drumming, and trances for contacting the spirits of the dead. It is generally used either to harm one's enemies or to ward off spells that others may have cast.

An object used in such spells is the *puchinga* doll. It is made of cloth stuffed with black feathers and is buried under the doorstep of the intended victim. Crosses are sometimes painted on children's foreheads to ward off the evil eye.

5 ● RELIGION

The Garifuna practice a version of Catholicism that uses many aspects of their traditional religion. It combines belief in saints with reverence toward *gubida* (the spirits of ancestors) and faith in shamans or "spirit helpers" (called *buwiyes*). Their religious practices—including dancing, singing, drumming, and use of alcohol—have long been considered suspicious by outsiders. Established churches and people living nearby have accused them of paganism and devil worship. Some buwiyes, however, have served as Roman Catholic priests or nuns.

Among the most important traditional religious practices is the *dugu*. It is a ceremonial feast, held to please the gubida when they seem to be angry at a living relative. The sign of this anger usually is illness. A dugu lasts from two to four days. It is attended by friends and relatives of the affected person. Sometimes that person will come all the way from the United States in order to be healed. Participants engage in ritual song and dance, led by a buwiye, who calls forth the gubida. After the food prepared for the feast and rum have been ceremonially offered to the ancestral spirit, all of it is either thrown into the sea or buried in the ground.

6 ● MAJOR HOLIDAYS

Many Garifuna ritual observances are held on the holy days of the Christian calendar, but some occur on the dates of nonreligious holidays as well. Festivities usually include processions and street dancing, often in masks and costumes. John Canoe *(Yankunu)* dancers (named for a Jamaican folk hero) perform at Christmastime and receive money, drinks, or homemade candies.

On November 19, the Garifuna of Belize celebrate Settlement Day, marking the beginning of a larger Garifuna presence in that country in 1823. It was then that their ancestors who had been forced out of Honduras, arrived in the area to join the small band that had already settled in the town of Stann Creek. In the town of Dangriga, the center of Belize's Garifuna community, there is a ceremony on Settlement Day. It reenacts the settlers' arrival. Some people row in from the ocean in dugout canoes. Their cargo is the same as their ancestors'. It includes simple cooking utensils, drums, cassava roots, and young banana trees. When they land on the shore, they are joined by hundreds of spectators. There is a lively procession that winds through the streets of Dangriga. The people go to the Catholic church for a special service. Afterward, the crowd enjoys dancing and feasting on traditional foods.

7 ● RITES OF PASSAGE

Major life changes (such as birth, becoming an adult, and death) are marked by religious ceremonies. They combine Catholic traditions with rites from the ancestral religion.

8 ● RELATIONSHIPS

Physical violence is rare among the Garifuna. An angry person almost always uses such practices as name-calling, cursing, gossip, and mocking songs. Sometimes a person who has been wronged will even use witchcraft *(obeah)* to gain revenge.

9 ● LIVING CONDITIONS

Houses are either wooden or made of wattle and daub (woven sticks and twigs plastered with clay). They have thatched roofs. Wooden houses are raised several feet off the ground on posts. Many villages still have no electricity, and even in the towns with electricity there are frequent power outages.

To Make Wattle and Daub

Materials for a 4x6-inch structure

About ten sticks, approximately ten inches long and between ¼- and ½- inch thick
Several dozen flexible twigs, varying in length, but all less than ¼-inch thick
Modeling clay
Cardboard (a large shoebox top or similar box top work well)

Directions

1. Using golfball-size lumps of clay, secure the large sticks vertically to form the posts of a rectangle 4 by 6 inches.

2. Using the flexible, thin twigs, begin weaving in and out between the upright sticks. Work carefully to keep the posts vertical. This woven siding is the "wattle."

3. Mix the clay with a little water until it is the consistency of very thick oatmeal. This is the "daub."

4. Slather the daub over the surface of the wattle, attempting to seal any cracks to make the structure "weatherproof."

5. Add a roof of heavy paper of light cardboard, covered with grass clippings or artifical grass to simulate thatch.

Garbage is often thrown into the sea or into open ditches and streams. In some cases, it is tossed out of the back door. Most houses have no toilet facilities.

With the increase of "junk food" in developing areas, the Garifuna diet has become less nutritious. Obesity has increased, especially among women. Preschool children do not get enough protein.

The Garifuna use both modern medicine and traditional remedies. But they hold to their belief that the most important thing determining people's health is the power of the spirits of their ancestors.

10 ● FAMILY LIFE

Among the Garifuna, many women bear children without having a permanent or legal relationship with the children's father. Legal marriage occurs in a minority of households. The Garifuna are generally seen as a *matrifocal* society (where women are central to family life). Family lines are determined by the mother, rather than the father. In the past, households often had three generations of women. Increasingly, however, only the oldest and youngest generations remain. Working-age people often go away seeking better jobs. The grandparents stay to raise the children. Since the 1960s, many women have gone to major cities in Central America or the United States. There they find jobs in the textile industry or as maids.

Garifuna mothers are not as directly and physically involved with their children as mothers in many similar cultures. Some observers connect this fact with a tendency toward independence and individualism among the Garifuna. Mothers wean children early and in some cases do not breast-feed at all. They also feel comfortable in leaving them with caregivers for short or long periods of time. In keeping with the nonviolent nature of the Garifuna, children are raised with little or no corporal punishment—they are not punished by being hit or spanked. Fights among children themselves are frowned upon and broken up. Violence among family members is also extremely rare.

11 ● CLOTHING

Most Garifuna wear modern Western-style clothing. Even among the older women, very few still wear the traditional costumes trimmed with shells. But they do wear brightly colored full skirts and kerchiefs, making them look very different from younger women, who wear jeans, tee-shirts, and tight skirts, much like young women everywhere.

The men also wear jeans, and the traditional straw hats have been replaced by baseball caps. Young people's clothing has been influenced by the places where their parents have settled. In the towns one can see some young people in the latest fashions from New York, paid for with money sent by relatives living abroad.

12 ● FOOD

Dietary staples include rice, fish, green bananas, plantains (which resemble bananas), and coconut milk. Coconut milk is used to prepare many dishes, such as *hudut,* in which it is mixed with crushed, boiled plantains. The green bananas are boiled and served as a starchy vegetable. "Boil-up," or *falmou,* is a spicy traditional soup or stew containing fish, coconut milk, spice, and other ingredients.

Manioc, or *cassava,* plays an important role in the diet of the Garifuna in Honduras, who eat it boiled as a vegetable. But it is important throughout the culture as the basic ingredient of *areba,* the flatbread. This food, and the customs for preparing it, have helped to unify Garifuna. Their name

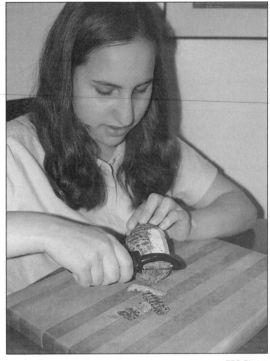

EPD Photos

This American student is trying her hand at shaving a cassava root. In the past, the Garifuna would have used a board studded with stones to accomplish the task. Modern Garifuna use electric graters.

is based on the term *karifuna,* which means "of the cassava clan."

Cassava roots were traditionally grated by hand on stone-studded wooden boards, a tedious job. Today, people often use electric graters. Then the pulp is strained by hand in bags made from woven leaves. The bags are hung from a tree and weighted at the bottom. This squeezes out the starch and juices (which are poisonous). The white meal that is left dries overnight, is sifted and made into flatbread.

The most popular beverages are coffee and various "bush teas," sweetened by generous amounts of sugar. Desserts include cakes and puddings made from sweet potatoes, rice, and bread scraps. A very popular dessert is the candy called *tableta,* made with grated coconut, ginger root, and brown sugar. The mixture is boiled, poured into a greased pan to cool, and cut into squares. Children sell this confection, a favorite among tourists, at bus stops and in other public places.

13 ● EDUCATION

School attendance is generally low after the primary grades. But the basic ability to read and write is valued, and most Garifuna do get enough schooling to learn that much. Most are also interested in improving their Spanish (in Honduras and Guatemala) or English (in Belize). Many Garifuna in Belize are well educated and have become respected schoolteachers.

14 ● CULTURAL HERITAGE

The Garifuna have a rich heritage with roots in both African and local cultures. Their traditional music includes work songs, hymns, lullabies, ballads, and healing songs. It shows an African influence in call-and-response song patterns and complex drum rhythms. Some songs are sung during daily tasks, such as the baking of cassava bread *(areba).*

The most typical Garifuna dance is the *punta,* which has its roots in African courtship dances. It is performed by couples, who compete for attention from spectators and from other dancers by making fancy flirtatious moves. The *paranda* is a slow dance performed by women, who move in a circle performing traditional hand movements, and sing as they dance.

A sacred dance, the *abaimahani,* is performed at the *dugu,* a feast held for the spirit of a deceased ancestor. The dancers—all women—form a long line, link little fingers, and sing special music. The *Wanaragua,* or John Canoe dance, performed at Christmastime, includes sad songs about the absence of loved ones.

While holding on to the older cultural traditions, the Garifuna are also developing some new ones. Modern musicians have transformed the ancient music of the *punta,* creating the popular "punta rock."

The paintings of internationally acclaimed artist Benjamin Nicholas depict aspects of Garifuna history and culture in bold, modern styles.

15 ● EMPLOYMENT

The Garifuna have traditionally lived by fishing and by basic small-scale farming. In the twentieth century, the banana industry became a major employer. This created jobs both in agriculture and in the major ports that sprang up along the coast. Since World War II, many Garifuna have worked in the merchant marine. However, the largest of the work force consists of underemployed wage laborers.

The Garifuna who live in towns but still farm often travel 5 to 10 miles (8 to 16 kilometers) to their plots, leaving early in the morning by bus and returning late in the afternoon. The civil service, especially the teaching profession, has been a major employer of Garifuna in Belize. Many children of Garifuna in the United States enter fields of medicine, engineering, and education. Some return home and others remain abroad permanently.

16 ● SPORTS

Soccer is a popular sport among the Garifuna. Young people organize games on flat open areas in their towns or villages, even on the beach.

17 ● RECREATION

Punta parties, named for the traditional dance that is performed at them, are a favorite form of entertainment. Pop musicians have developed "punta rock," which combines the beat of traditional punta music with the electric guitar sounds of rock music and modern Garifuna lyrics. This music, which originated in Belize, is becoming popular throughout the Caribbean. In a reverse development, the Garifuna have adapted the West Indian reggae music to a form of their own called *cungo*.

Today, many Garifuna households in the larger towns have television sets. A TV is also one of the first purchases of Garifuna who come to the United States.

18 ● CRAFTS AND HOBBIES

Few of the Garifuna still practice their traditional crafts. These include hat-making, drum-making, basket-weaving, and the carving of dugout canoes. To prevent the loss of this heritage, the National Garifuna Council of Belize held a workshop in 1987. In it, young people were taught the crafts of their ancestors.

19 ● SOCIAL PROBLEMS

The lack of opportunities at home has led many Garifuna to go to other parts of Central America and to the United States. It has been estimated that as many as 50 percent of the men are absent from the average Garifuna community at any given time. With growing numbers of women also traveling, communities are losing a whole generation of working-age adults. The elderly and very young are left to survive together. They often live on money sent by absent family members, until the young people are old enough to leave as well.

There is increased concern about alcoholism among the Garifuna. Alcohol consumption itself has increased, a fact that some people relate to the social problems caused by unemployment and the absence of adults. Marijuana use, mainly by young men, has become common among Garifuna living in the towns.

20 ● BIBLIOGRAPHY

Gonzalez, Nancie. "Garifuna." In *Encyclopedia of World Cultures.* Boston: G. K. Hall, 1992.

Kerns, Virginia. *Women and the Ancestors: Black Carib Kinship and Ritual.* Urbana, Ill.: University of Illinois Press, 1983.

Olson, James S. *The Indians of Central and South America: An Ethnohistorical Dictionary.* New York: Greenwood Press, 1991.

WEBSITES

Belize Tourism Industry Association. [Online] Available http://www.belize.com/, 1998.

Green Arrow Advertising. Belize. [Online] Available http://www.greenarrow.com/belize/belize.htm, 1998.

World Travel Guide. [Online] Available http://www.wtgonline.com/country/bz/gen.html, 1998.

Benin

The people of Benin are called the Beninese. There are more than forty-two ethnic groups in Benin. The Fon make up 40 percent of the population.

Beninese

PRONUNCIATION: ben-uh-NEEZ
ALTERNATE NAME: (former) Dahomey
LOCATION: Benin
POPULATION: 5.7 million
LANGUAGE: French (official language); Fon and Yoruba in the south; Bariba and Fulani in the north; over 40 other languages
RELIGION: Animism; Christianity (Catholicism); Islam

1 ● INTRODUCTION

Until 1972, Benin was called "Dahomey," named after the ancient Kingdom of Dan Homey. The French and Portuguese colonized Dahomey. They took part in the slave trade in Dahomey until it was ended in 1885. In the 1880s the French overthrew the kings of Dahomey. Dahomey gained independence from the French on August 1, 1960. Since then the country has suffered ethnic conflict and army revolts. In 1990 prodemocracy protests helped end military rule. Since then, a president was elected, and the economy and armed forces were reorganized. However, student protests and strikes by government employees show that people are still unhappy with Benin's weak economy.

2 ● LOCATION

Benin is a small west African country about the size of Pennsylvania. It has a flat and sandy coastal plain with warm temperatures (70°F to 85°F) and two rainy seasons. The northern, thinly wooded savanna has one short rainy season, and temperatures reach over 110°F.

In 1996, Benin's population was about 5.7 million people. Over half of them were under fifteen years old. Many people have moved to cities, but most still live in villages. There are more than forty-two ethnic groups in Benin: the Fon make up 40 percent of the population; the Adja, Bariba, Yoruba, and Aizo/HouJda make up another 40 percent; the Fulani, Kotokoli, and Dendi comprise the rest (20 percent).

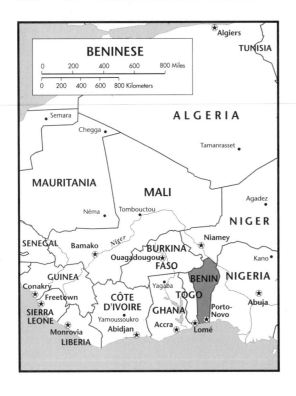

BENINESE

0 200 400 600 800 Miles

0 200 400 600 800 Kilometers

Algiers

TUNISIA

ALGERIA

Semara

Chegga

Tamanrasset

MAURITANIA

MALI

Néma Tombouctou

Agadez

NIGER

SENEGAL Bamako Niger Niamey

Ouagadougou BURKINA FASO Kano

GUINEA Yagaba BENIN NIGERIA

Conakry

Freetown CÔTE TOGO

SIERRA D'IVOIRE GHANA Porto- Abuja

LEONE Yamoussoukro Novo

Monrovia Abidjan Accra Lomé

LIBERIA

3 ● LANGUAGE

The peoples of Benin speak fifty-one languages. French is the official language. The two major languages in the south are Fon and Yoruba. In the north, they are Bariba and Fulani.

These are some common greetings in Fon.

ENGLISH	PRONUNCIATION
Good morning	AH-FON ghan-jee-ah
How are you?	AH-DOH ghan-jee-ah
Thank you	AH-WAH-nou
Good bye	OH-dah-boh

4 ● FOLKLORE

Benin's nickname is "Land of Songs" because singing is important in daily life. Through singing, people express their feelings and tell their history. Songs vary from pleasant to dramatic in order to convey the proper emotion. Each ethnic group has its own songs and dances.

5 ● RELIGION

The majority of Beninese practice animist religion. About 15 percent are Christian, and about 13 percent are Islamic. Beninese animists include the Fon, Yoruba, and Mina groups. Animists recognize some 5,000 to 6,000 gods or spirits. The animist leaders worship spirits, predict the future, and use many kinds of spiritual objects. One of the most famous cults is the Python Cult, also called the Cult of the Great Serpent. The Python Cult worships a deity from the ancient kingdom of Ouidah. Their main temple contains huge, living, defanged pythons.

6 ● MAJOR HOLIDAYS

Benin has a mix of animist, Muslim, Christian, and secular holidays. Beninese celebrate the Muslim Tabaski feast and the month-long fast of Ramadan. They also observe the Christian holidays of Christmas and Easter. Benin celebrates its Independence Day on August 1. In the past, the Beninese held parades, native dances, and evening balls. But since living conditions have been difficult under the military rule that followed independence, citizens don't have much enthusiasm for patriotic celebrations. Consequently, most Beninese now spend holidays quietly with their families, enjoying a good meal if they can afford it.

7 ● RITES OF PASSAGE

Beninese place great importance on rites of passage. Their families, society, and tradi-

Cory Langley

Many houses do not have safe drinking water or proper toilets.

tions depend on them. Rites of passage can be joyful. For example, baptisms are community celebrations that involve feasting and dancing. Weddings are cause for feasting and celebration. Traditional weddings can last weeks. When someone dies, the rituals involve helping the survivors.

8 ● RELATIONSHIPS

In Benin, people usually greet each other even if they are strangers. Muslims ask about the other person's family. Visitors are always offered a glass of water, and if it is mealtime, they are expected to eat. When they wake up, children directly greet their parents. People kneel in front of older family members or important members of the community. This is a sign of respect.

9 ● LIVING CONDITIONS

Compared to the rest of the world, living standards in Benin are low. Outside of cities, many houses do not have safe drinking water or proper toilets. Medical problems like malaria, measles, and malnutrition kill many infants. Many young children and pregnant women are malnourished. These are serious health problems. However, Benin is improving the health and living conditions of its people. The constitution of 1990 helps and protects children. Benin takes part in a health plan known as the Bamako Health Initiative, which brings medicines to rural health clinics and immunizes children.

The main roads in Benin are paved. It is easy to travel from the coast to the north by bush taxi or minivan. Secondary roads can be rugged and can tear up vehicles. Benin has 600 miles (1,000 kilometers) of paved roads and another 5,000 miles (8,000 kilometers) of unpaved roads.

10 ● FAMILY LIFE

Beninese women play leading roles in the home. They make many decisions about home economics and child care. Traditionally, the husband's job has been to support the family. Nowadays, more Beninese women work outside the home. They tend small gardens or work in small businesses.

On average, Beninese women have seven pregnancies in their lifetime. But families of four to six children are becoming more common. Usually, if a child is born out of wedlock, the parents will marry to take care of the child. Some marriages are polygamous, where there is one husband but more than one wife. In polygamous marriages, each wife has her own apartment in a large family house. The wives share a common kitchen and other facilities.

11 ● CLOTHING

On the coast, women usually wear African *pagnes*. These are of dazzling colors and patterns, and often have a matching head scarf.

Muslim women wear a three-piece cloth outfit. One piece wraps around the waist, one around the chest, and one covers the head. Once married, Muslim women in

Cory Langley

There are not enough acceptable jobs in Benin. About three-fourths of people in cities have menial jobs like peddler or pushcart operator.

Benin always cover their heads in public. Men traditionally wear *boubou*-style (loose, long, and flowing) cotton shirts over pants. The west African embroidered boubou is becoming popular with both men and women. The boubou requires many hours to sew and embroider and is very expensive, costing as much as hundreds of dollars. Therefore, boubou are worn only for special occasions.

12 ● FOOD

There is a great variety of food in Benin. The main food is *la pate,* bread made of various kinds of flour. La pate is dipped into sauces and is eaten with the right hand. Traditional households eat porridge for breakfast, which is made from millet, corn, yams,

Recipe

African Vegetable Stew

Ingredients

olive oil
1 large onion, chopped
1 bunch Swiss chard, white stems and
    greens separated and chopped
1 can garbanzo beans (known also as
    chick peas)
½ cup raisins
½ cup uncooked rice
several fresh tomatoes (or 1 large can of
    tomatoes)
1 clove garlic
2 yams
salt and pepper to taste
Tabasco sauce to taste

Directions

1. Saute onion, garlic, and white stems of chard in small amount of olive oil until barely limp.
2. Add chopped greens and saute until limp.
3. Either peel the yams or scrub them well with a vegetable brush. Then slice them into thick slices.
4. Add garbanzos, raisins, yams, tomatoes, salt, and pepper to frying pan. Heat for 2 to 3 minutes.
5. Make a well in the center of the mixture in the pan. Put the rice in this well and pat it down until it is thoroughly moistened.
6. Cover and cook until rice is done (about 25 minutes).
7. Add a drop or two of Tabasco sauce to taste. Add more Tabasco if desired.

This recipe takes about 15 minutes for preparation, and 30 minutes for cooking.

or manioc. *Gari* is made of grated manioc and is enjoyed with peanut-cake snacks. Merchants on street corners in southern towns sell deep-fried dumplings made from pounded bananas or beans. Many Beninese enjoy soft drinks and beer, but these require spare cash. Local drinks include natural lemonade and limeade, palm wine (*sodabi*), and beer and gin made from millet (*chapalo*).

13 ● EDUCATION

Benin has low enrollment in its primary schools. In 1989, only 59 percent of the children were enrolled. About 30 percent reached sixth grade and only 64 children graduated. However, Benin is working to improve adult literacy. In 1995, the government estimated that about 37 percent of adults could read and write. This was much better than in the past.

14 ● CULTURAL HERITAGE

Beninese animism, dance, and music have a long and rich history. The traditional dances of the Fon people are well-known. Now, Fon dance is becoming modernized. The music is played on a mix of traditional drums and modern instruments such as electric guitars and synthesizers. Skilled craftspeople produce traditional instruments of high quality.

Many Beninese cultural traditions are derived from ancient kingdoms. For example, Nikki is the capital of a kingdom that began in the fifteenth century. The Baribas live where that kingdom once existed. They are wonderful riders who like to show off their horsemanship.

15 ● WORK

There are not enough acceptable jobs in Benin. In the cities, about 75 percent of people have low-paying, menial jobs like peddler and pushcart operator. In the villages, most Beninese (62 percent) work in agriculture, forestry, and fishing. The main crops are manioc, maize, and yams. Other crops, like coconut palms, and cotton, are sold for cash. As of the late 1990s, Beninese hoped that a planned hydroelectric dam on the Mono River would bring factories. They also hoped that mineral deposits and offshore oil would provide new and better jobs.

16 ● SPORTS

The Beninese national sport is soccer. It is watched by Beninese everywhere and is played mainly by boys and young men.

17 ● RECREATION

Entertainment is different in the cities and villages of Benin. In the towns and cities where electricity is available, Beninese can watch state-run television. Many people are also buying satellite dishes. Few people have video cassette recorders. Movies are always popular.

Beninese also enjoy traditional dancing. Because of their cultural heritage, dancing, music, and cultural performances may be considered a type of sport. As in sports, teamwork is very important. Beninese compare and rate dancers and musicians for their agility, creativity, skill, and stamina.

Electricity is not available in most villages. There, people make their own fun. Ceremonies, holidays, and traditional feasts make up most of the recreation. For exam-ple, baptisms happen often and are one of the most common forms of entertainment. A village of 300 to 400 people may have as many as thirty baptisms a year.

18 ● CRAFTS AND HOBBIES

Beninese artists produce fine weaving and traditional sculptures. Sculptors also make masks, tables, boxes, scepters (a baton or staff that symbolizes authority), and arm-chairs. Crafts are both artistic and practical. For example, craftswomen make pots of all sizes for carrying and storing water. Black-smiths not only produce works of art, but also repair bicycles, motorcycles, and auto-mobiles. Beninese also make a wide range of handmade instruments, from twin drums to small Beninese guitars.

19 ● SOCIAL PROBLEMS

At this time, Benin's major social problems are mainly caused by the poor economy. Benin has high unemployment and low wages. Even educated people have to take manual jobs such as driving motorcycle-taxis. But social problems like crime, mur-der, and drug abuse are rare. However, some countries are starting to ship illegal drugs through Benin. This might cause more drug crime in the future.

20 ● BIBLIOGRAPHY

Africa on File. New York: Facts on File, 1995.
Decalo, Samuel. *Historical Dictionary of Benin.* Lanham, Md.: The Scarecrow Press, Inc., 1995.

WEBSITES
Internet Africa Ltd. [Online] Available http://www.africanet.com/africanet/country/benin/, 1998.
World Travel Guide. Benin. [Online] Available http://www.wtgonline.com/country/bj/gen.html, 1998.

Bhutan

The people of Bhutan are known as Bhutanese. There are three major ethnic groups: the Bhutia (also Bhotia, or Bhote), comprising roughly 50 percent of the population; the Nepalese, accounting for another 35 percent; and the Assamese, making up 15 percent. Small numbers of aboriginal (native) people live in villages scattered throughout Bhutan. For more information on the Nepalese, consult the chapter on Nepal in Volume 6.

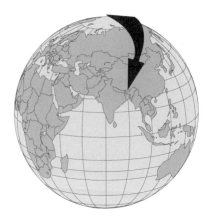

Bhutanese

PRONUNCIATION: BOOT-un-eez

LOCATION: Bhutan

POPULATION: 816,000–1.8 million (including Nepalese immigrants and other minorities)

LANGUAGE: Dzongkha (official); Nepali; Assamese; Gurung; Tsangla; Hindi

RELIGION: Mahayana Buddhism (official); Bon (shamanism); mix of Hinduism and Buddhism; Islam

1 ● INTRODUCTION

Bhutanese is the name given to the people who live in the Kingdom of Bhutan. Bhutan is a small, landlocked country in the mountainous area north of India. The name *Bhutan* is derived from a word that means the "borderland" of Bhot, or Tibet. The Bhutanese themselves call their country *Druk-Yul* or the "Land of the Thunder Dragon." The ruling monarch of the country carries the title *Druk Gyalpo* or "Dragon King."

From the beginning of the ninth century AD, the region was settled by Tibetans migrating south. Bhutan was born in the early seventeenth century when a Tibetan Buddhist monk established his authority as king, taking the title of *Dharma Raja*. As of the late 1990s, the king was Druk Gyalpo Jigme Singye Wangchuk.

The British held colonial power over India in the early nineteenth century. In 1910, Bhutan's relations with other countries were controlled by British India. In return, Britain agreed not to interfere in Bhutan's internal affairs. In 1949 when India gained its independence, India took control of Bhutan's relations with other countries. Chinese forces took control of Bhutan's neighbor, Tibet, in 1950. Bhutan saw its ties with India as a way to fight off a threat from China. During the 1960s, Bhutan started to modernize and allowed people from other countries to visit without a special invitation from the king.

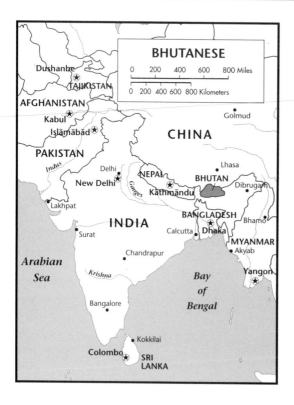

eastern Himalayan Mountain Range. Bhutan has three distinct geographic regions. In the south is a narrow strip of lowland known as the Duars Plain. The area receives between 200 and 300 inches (500 and 760 centimeters) of rain a year. It is covered with dense subtropical forest and undergrowth and is hot, humid, and a generally unhealthy atmosphere in which to live. North of the Duars is the Inner Himalaya, a region of mountains extending southward from the main Himalayan Range. Between these spurs lie fertile valleys at elevations between 5,000 and 9,000 feet (1,500 and 2,700 meters). With a relatively moderate climate, these valleys support agriculture. Most of Bhutan's population lives in these valleys. Further to the north, along the Tibetan border, are the main ranges of the Great Himalaya. The highest peaks approach 24,000 feet (7,300 meters), with Kula Kangra soaring to 24,784 feet (7,554 meters). Below the high peaks are alpine meadows used for grazing yaks in the summer months.

3 ● LANGUAGE

The official language of Bhutan is Dzongkha, a dialect of Tibetan. In its written form, Dzongkha is identical to Tibetan. Other languages spoken in Bhutan include Nepali, Assamese, and Gurung. Some Hindi is spoken in southern areas that border India.

4 ● FOLKLORE

There are many folktales in Bhutan that relate to events and personalities of the past. One tradition tells of a prince from India who settled in Bhutan in the eighth century AD. He invited the monk Padmasambhava to his kingdom. Known in Tibet as *Guru Rim-*

2 ● LOCATION

There is no reliable census of the population of Bhutan. The government estimates the total population at over 800,000 people, but they do not include immigrants. If immigrants from Nepal and other minorities are included, the population is estimated to be over 1.8 million. There are three major ethnic groups in Bhutan: the Bhutia (also Bhotia, or Bhote), Nepalese, and Assamese. Bhutia comprise roughly 50 percent of Bhutan's population. The Nepalese account for another 35 percent, while the Assamese make up 15 percent of the country's inhabitants.

Bhutan, with an area of 18,217 square miles (47,182 square kilometers), lies in the

poche ("Precious Teacher"), Padmasambhava was primarily responsible for introducing Buddhism in Bhutan. Other stories center on the fifteenth-century lama Pemalingpa, who is seen as an incarnation of Padmasambhava. Another heroic figure of Bhutan is Shabdrung, the lama who assumed the title of Dharma Raja in the seventeenth century and laid the political foundations of Bhutan State.

5 ● RELIGION

Approximately three-fourths of Bhutanese are Buddhist. The dominant religious order in the country is the Red-Hat sect (Kargyupa). Belief in sorcerers, spirits, demons, and the need for exorcisms as undertaken in the "devil dances" are a part of everyday Bhutanese religious practices. Lamas (religious leaders) skilled in rituals perform the necessary religious observances. Animal sacrifice has been replaced in Bhutan by the offering of *torma,* ritual figures made from dough and butter. Hinduism, or a mix of Hinduism and Buddhism, is the religion of the Nepalese peoples of Bhutan.

6 ● MAJOR HOLIDAYS

Losar, the Tibetan New Year, is one of the most important festivals in Bhutan. It is celebrated in February with feasting and drinking. Folk dances, including masked dances, are performed and archery competitions held. Friends and relatives exchange greeting cards. Domchheo and Tsechu are annual religious festivals marked by worship ceremonies and performances of the ritual masked dances by monks. These are held at monasteries and *dzongs,* the forts around which many Bhutanese villages are built. Various other Buddhist and Hindu festivals

are observed. The king's birthday (September 22) and the National Day of Bhutan (December 17) are celebrated as public holidays.

7 ● RITES OF PASSAGE

Birth and marriage in Bhutan are social or family events. Funerals, on the other hand, are elaborate religious affairs. After a death, a lama (Buddhist religious leader) is called in to extract the *sem* (spirit) from the body and speed it on its way. The body is placed in a sitting position before an altar, on which various ritual objects—including *torma* (figurines made of dough and butter)—are placed. A lama leads the service for the dead, reciting passages from various Buddhist texts. Cremation is the usual form of disposal of the corpse, although bodies may be buried or thrown in a river. Rituals are performed for forty-nine days after death. During this period an effigy (symbolic model) of the dead person is kept in the house. Both the end of the mourning period and the one-year anniversary of the death are celebrated with a feast.

8 ● RELATIONSHIPS

A Bhutanese host greets a guest by bowing slightly, extending his or her hands towards the ground with palms facing the visitor, and moving the hand in a gesture inviting the guest into the house. The host may also say, *"Yala! Yala! Kuzu zangpola?"* ("Hello! Hello! How do you do?"). The guest, after responding in an appropriate manner, is then seated in the drawing room. She or he is served tea, beer, or other refreshments. Men and women mix and converse freely, without restrictions.

9 ● LIVING CONDITIONS

Bhutan was isolated from the outside world until around 1960. As a result, health care services in Bhutan are not very well developed. Leading causes of death include respiratory infections, diarrhea and dysentery, skin infections, infections from parasites, and malaria. Over 10 percent of all babies die shortly after birth.

Ninety percent of Bhutan's population live in villages scattered throughout the country. Although there are a handful of small towns in Bhutan, only Thimphu, the capital, exceeds 20,000 inhabitants in size. Living standards are generally low, with per capita income (money earned by one person) less than $200 per year. Bhutan's mountainous terrain makes communications difficult.

10 ● FAMILY LIFE

Most people in Bhutan marry within their own ethnic group. The legal age for marriage is set by the government at sixteen years for women and twenty-one years for men. In the past, marriages were arranged by the parents. By the 1990s, more and more young couples were selecting their own marriage partners. Bhutanese marriages are relatively simple. A lama (Buddhist religious leader) officiates at the ceremony. Offerings of *chang* (beer) are made to ghosts and spirits. Betel leaves, areca nuts, and fruits are distributed to wedding guests and observers. More food and entertainment follow the ceremony.

The Bhutanese are essentially monogamous (have only one husband or wife). Polyandry (more than one husband) has

AP/Wide World Photos

Some 20 percent of primary-school-age children, and only 2 percent of secondary-school-age children, are enrolled in school.

been abolished (made illegal). Polygyny (more than one wife) is restricted to a maximum of three wives per husband. A bride does not necessarily move into her husband's household. The new husband may live with his wife's family, if her family needs laborers to help with their work. Alternatively, the new couple may set up their own household on their own plot of land. Divorce is permitted, but the spouse who wants the divorce must compensate the other with money or goods.

11 ● CLOTHING

Bhutanese dress for men consists of a *ko* (long, loose robe) that reaches the ankles.

During the day, the *ko* is hoisted up and fastened at the waist by a woven belt so that it reaches the knees. At night, it is let down to the ankles. A coat, worn over the ko, fastens at the neck but is worn open during the day. The sleeves are long and loose. Bhutanese men seldom wear a hat, but they sometimes wrap a scarf around the head at night. Shoes are rarely worn, though some men wear sandals. Wealthier men wear woolen boots. Every man carries a long knife slung from his belt. When the ko is tied in the "up" position, it forms a pouch that is used for carrying objects.

Bhutanese women wear the *kira,* a woven dress that is fastened at each shoulder by silver buckles. A woven belt is tied around the waist. Women commonly wear necklaces of coral and turquoise, strung together with silver amulets (charms). The hair is usually cut short.

12 ● FOOD

Rice is the main food in Bhutan. Rice is accompanied by meat whenever it is available. Though most Bhutanese are Buddhists, they are not vegetarians. They eat beef, pork, goat, chicken, and eggs. A typical Bhutanese meal might consist of *thugpa,* a meat soup prepared with herbs, rice (of the round, red variety), and a meat curry or omelet. Sweet rice (white rice cooked in milk and sugar) is served on special occasions. Tea, made with salt and butter, is a Bhutanese staple. *Chang* (beer) is made from grain and is served to guests and offered to the gods.

At high altitudes, barley and buckwheat (cereal grains) are grown. The cereals are ground, then roasted or fried, and stored for future use. Fried corn powder is popular among the Bhutanese. Milk is scarce and of poor quality, although a hard cheese is made from yak milk.

13 ● EDUCATION

No formal schools existed in Bhutan before the early 1960s, except for those associated with religious institutions. The government has tried to improve education, but Bhutan still lags behind its neighbor countries in education. Only about 20 percent of children from ages five to twelve are enrolled in school. Only 2 percent of children thirteen to eighteen are enrolled in high school. About 20 percent of adults can read and write.

14 ● CULTURAL HERITAGE

Bhutan's culture is deeply rooted in Tibetan Buddhism. The country began as a theocracy (its ruler was a religious leader). Even in the 1990s, lamas (Buddhist religious leaders) influence government affairs. The *dzongs* (forts) and monasteries remain centers of political, economic, social, and religious life. It is in these places that festivals are celebrated with religious music and masked dances. Lamas continue the traditions of Buddhist learning. Religion finds architectural expression in numerous *chorten* (mounds of relics) and temples. Dzongs are often patterned after the Potala in Lhasa, Tibet (part of China since the 1950s). The Potala is the home of the Buddhist leader, the Dalai Lama. Religious objects such as the *mandala* (Buddhist Wheel of Life) and *thanka* (a painted religious scroll) are works of art in their own right.

15 ● EMPLOYMENT

Bhutan is essentially an agrarian (farming) country. Over 90 percent of all workers are involved in subsistence agriculture (growing enough food for the family's use, with little left to sell) and raising livestock. Only 3 percent of Bhutan's area is used for farming, since much of the land is mountainous or heavily forested. Rice, wheat, maize (corn), and millet are the main crops grown in the country. Fruit production is important, with apples, peaches, plums, and apricots among the varieties grown. Livestock raised in the region include cattle, sheep, pigs, chickens, and the yak, an animal adapted to high altitudes.

16 ● SPORTS

The Bhutanese are well known for their archery skills, and archery competitions are commonly held at the time of festivals and national holidays.

17 ● RECREATION

Bhutanese have limited access to modern forms of entertainment. For radio, FM broadcasts are aired in Thimphu, and short-wave broadcasts can be received in the rest of the country. In 1989 the government banned the viewing of television by ordering all TV antennas in the country to be dismantled. The government publishes a weekly newspaper, *Kuensel,* but with the country's low literacy rate, the paper has a very small circulation. Religious festivals and folk traditions such as singing and dancing are the primary forms of entertainment and recreation.

18 ● CRAFTS AND HOBBIES

Bhutanese women are skilled at weaving. They make their own clothing, bedding, tablecloths, floor coverings, and items for religious use. Embroidery is a favorite art. Much effort goes into making costumes and masks for the ritual dances performed at festivals. Smiths excel in working gold, silver, brass, and other metals.

19 ● SOCIAL PROBLEMS

The Bhutanese live in the least-developed country in all of South Asia. Despite efforts at modernization, poverty, lack of potable (clean) water, inadequate health care, illiteracy, and difficulties in transportation remain serious problems. Tensions between the Bhutanese and Nepalese minority have created a problem in the country. Since 1990, antigovernment extremists among the Nepalese have been waging a terrorist war in Bhutan.

20 ● BIBLIOGRAPHY

Chakravarti, B. *A Cultural History of Bhutan.* Chittraranjan, India: Hilltop Publishers, 1980.

Karan, P. P. *Bhutan: A Physical and Cultural Geography.* Lexington, Ky.: University of Kentucky Press, 1967.

Matles, Andrea, ed. *Nepal and Bhutan: Country Studies.* Washington, D.C.: Federal Research Division, Library of Congress, 1993.

WEBSITES

Bhutan Tourism Corp., Ltd. [Online] Available http://www.kingdomofbhutan.com/1998.

World Travel Guide. Bhutan. [Online] Available http://www.wtgonline.com/country/bt/gen.html, 1998.

Bolivia

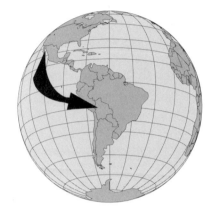

The people of Bolivia are called Bolivians. About 50 percent are Amerindian (native people). About 25 percent are white of European descent; and about 25 percent are *cholo* or *mestizo* (of mixed lineage). The Amerindian population is made up of Quechua and Aymara. For more information on the Quechua, consult the chapter on Peru in Volume 7.

Bolivians

PRONUNCIATION: bow-LIV-ee-yuhns
LOCATION: Bolivia
POPULATION: 7 million
LANGUAGE: Spanish; Quechua; Aymara
RELIGION: Roman Catholicism; Protestantism

1 ● INTRODUCTION

The highlands and jungles of Bolivia have been inhabited for thousands of years, long before the Spanish arrived in the fifteenth century. As a Spanish colony, Bolivia was part of the Viceroyalty of Peru. The city of La Paz was founded by Alonso de Mendoza in 1548. It is modern Bolivia's political capital. General Antonio José de Sucre gained Bolivian independence from Spain in 1825. He founded the República de Bolívar (Republic of Bolivia) in honor of Simon Bolívar, the fighter for South American independence. The new republic had a senate and a house of representatives.

Bolivia has been a mining country. First, it was famous for its silver mines in the city of Potosí. The mines provided great riches for Spain in the sixteenth and seventeenth centuries. Later Bolivia was one of the first providers of tin for the world market. Miserable conditions for miners led to the founding of a radical workers' party, the National Revolutionary Movement (MNR). It came to power under President Victor Paz Estenssoro in the 1950s. The government then took over the mines, and introduced agricultural, industrial, and social reforms.

Bolivia later suffered under a number of military dictators. Then it suffered by disastrous economic conditions under President Siles Zuazo, who was a leftist. Democratic elections have been held more recently. Today Bolivia is considered to be a working democracy.

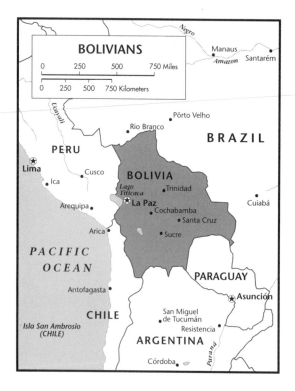

BOLIVIANS

0   250   500   750 Miles

0   250   500   750 Kilometers

part, the Andean *cordillera* (system of mountain ranges) extends from north to south. It has some of the highest peaks in South America. The center of the country consists of fertile valleys. The lowlands extend east toward the Amazon rain forest.

3 ● LANGUAGE

The official language of Bolivia is Spanish, although many Indians speak either Quechua (the language spoken originally by the Incas) or Aymara (a language spoken by Indians before the arrival of the Incas). Most Indians speak Spanish as well, although peasants in isolated parts of the country do not speak any Spanish.

2 ● LOCATION

Bolivia is a landlocked South American country of almost seven million people. More than 50 percent are Amerindians who speak mainly Quechua or Aymara as well as Spanish. The others are mainly descendants of Spaniards and mestizos (part Indian, part Spanish). There are a few other Indian groups, some in the rain forest of the Amazon River basin.

Bolivia shares a border to the north and east with Brazil, to the west with Peru, to the southwest with Chile, to the south with Argentina, and to the southeast with Paraguay.

Bolivia has a varied climate and terrain, or set of geographic features. In the western

4 ● FOLKLORE

A myth of the early Incas and other Indians was that a bearded white man had come to teach the Indians and would return. He was known as the Creator God, *Viracocha*. When the Spanish arrived, the Incas mistook the white Spanish conquerors for Viracocha. This belief was widespread. In Mexico, the Aztecs called this figure Quetzalcoatl. It is thought that this myth contributed to the ease with which the Spaniards entered the major Indian cities.

5 ● RELIGION

Most Bolivians are Roman Catholic. However, among the Indian groups, certain beliefs and rituals remain from the time before Christopher Columbus. Their respect for nature is embodied in the belief in Mother Earth, known as *Pachamama*.

Cory Langley

Many people do not have a car and use buses for local and long-distance travel. Practically all towns are connected by bus routes. In the major cities, such as La Paz, pictured here, Bolivians live a more modern lifestyle.

6 ● MAJOR HOLIDAYS

Bolivians celebrate the main Catholic holidays such as Easter, Christmas, and Corpus Christi. They also celebrate Labor Day, and their Independence Day is August 6.

A major festival celebrated in March is *Pookhyái,* which is held in the Andean town of Tarabuco. There the famous heroine Juana Azurduy led her people against the Spanish in the Battle of Jambati on March 12, 1816, and liberated the town. *Pookhyái* is a Quechua word meaning "entertainment." During the festival, dozens of groups in local costume dance and sing. The whole town, together with thousands of visitors,

takes part in a special Quechua mass and procession. It is a joyful celebration in which Bolivians give thanks for their freedom as a nation.

Carnival is celebrated throughout Bolivia the week before Lent. The *Diablada,* one of the most typical dances, has elaborate costumes and masks of the devil. It is arranged to represent a battle between good and evil. The dancers celebrate the victory of good, represented by the Archangel Michael, over evil, represented by Lucifer and his devils. Other groups reenact the Conquest, in which Spanish conquerors such as Francisco Pizarro fight with the

Cory Langley

Education is officially available to all children of Bolivia, but not all school-aged children are able to attend. Schools may be too far away or the child is needed to help at home. The most pressing social problem in Bolivia is poverty.

Incas. The feasting and dancing last several days.

7 ● RITES OF PASSAGE

Most children in Bolivia receive the Catholic sacrament of baptism at birth. They receive First Communion at the age of seven and confirmation at the beginning of adolescence. These ceremonies are regarded as important events.

During the teenage years, Bolivian boys and girls are expected to maintain close ties with their families. Many Bolivians marry in church, but they have to have a civil marriage as well. When a person dies, he or she receives a Catholic funeral. A dying person sometimes makes a final confession to a priest.

In many Indian communities, Catholic and Indian beliefs exist together.

8 ● RELATIONSHIPS

A formal greeting will include the words *"Mucho gusto,"* equivalent to the English "Pleased to meet you." There is also an informal greeting, *"Qué tal?"* which means, "How are you?" But Bolivians do not stop there. It is also considered polite to ask about other family members, and the greetings can become quite extensive.

Men shake hands, but in the cities men and women greet each other with a kiss. When people visit, they are served a small cup of black coffee.

In some small cities, Bolivians are very traditional about dating. Families keep a close watch on their daughters' friends and social contacts. In many places, girls are not supposed to date boys who do not know their parents. Parents will first find out about the boy's family if they do not already know his family. Many people marry when they are still quite young.

9 ● LIVING CONDITIONS

Bolivia is one of the poorest countries of the Americas. Many Bolivians, particularly in rural areas, live completely outside the cash economy. They have a very simple lifestyle. In the major cities, such as La Paz, Bolivians live a more modern lifestyle.

Many people do not have a car and use buses and trucks for local and long-distance travel. Practically all towns are connected by extensive bus routes. Pack animals are used in the more remote highland areas.

10 ● FAMILY LIFE

In one sense, women have a lower status than men in Bolivia, but in another sense they are seen as very important. They are at the center of family life in their role as mother, wife, and member of the extended family. In the lower social and economic classes, women provide the economic support of the family. Since colonial times, Indian women have been part of the business and trade activities of Bolivia.

Although this is changing, Bolivian families have traditionally been quite large. Having six or seven children is not uncommon. A family is not only a father, a mother, and their children, but includes other relatives such as grandparents, aunts, uncles, and cousins. This traditional extended family is the main social-support system in Bolivia.

11 ● CLOTHING

In the cities, men wear trousers and shirts, or suits. Women wear skirts and blouses, or dresses. Men in the countryside often wear ponchos, which developed from the Spanish cape.

12 ● FOOD

The foundation of the Bolivian diet in the Andean highlands or *altiplano* is the potato. Main meals in the major towns include some meat, but there is also rice. Often both rice and potatoes are served, as well as salad or vegetables. Bolivian food tends to be plain and filling.

A typical Bolivian snack is the *salteña,* a spicy version of the *empanada,* a type of turnover popular all over South America. The salteña is spicy, and is filled with a mixture of chopped chicken or meat, potatoes, raisins, olives, onions, hard-boiled eggs, and spices. Both salteñas and empanadas are shaped like half moons and are fried or sometimes baked.

In La Paz, pieces of beef heart grilled on skewers are popular. They are known as *anticuchos.* A hot, peppery sauce called *llajua* is often served with meats.

Recipe

Salteñas

Ingredients

For pastry

3-ounce package of cream cheese
½ cup butter
Dash of Tabasco sauce
Pinch of salt
2 Tablespoons toasted sesame seeds
¼ cup Parmesan cheese
1 cup flour

For the filling

1/3 pound ground beef
½ onion, finely chopped
2 cloves garlic, finely chopped
1 can chopped green chilies, or 3 serrano
  chiles, seeded and finely chopped
1 Tablespoon ground cumin
½ cup canned chopped tomatoes, drained
2 Tablespoons chopped fresh parsley, or 2
  teaspoons dried parsley
2 Tablespoons chopped fresh cilantro, or 2
  teaspoons dried cilantro
½ cup raisin
2 hard-boiled eggs, sliced crosswise
10 to 12 green olives, stuffed with pimien-
  tos, cut in half crosswise

Directions

Make the pastry

1. Combine cream cheese, butter, Tabasco
   sauce, salt, and sesame seeds. (Use a
   food processor or mix with a wooden
   spoon.)
2. Add the Parmesan cheese and flour, and
   combine well. Wrap dough with plastic
   wrap and chill for at least 30 minutes or
   up to three days.
3. Roll dough out to a uniform thickness of
   about ¼ inch. Cut into 3-inch circles.

Make filling

1. Brown meat in a frying pan, breaking up
   lumps.
2. Add onion, garlic, chilies, cumin, and
   salt and pepper to taste, and continue
   cooking until onion is softened.
3. Add parsley, cilantro, tomatoes, and raisins, and continue cooking until all liquid evaporates.

Assemble salteñas

1. Place a slice of olive and hard-boiled
   egg in the center of each round of
   dough. Top with a spoonful of filling.
2. Fold dough circle in half to form a half-
   moon, and seal edges. Optional: press a
   pattern into the edge of the half-moon
   with a fork.
3. Bake at 375°F for 25 minutes, or until
   browned.

13 ● EDUCATION

Primary education is officially available to all Bolivian children. However, it did not really come to the villages until the 1950s. Since then, high school education has been more attainable. Most Bolivian cities, including La Paz, Cochabamba, and Sucre, have universities, some of which have existed for hundreds of years. The largest universities are funded by the government and are practically free to students who qualify. There are also many private universities.

14 ● CULTURAL HERITAGE

Bolivia has many fine churches that date from colonial times. One of the painters who was an expert at portraying religious subjects is Holguín. His paintings of the birth of Christ and the birth of the Virgin Mary are in the Church of Merced in the city of Sucre. The church was built in 1581.

One of the best known Bolivian writers is Alcides Arguedas (1879–1946). He was also a sociologist and a diplomat (representing Bolivia to the governments of other countries). He even served for a time as Bolivia's minister for agriculture. He wrote about major aspects of Bolivian Indian life. His novels include *Raza de Bronce* (The Bronze Race), *Vida Criolla* (Creole Life), *Pisagua,* and *Wata-wara.*

Another important modern writer is Augusto Céspedes. In a novel called *El Metal del Diablo* (The Devil's Metal) he examined the lives of the very wealthy men who controlled the tin business.

15 ● EMPLOYMENT

In rural areas, many Bolivians work as farmers on small plots of land. Mining has a long history in Bolivia, from the colonial silver mines of the Potosí to the tin mines of today. When the international tin market collapsed in 1985, thousands of tin miners were lost their jobs. So as not to starve to death, many miners moved to the lowlands. They began growing coca leaves for the illegal cocaine industry.

In the towns, people work as street vendors, in the construction industry, as maids and housekeepers, or as plumbers, electricians, or carpenters. There is also a middle class of professionals. In addition to doctors and lawyers, there are more and more engineers and technicians of various types.

16 ● SPORTS

All kinds of modern sports are played by Bolivian young people. There are interschool athletic competitions. There are also professional basketball, volleyball, and soccer teams. Probably the most popular sport is soccer, and major towns have stadiums filled with enthusiastic crowds during matches. One of the best-known stadiums is the Hernando Siles in the city of La Paz.

17 ● RECREATION

As in many other Latin American countries, there are many movie theaters in Bolivia and people enjoy going to the movies. Most of the main cities also have theaters where plays are performed.

In the town of Santa Cruz, there are modern discos, which are very popular

Anne Kalosh

In rural areas, many Bolivians work as farmers on small plots of land.

among the young people. There are also discos in La Paz, Cochabamba, and Sucre.

One of the most enjoyable events in Bolivia is *Carnival*, the period preceding Lent. It is celebrated everywhere, but with interesting variations according to local costumes, dancing, and music.

18 ● CRAFTS AND HOBBIES

One of Bolivia's major crafts is weaving. Most young girls in rural areas learn to weave and spin. Patterns and colors vary according to the region. Patterns use geometric shapes or depict animals. Occasionally they show aspects of daily home life. Alpaca and llama wool have been used tra-ditionally, but sheep's wool is also used today.

Many interesting musical instruments are made in Bolivia, including the *charango*, a type of guitar, as well as native violins and a wide variety of woodwind instruments.

19 ● SOCIAL PROBLEMS

The most pressing social problem in Bolivia is poverty. Despite many efforts to stamp out the production of coca (from which cocaine is made), hundreds of thousands of people are employed in growing and distributing it. Many peasant farmers, who are often desperately poor, have attempted to grow other types of crops. The crop-substitution programs begun by the Bolivian government offer crops to replace the coca, such as coffee and bananas. Unfortunately, these crops cannot produce anything like the income that coca farming provides.

20 ● BIBLIOGRAPHY

Blair, David Nelson. *The Land and People of Bolivia.* New York: J.B. Lippincott, 1990.
Bolivia in Pictures. Minneapolis: The Company, 1987.
Crowther, Geoff. *South America on a Shoestring.* Hawthorn, Australia: Lonely Planet Publications, 1994.
Jacobsen, Karen. *Bolivia.* Chicago: Childrens Press, 1991.
Pateman, Robert. *Bolivia.* New York: Marshall Cavendish, 1995.
Schimmel, Karen. *Bolivia.* New York: Chelsea House, 1990.

WEBSITES
Bolivia Web. [Online] Available http://www.boliviaweb.com/, 1998.
World Travel Guide. Bolivia. [Online] Available http://www.wtgonline.com/country/bo/gen.html, 1998.

Aymara

PRONUNCIATION: eye-MAHR-ah
LOCATION: Bolivia; Peru; Chile
POPULATION: About 2 million (Bolivia); 500,000 (Peru); 20,000 (Chile)
LANGUAGE: Aymara; Spanish
RELIGION: Roman Catholicism combined with indigenous beliefs; Seventh Day Adventist

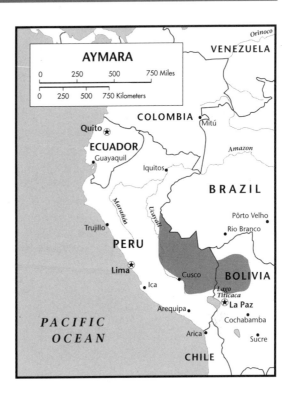

1 ● INTRODUCTION

The Aymara are the indigenous (native) people who live in the *altiplano* (high plains) of the Andes Mountains of Bolivia. Bolivia has the highest proportion of indigenous peoples of any country in South America. It is also the poorest country on the continent.

Bolivia was colonized by Spain. The Aymara faced great hardships under Spanish colonial rule. In 1570, the Spanish decreed that the natives would be forced to work in the rich silver mines on the altiplano. The city of Potosí was once the site of the richest silver mine in the world. Millions of Aymara laborers perished in the wretched conditions in the mines.

2 ● LOCATION

The Aymara live on high-altitude plains in the Bolivian Andes, on the Lake Titicaca plateau near the border with Peru. The altiplano is at an elevation of 10,000 to 12,000 feet (3,000 to 3,700 meters) above sea level. Weather conditions are cold and harsh, and agriculture is difficult.

An ethnic group closely related to the Aymara lives among the Uru islands on Lake Titicaca. These communities live not on land but on islands that are made of floating reeds.

An estimated two million Aymara live in Bolivia, with five hundred thousand residing in Peru, and about twenty thousand in Chile. The Aymara are not confined to a defined territory (or reservation) in the Andes. Many live in the cities and participate fully in Western culture.

3 ● LANGUAGE

The Aymara language, originally called *jaqi aru* (the language of the people), is still the major language in the Bolivian Andes and in southeastern Peru. In the rural areas, one finds that the Aymara language is predominant. In the cities and towns the Aymara are bilingual, speaking both Spanish and

Cory Langley

The Aymara live in the altiplano *(high plains) of the Andes Mountains of Bolivia. Bolivia has the highest proportion of indigenous peoples of any country in South America.*

Aymara. Some are even trilingual—in Spanish, Aymara, and Quechua—in regions where the Incas predominate.

4 ● FOLKLORE

Aymara mythology has many legends about the origin of things, such as the wind, hail, mountains, and lakes. The Aymara share with other ethnic groups some of the Andean myths of origin. In one of them, the god Tunupa is a creator of the universe. He is also the one that taught the people customs: farming, songs, weaving, the language each group had to speak, and the rules for a moral life.

5 ● RELIGION

The Aymara believe in the power of spirits that live in mountains, in the sky, or in natural forces such as lightning. The strongest and most sacred of their deities is Pachamama, the Earth Goddess. She has the power to make the soil fertile and ensure a good crop.

Catholicism was introduced during the colonial period and was adopted by the Aymara, who attend Mass, celebrate baptisms, and follow the Catholic calendar of Christian events. But the content of their many religious festivals shows evidence of their traditional beliefs. For example, the

Aymara make offerings to Mother Earth, in order to assure a good harvest or cure illnesses.

6 ● MAJOR HOLIDAYS

The Aymara celebrate the same holidays as other Bolivians: the civic holidays such as Independence Day and the religious ones such as Christmas and Easter. Another important holiday is *Día del Indio,* on August 2, which commemorates their cultural heritage.

The Aymara also celebrate *Carnival.* Carnival is a festival held just before Lent begins. It is widely celebrated throughout South America. Dancing to drums and flutes accompanies a week-long celebration. Also important is the festival *Alacistas,* which features the God of Good Luck. Most households have a ceramic figure of the Good Luck spirit, known as *Ekeko.* This spirit is believed to bring prosperity and grant wishes. The doll is a round, plump figure, carrying miniature replicas of household goods such as cooking utensils and bags of food and money.

7 ● RITES OF PASSAGE

An Aymara child is introduced gradually to the social and cultural traditions of the community. A significant event in the life of an Aymara child is the first haircut, known as *rutucha.* A baby's hair is allowed to grow until the child is able to walk and talk. At about two years of age, when it is unlikely that he or she will be stricken with the many childhood diseases in the Andes, the child's head is shaved bare.

8 ● RELATIONSHIPS

An important feature of the Aymara culture is the social obligation to help other members of the community. The exchange of work and mutual aid play a basic role within an *ayllu* or community. Such exchanges occur when more work is required than a single family can provide. An Aymara peasant might ask a neighbor for help building a house, digging an irrigation ditch, or harvesting a field. In return, he or she is expected to pay back the favor by donating the same number of days' labor to the neighbor.

9 ● LIVING CONDITIONS

Living conditions of the Aymara depend mainly on where they live and how much they have adopted the Western way of life. Many Aymaras reside in cities and live in modern houses or apartments. There are also large numbers of poor Aymaras in the cities who live in just one room. In rural areas, the construction of an Aymara house depends upon its location and the availability of materials. A typical Aymara house is a small oblong building made of adobe. Near the lake reeds are the primary building material. Thatched roofs are made of reeds and grasses.

The high altitude makes life in the altiplano very difficult. The decreased oxygen in the air can leave a person with *soroche* (altitude sickness), which causes headaches, fatigue, and nausea—and, sometimes, death. In order to adapt to life in the mountains, the Aymara have developed physical traits that enable them to survive. Most importantly, the Aymara and other

Cory Langley

Aymara women wear long skirts of homespun material, embroidered shawls, and bowler hats.

mountain peoples have a greatly increased lung capacity.

10 ● FAMILY LIFE

The central social unit of the Aymara is the extended family. Typically, a family will include parents, unmarried children, and grandparents in one house, or in a small cluster of houses. Large families with as many as seven or eight children are common.

There is a sharp division of labor within an Aymara household, but women's work is not necessarily seen as less valuable. Plant-ing, in particular, is a women's job that is highly respected.

Women in Aymara society also have inheritance rights. Property owned by women will be passed down from mother to daughter. This ensures that not all land and property goes to the sons.

Marriage is a long process with many steps, such as inheritance feasts, a planting ceremony, and the building of the house. Divorce is accepted and is relatively simple.

11 ● CLOTHING

Clothing styles vary greatly among the Aymara. Men in the cities wear regular

Western clothes, and women wear their traditional *polleras* (skirts) made of fine materials, such as velvet and brocade. They wear embroidered shawls and bowler hats (some of which are made in Italy).

In the altiplano, the story is different. The strong cold winds require warm woolen clothing. Women wear long, homespun skirts and sweaters. The skirts are worn in layers. For festivals or important occasions, women wear as many as five or six skirts on top of each other. Traditional weaving techniques date back to pre-Inca times. Brightly colored shawls are used to strap babies to their mothers' backs or to carry loads of goods.

Aymara men in the altiplano wear long cotton trousers and woolen caps with ear flaps. In many regions, men also wear ponchos. Both sexes may wear sandals or shoes, but many go barefoot despite the cold.

12 ● FOOD

In cities, the Aymara diet is varied, but it has one distinctive ingredient: *aji,* a hot pepper is used to season the dishes. In the countryside, potatoes and grains, such as quinoa, form the staple diet. Quinoa, which has become popular in U.S. health food stores, is a nutritious, high-protein grain. It has been grown in the Andes for centuries.

The extremes of temperature in the high Andes make it possible to freeze-dry and preserve potatoes naturally. The cold air at night freezes the moisture from the potato, while the sun during the day melts and evaporates it. After a week of lying outdoors, the potatoes are pounded. The result

is *chuño*—small, rock-hard pieces of potato that can be stored for years.

Meats are also freeze-dried. A traditional dish is *olluco con charqui—olluco* is a small, potato-like tuber, which is cooked with *charqui,* dried llama meat. But since llamas are important for their wool and as packing animals, they are rarely eaten. Fish from Lake Titicaca or neighboring rivers is also an important part of the diet.

13 ● EDUCATION

In Bolivia, primary school education is required until the age of fourteen. However, as in most developing countries, children of subsistence farmers are less likely to complete school. Children often have the responsibility of tending a herd or taking care of younger brothers and sisters. Boys are more likely to complete school than girls, who have more household tasks, even at a very young age.

14 ● CULTURAL HERITAGE

The Aymara have a rich musical tradition. Although there is a clear Spanish influence, the main musical influences date back to the pre-Inca ancestors. Drums and flutes are featured at festivals and celebrations. Panpipes *(zampoñas)* and the *pututu* horn, made out of a hollowed-out cow's horn, are traditional instruments that are still played. Homemade violins and drums are also common.

Traditional dances have been passed down through generations. Many dances feature large, bright masks and costumes. Some dances represent and parody the Spanish colonizers. The "old man dance," for example, features a bent-over Spanish

Cory Langley

The Aymara celebrate the same civic and religious holidays as other Bolivians.

tion. The most important crop is the potato, which first grew in the Andes. Corn, quinoa, and barley are also important. Many families own land at different altitudes. This enables them to grow several different crops.

Tractors and even oxen teams are rare in the high Andes. Traditional agricultural implements, such as the foot plow, are still widely used. While the men do the plowing and digging, the sacred task of planting is reserved for women, since only they have the power to give life. This tradition is maintained in deference to *Pachamama,* the Earth Goddess.

The Aymara are also herders. They get both wool and meat from herds of llamas, alpacas, and sheep. A family may also supplement its grazing herd with cows, frogs, or chickens.

The growing tourist trade has increased the demand for the luxurious wool of the alpaca, and some people knit sweaters for the tourists. This has provided the Aymara with some badly needed cash.

Some Aymara also work as laborers in silver or tin mines. This work can be very dangerous.

Many Aymara have entered politics. They have founded a political party, *Katarista,* and they have elected Aymara senators and representatives to the Bolivian congress.

nobleman with a large top hat. The dancer imitates in a comic manner the gestures and mannerisms of old Spanish gentlemen.

15 ● EMPLOYMENT

Many Aymara are subsistence farmers in the harsh, high-altitude environment. The altitude, cold nights, and poor soil greatly limit the types of crops that can be grown. The Aymara follow traditional patterns of agriculture. Some still use the terraced fields used by their ancestors before Christopher Columbus arrived in the New World. They also follow a careful pattern of crop rota-

16 ● SPORTS

There are no sports that are strictly Aymara. However, soccer is the Bolivian national sport and many Aymara participate in it.

Cory Langley

The Aymara use a great many materials in their weaving, including cotton, as well as wool from sheep, alpacas, and llamas.

17 ● RECREATION

The Aymara now enjoy their own TV shows, both as viewers and as performers. Some Aymara musical groups have made recordings that are very popular. In the cities, Aymara are frequent moviegoers.

One of the favorite activities is dancing in folk festivals. Young people use these occasions to socialize.

18 ● CRAFTS AND HOBBIES

The Aymara are skilled weavers, a tradition dating back to the time before the Incas.

Many anthropologists believe that the textiles of the Andes are among the most highly developed and complex in the world. The Aymara use a great many materials in their weaving, including cotton, as well as wool from sheep, alpacas, and llamas. The Aymara also use *totora* reeds to make fishing boats, baskets, and other articles.

19 ● SOCIAL PROBLEMS

The most significant social problems faced by the Aymara stem from colonial times. European colonizers and their descendants have treated the Aymara as insignificant, taking their land and resources and giving nothing in return. The decreased standard of living among the Aymara and the anger between groups have weakened the social structure of the region.

Only in the second half of the twentieth century has Bolivian society been open to accepting the Aymara heritage. In 1952 (almost five hundred years after Europeans arrived), the Aymara and other indigenous people were given some civil rights that every other Bolivian had had.

With access to education, the Aymara have begun participating more fully in the modern life of the country. There are still serious class and racial barriers, however, and unfortunately, many Aymara still remain in poverty in rural areas. Large numbers move to the cities, where life becomes even harder for them in many ways.

20 ● BIBLIOGRAPHY

Blair, David Nelson. *The Land and People of Bolivia.* New York: J.B. Lippincott, 1990.
Cobb, Vicki. *This Place Is High.* New York: Walker, 1989.

La Barre, Weston. *The Aymara Indians of the Lake Titicaca Plateau, Bolivia.* Memasha, Wisc.: American Anthropological Association, 1948.

Moss, Joyce, and George Wilson. *Peoples of the World: Latin Americas.* Detroit: Gale Research, 1989.

WEBSITES

Bolivia Web. [Online] Available http://www.boliviaweb.com/, 1998.

World Travel Guide. Bolivia. [Online] Available http://www.wtgonline.com/country/bo/gen.html, 1998.

Bosnia and Herzegovina

■ BOSNIANS 201

The people who live in Bosnia and Herzegovina are commonly referred to as Bosnians. About half are Muslim, one-third are Serbs, and almost 20 percent are Croats. Just over 5 percent of the population describe themselves as Yugoslavs.

Bosnians

PRONUNCIATION: BOZ-nee-uhns
LOCATION: Bosnia and Herzegovina
POPULATION: 4.5 million (1992)
LANGUAGE: Serbo-Croatian (Bosnian)
RELIGION: Muslim; Eastern Orthodox; Roman Catholicism; Islam

1 ● INTRODUCTION

"Bosnian" refers to someone who lives in Bosnia and Herzegovina. (This country is usually referred to just as "Bosnia.") In the early 1990s, Yugoslavia broke apart into Croatia, Bosnia and Herzegovina, Slovenia, and Serbia and Montenegro. Serbia and Montenegro reclaimed the name, Yugoslavia, in 1997.

Ancestors of the Bosnians, Slavic people of central Europe, first settled in the region that is modern Bosnia in the fifth century. The twelfth century brought domination by Hungary and Austria. These two countries later joined forces as the Hapsburg Empire. From 1328 to 1878, the region was occupied by the Turks of the Ottoman empire. During this time, many people converted to Islam, the religion of the Ottoman rulers. The Austro-Hungarian empire once again took over the region in 1878.

In June 1914, Archduke Franz Ferdinand, heir to the throne of the Austro-Hungarian Empire, was assassinated by a Bosnian Serb nationalist named Gavrilo Princip (1894–1918) in Sarajevo. This caused Germany and the Austro-Hungarians to declare war on Serbia and its allies (including Bosnia). Soon the world was involved in the worst war it had ever seen, now known as World War I (1914–18). When the war ended in December 1918, Bosnia became part of the newly created Kingdom of the Serbs, Croats, and Slovenes. In 1929, the kingdom was renamed Yugoslavia. During World War II (1939–

BOSNIANS

0   100   200   300 Miles

0   100   200   300 Kilometers

lim leader Alija Izetbegovic (1926–) was elected president in 1996.

2 ●LOCATION

Bosnia is located in the west-central region of the former Yugoslavia on the Balkan peninsula. The Balkan peninsula lies east of Italy and west of Turkey and the Black Sea. Mountain ranges cover much of the peninsula. Northern Bosnia consists of low-lying plains, changing to rolling hills and mountains to the south. Central Bosnia, where Sarajevo is located, is a mountainous region.

Before war began in 1992, Bosnia's population was 4.5 million, approximately 44 percent Muslim, 31 percent Serbian, and 17 percent Croatian, with smaller numbers from other ethnic groups.

3 ●LANGUAGE

The language of Bosnia is known as Serbo-Croatian. Serbo-Croatian belongs to the Slavic branch of the Indo-European language family.

The Croats and Muslims use the Roman alphabet to write Serbo-Croatian, while the Serbs use the Cyrillic alphabet. For example, the word "hello" is *zdravo* in the Roman alphabet and здраво in the Cyrillic alphabet. "Please" is *molim,* "thank you" is *hvala* (FAH-lah), "Yes" and "No" are *Da* (or *Jeste*) and *Ne.* The numbers one to ten in Serbo-Croatian are: *jedan (jedna, jedno), dva* (or *dvije* for feminine nouns), *tri, četiri, pet, šest, sedam, osam, devet,* and *deset.*

45), a leader named Josip Broz (1892–1980), known as Marshal Tito, emerged. When the war ended, Tito took full command of the country and created a communist state.

Slovenia and Croatia seceded from Yugoslavia in 1991. The Republic of Bosnia and Herzegovina declared its independence in 1992, with its capital at Sarajevo. Slovenia and Serbia and Montenegro were the other two countries created from the former Yugoslavia. War between Serbia and Bosnia began in 1992, and conflicts with Croatia followed. Fierce fighting continued until the end of 1995, when a peace agreement was signed in Paris, following U.S.-sponsored peace talks in Dayton, Ohio. Bosnian Mus-

4 ● FOLKLORE

Given the ethnic diversity in Bosnia and Herzegovina, there is no particular folklore that can be said to be Bosnian.

5 ● RELIGION

About 44 percent of Bosnians are Muslim. Some Islamic practices in Bosnia differ sharply from those in other Muslim countries. For many Bosnians, religion is something observed only on major religious holidays.

Serbs are mostly Eastern Orthodox, and Croatians are mostly Roman Catholic.

6 ● MAJOR HOLIDAYS

Bosnians celebrate a number of religious, secular, and family holidays. These include the state New Year holiday (January 1 and 2), both Eastern Orthodox and Catholic Christmases, Marshal Tito's birthday, and the Day of the Republic. Eastern Orthodox Christian families also celebrate the *slava,* or special day of their patron saint.

Muslim festivities center on Ramadan, the month of ritual fasting. During the three days at the end of Ramadan, called *Bajram* (known as *Eid al-Fitr* elsewhere), people visit and exchange gifts. During this period, the minarets (towers) of all the mosques are illuminated with strings of electric lights.

7 ● RITES OF PASSAGE

Major life transitions are marked by ceremonies appropriate to each Bosnian's religious tradition. Weddings are a major occasion for celebration.

8 ● RELATIONSHIPS

The warfare of the 1990s severely disrupted the social fabric of Bosnian society, pitting neighbor against neighbor in an atmosphere of violence, distrust, and fear. It is difficult, therefore, to characterize typical interpersonal relations in Bosnia at present.

People try to be polite to one another, and to avoid topics in conversation that might trigger conflict or even violence. Many people living in Bosnia try to use humor in interpersonal relationship to ease tension.

9 ● LIVING CONDITIONS

Before the war in the 1990s, about three-fourths of village homes had electricity, and nearly all had running water. After the war began in 1992, many villages were destroyed and people were forced to leave.

Cities were also hard hit. In Sarajevo, many people had no electricity or running water, and little food. Before the war, life in the big cities was quite modernized. People lived in apartments with televisions and modern appliances. By the time the war ended, many apartments had been reduced to rubble. Nearly three-fourths of the population (over three million people) lost their homes.

10 ● FAMILY LIFE

Emphasis is on the nuclear family. However there is still some evidence of the Slavic extended family social pattern, called *zadruga.* Women commonly hold both an office or factory job and the job of managing the household. Men rarely do any housework. In the 1990s, family size has been decreasing.

11 ● CLOTHING

Most urban Bosnians dress in Western-style clothing. Blue jeans are extremely popular. In large cities like Sarajevo, older men can occasionally be seen in the traditional Muslim costume of breeches, cummerbund, striped shirt, vest, and fez. Formerly, the traditional baggy Muslim trousers (*dimija*) were worn by women of various Bosnian ethnic groups. Today, they are rarely seen in the cities but are still common in rural districts.

Even the most devout Muslim women in Bosnia do not wear the traditional *chador* (or *chadri*) worn by women in Arab countries. This one-piece cloth sack is worn over the head and reaches to the ground. It has a mesh insert over the eyes and nose area.

12 ● FOOD

The cuisine of Bosnia shows influences from Central Europe, the Balkans, and the Middle East. Meat dishes are based on mixtures of lamb, pork, and beef. These are commonly eaten as sausages (called *c'evapčic'i*) or hamburger-like patties (called *pleskavica*). They are grilled along with onions and served hot on fresh *somun* (a thick pita bread). Bosnian hotpot stew (*Bosnanki lonac),* a slow-roasted mixture of layers of meat and vegetables, is the most typical regional specialty. Turkish dishes, such as *kebabs* (marinated pieces of meat cooked on a skewer), *burek* (meat- or vegetable-filled pastry), and *baklava* (a sweet, layered dessert pastry) are common. Homemade plum brandy, called *rakija,* is a popu-

EPD Photos
Sweet pastries like baklava are popular treats in Bosnia. Also enjoyed by people living around the Mediterranean Sea, baklava is available in bakeries around the world.

lar drink. Turkish coffee and a thin yogurt drink are also popular.

13 ● EDUCATION

In the former Yugoslavian state system, education through the eighth grade was free and compulsory. Then a student could choose either a vocational school or the more academically oriented *gymnasium* for secondary education. Post-secondary education was available at a number of universities in the larger cities.

14 ● CULTURAL HERITAGE

The arts are highly developed in Bosnia and Herzegovina. With three major ethnicities to draw on (Serbian, Croatian, and Muslim), a great wealth of song, dance, literature, and poetry is available.

In cities, many variations on the *sevdalinka* (love song) may be heard in cafes and on street corners. Sevdalinka are often melancholy, relating tragic stories of lovers who must be separated.

Rural folksongs include the *ravne pesme,* literally, a flat song with a single, simple melody; the *ganga,* an almost-shouted song; and other types of songs. They may be accompanied on the *šargija* (a simple, long-necked lute), wooden flute, or the *diple* (a droneless bagpipe). Urban folksongs show a much heavier Turkish influence. They feature chant-like singing accompanied on the *saz,* a larger and more elaborate version of the šargija.

Bosnian folk dances include the silent *kolo* (accompanied only by the sound of stomping feet and the clash of silver coins on the women's aprons). Men and women dance separately in Bosnian line dances.

15 ● EMPLOYMENT

Before the 1992–95 war, about 40 percent of Bosnians worked in industry. Major industries were textiles, food-processing, coal and iron mining, and steel manufacturing. As of the late 1990s, these industries had not made a full recovery, since many factories, power plants, and other buildings were destroyed during the fighting. Bosnia's rural population engages in agriculture and related industries. Many city dwellers have service-related or professional jobs.

16 ● SPORTS

Soccer is the favorite sport of Bosnians. Official matches draw spectators from all over the country, and informal games spring up in parks, on playgrounds, and in the streets. Makeshift goals are created from old netting, clothes, rags, and even plastic bags. Outdoor sports such as hiking, skiing, swimming, and fishing are also very popular in Bosnia. The 1984 Winter Olympics were held in Sarajevo, a city that was then in Yugoslavia.

17 ● RECREATION

Bosnians enjoy watching television, listening to pop music, going to movies, and other typical modern forms of recreation. A traditional form of recreation is *korzo*—taking a walk in the evening and stopping to chat with friends or to have a cup of coffee in the *kafana,* or coffeehouse.

18 ● CRAFTS AND HOBBIES

The main folk art in Bosnia is carpet-weaving. The cities of Mostar and Sarajevo are famous for their *kilims* (handwoven carpets). They are made from brightly colored wools in a variety of complicated designs.

19 ● SOCIAL PROBLEMS

The worst social problem for Bosnians is the effects of the war that raged in their country from 1992 through 1995. Over 60 percent of the homes in Sarajevo, the capital, were destroyed, as well as many historic buildings. The environment suffered heavy damage from bombing and fires.

20 ● BIBLIOGRAPHY

Clark, Arthur L. *Bosnia: What Every American Should Know.* New York: Berkley Books, 1996.

Filipovic, Zlata. *Zlata's Diary.* London: Viking, 1994.

Fireside, Harvey, and Bryna J. Fireside. *Young People from Bosnia Talk About War.* Springfield, N.J.: Enslow Publishers, 1996.

Flint, David. *Bosnia: Can There Ever Be Peace?* Austin, Tex.: Raintree Steck-Vaughn, 1995.

Ganeri, Anita. *I Remember Bosnia.* Austin, Tex.: Raintree Steck-Vaughn, 1994.

Reger, James P. *The Rebuilding of Bosnia.* San Diego, Calif.: Lucent Books, 1997.

Tekavec, Valerie. *Teenage Refugees from Bosnia-Herzegovina Speak Out.* New York: Rosen Publishing Group, 1994.

Yancey, Diane. *Life in War-Torn Bosnia.* San Diego, Calif.: Lucent Books, 1996.

WEBSITES

Embassy of Bosnia, Washington, D.C. [Online] Available http://www.bosnianembassy.org/, 1998.

George Mason University, Geography Department. Bosnian Virtual Fieldtrip. [Online] Available http://geog.gmu.edu/projects/bosnia/default.htm, 1998.

Irfanoglu, Ayhan, and Ahmet Kirag. Bosnia Homepage. [Online] Available http://www.cco.caltech.edu/~bosnia, 1997.

NTG Sarajevo. Saray.net (Sarajevo). [Online] Available http://www.saray.net, 1998.

World Travel Guide, Bosnia. [Online] Available http://www.wtgonline.com/country/ba/gen.html, 1998.

Glossary

aboriginal: The first known inhabitants of a country.

adobe: A brick made from sun-dried heavy clay mixed with straw, used in building houses.

Altaic language family: A family of languages spoken in portions of northern and eastern Europe, and nearly the whole of northern and central Asia, together with some other regions.

Amerindian: A contraction of the two words, American Indian. It describes native peoples of North, South, or Central America.

Anglican: Pertaining to or connected with the Church of England.

animism: The belief that natural objects and phenomena have souls or innate spiritual powers.

apartheid: The past governmental policy in the Republic of South Africa of separating the races in society.

arable land: Land that can be cultivated by plowing and used for growing crops.

archipelago: Any body of water abounding with islands, or the islands themselves collectively.

Austronesian language: A family of languages which includes practically all the languages of the Pacific Islands—Indonesian, Melanesian, Polynesian, and Micronesian sub-families.

average life expectancy: In any given society, the average age attained by persons at the time of death.

Baha'i: The follower of a religious sect founded by Mirza Husayn Ali in Iran in 1863.

Baltic states: The three formerly communist countries of Estonia, Latvia, and Lithuania that border on the Baltic Sea.

Bantu language group: A name applied to the languages spoken in central and south Africa.

Baptist: A member of a Protestant denomination that practices adult baptism by complete immersion in water.

barren land: Unproductive land, partly or entirely treeless.

barter: Trade practice where merchandise is exchanged directly for other merchandise or services without use of money.

Berber: a member of one of the Afroasiatic peoples of northern Africa.

Brahman: A member (by heredity) of the highest caste among the Hindus, usually assigned to the priesthood.

bride wealth (bride price): Fee, in money or goods, paid by a prospective groom (and his family) to the bride's family.

Buddhism: A religious system common in India and eastern Asia. Founded by Siddhartha Gautama (c.563–c.483 BC), Buddhism asserts that suffering is an inescapable part of life. Deliverance can only be achieved through the practice of charity, temperance, justice, honesty, and truth.

Byzantine Empire: An empire centered in the city of Byzantium, now Istanbul in present-day Turkey.

cassava: The name of several species of stout herbs, extensively cultivated for food.

caste system: Heriditary social classes into which the Hindus are rigidly separated according to the religious law of Brahmanism. Privileges and limitations of each caste are passed down from parents to children.

Caucasian: The white race of human beings, as determined by genealogy and physical features.

census: An official counting of the inhabitants of a state or country with details of sex and age, family, occupation, possessions, etc.

Christianity: The religion founded by Jesus Christ, based on the Bible as holy scripture.

Church of England: The national and established church in England.

civil rights: The privileges of all individuals to be treated as equals under the laws of their country; specifically, the rights given by certain amendments to the U.S. Constitution.

coastal plain: A fairly level area of land along the coast of a land mass.

coca: A shrub native to South America, the leaves of which produce organic compounds that are used in the production of cocaine.

colonial period: The period of time when a country forms colonies in and extends control over a foreign area.

colonist: Any member of a colony or one who helps settle a new colony.

colony: A group of people who settle in a new area far from their original country, but still under the jurisdiction of that country. Also refers to the newly settled area itself.

commonwealth: A free association of sovereign independent states that has no charter, treaty, or constitution. The association promotes cooperation, consultation, and mutual assistance among members.

communism: A form of government whose system requires common ownership of property for the use of all citizens. Prices on goods and services are usually set by the government, and all profits are shared equally by everyone. Also, communism refers directly to the official doctrine of the former Soviet Union.

compulsory education: The mandatory requirement for children to attend school until they have reached a certain age or grade level.

Confucianism: The system of ethics and politics taught by the Chinese philosopher Confucius.

constitution: The written laws and basic rights of citizens of a country or members of an organized group.

copra: The dried meat of the coconut.

cordillera: A continuous ridge, range, or chain of mountains.

coup d'ètat (coup): A sudden, violent overthrow of a government or its leader.

cuisine: A particular style of preparing food, especially when referring to the cooking of a particular country or ethnic group.

Cushitic language group: A group of languages that are spoken in Ethiopia and other areas of eastern Africa.

Cyrillic alphabet: An alphabet invented by Cyril and Methodius in the ninth century as an alphabet that was easier for the copyist to write. The Russian alphabet is a slight modification of it.

deity: A being with the attributes, nature, and essence of a god; a divinity.

desegregation: The act of removing restrictions on people of a particular race that keep them socially, economically, and, sometimes, physically, separate from other groups.

desertification: The process of becoming a desert as a result of climatic changes, land mismanagement, or both.

Dewali (Deepavali, Divali): The Hindu Festival of Lights, when Lakshmi, goddess of good fortune, is said to visit the homes of humans. The four- or five-day festival occurs in October or November.

dialect: One of a number of regional or related modes of speech regarded as descending from a common origin.

dowry: The sum of the property or money that a bride brings to her groom at their marriage.

Druze: A member of a Muslim sect based in Syria, living chiefly in the mountain regions of Lebanon.

dynasty: A family line of sovereigns who rule in succession, and the time during which they reign.

Eastern Orthodox: The outgrowth of the original Eastern Church of the Eastern Roman Empire, consisting of eastern Europe, western Asia, and Egypt.

Eid al-Adha: The Muslim holiday that celebrates the end of the special pilgrimage season (hajj) to the city of Mecca in Saudi Arabia.

Eid al-Fitr: The Muslim holiday that begins just after the end of the month of Ramadan and is celebrated with three or four days of feasting.

emigration: Moving from one country or region to another for the purpose of residence.

empire: A group of territories ruled by one sovereign or supreme ruler. Also, the period of time under that rule.

Episcopal: Belonging to or vested in bishops or prelates; characteristic of or pertaining to a bishop or bishops.

exports: Goods sold to foreign buyers.

Finno-Ugric language group: A subfamily of languages spoken in northeastern Europe, including Finnish, Hungarian, Estonian, and Lapp.

fjord: A deep indentation of the land forming a comparatively narrow arm of the sea with more or less steep slopes or cliffs on each side.

folk religion: A religion with origins and traditions among the common people of a nation or region that is relevant to their particular life-style.

Former Soviet Union: Refers to the republics that were once part of a large nation called the Union of Soviet Socialists Republics (USSR). The USSR was commonly called the Soviet Union. It included the 12 republics: Russia, Ukraine, Belarus, Moldova, Armenia, Azerbaijan, Uzbekistan, Turkmenistan, Tajikistan, Kazakhstan, Kyrgizstan, and Georgia. Sometimes the Baltic republics of Estonia, Latvia, and Lithuania are also included.

fundamentalist: A person who holds religious beliefs based on the complete acceptance of the words of holy scriptures as the truth.

Germanic language group: A large branch of the Indo-European family of languages including German itself, the Scandinavian languages, Dutch, Yiddish, Modern English, Modern Scottish, Afrikaans, and others. The group also includes extinct languages such as Gothic, Old High German, Old Saxon, Old English, Middle English, and the like.

Greek Orthodox: The official church of Greece, a self-governing branch of the Orthodox Eastern Church.

guerrilla: A member of a small radical military organization that uses unconventional tactics to take their enemies by surprise.

hajj: A religious journey made by Muslims to the holy city of Mecca in Saudi Arabia.

Holi: A Hindu festival of processions and merriment lasting three to ten days that marks the end of the lunar year in February or March.

Holocaust: The mass slaughter of European civilians, the vast majority of whom were Jews, by the Nazis during World War II.

Holy Roman Empire: A kingdom consisting of a loose union of German and Italian territories that existed from around the ninth century until 1806.

homeland: A region or area set aside to be a state for a people of a particular national, cultural, or racial origin.

homogeneous: Of the same kind or nature, often used in reference to a whole.

Horn of Africa: The Horn of Africa comprises Djibouti, Eritrea, Ethiopia, Somalia, and Sudan.

human rights issues: Any matters involving people's basic rights which are in question or thought to be abused.

immigration: The act or process of passing or entering into another country for the purpose of permanent residence.

imports: Goods purchased from foreign suppliers.

indigenous: Born or originating in a particular place or country; native to a particular region or area.

Indo-Aryan language group: The group that includes the languages of India; also called Indo-European language group.

Indo-European language family: The group that includes the languages of India and much of Europe and southwestern Asia.

Islam: The religious system of Muhammad, practiced by Muslims and based on a belief in Allah as the supreme being and Muhammed as his prophet. Islam also refers to those nations in which it is the primary religion. There are two major sects: Sunni and Shia (or Shiite). The main difference between the two sects is in their belief in who follows Muhammad, founder of Islam, as the religious leader.

Judaism: The religious system of the Jews, based on the Old Testament as revealed to Moses and characterized by a belief in one God and adherence to the laws of scripture and rabbinic traditions.

khan: A sovereign, or ruler, in central Asia.

khanate: A kingdom ruled by a khan, or man of rank.

literacy: The ability to read and write.

Maghreb states: Refers to Algeria, Morocco, and Tunisia; sometimes includes Libya and Mauritania.

maize: Another name (Spanish or British) for corn or the color of ripe corn.

manioc: The cassava plant or its product. Manioc is a very important food-staple in tropical America.

matrilineal (descent): Descending from, or tracing descent through, the maternal, or mother's, family line.

Mayan language family: The languages of the Central American Indians, further divided into two subgroups: the Maya and the Huastek.

mean temperature: The air temperature unit measured by the National Weather Service by adding the maximum and minimum daily temperatures together and diving the sum by 2.

Mecca: A city in Saudi Arabia; a destination of Muslims in the Islamic world.

mestizo: The offspring of a person of mixed blood; especially, a person of mixed Spanish and American Indian parentage.

millet: A cereal grass whose small grain is used for food in Europe and Asia.

monarchy: Government by a sovereign, such as a king or queen.

Mongol: One of an Asiatic race chiefly resident in Mongolia, a region north of China proper and south of Siberia.

Moors: One of the Arab tribes that conquered Spain in the eighth century.

Moslem *see* **Muslim.**

mosque: An Islam place of worship and the organization with which it is connected.

Muhammad (or Muhammed or Mahomet): An Arabian prophet (AD 570–632), known as the "Prophet of Allah" who founded the religion of Islam in 622, and wrote the Koran, (also spelled Quran) the scripture of Islam.

mulatto: One who is the offspring of parents one of whom is white and the other is black.

Muslim: A follower of Muhammad in the religion of Islam.

Muslim New Year: A Muslim holiday also called Nawruz. In some countries Muharram 1, which is the first month of the Islamic year, is observed as a holiday, in other places the new year is observed on Sha'ban, the eighth month of the year. This practice apparently stems from pagan Arab times. Shab-i-Bharat, a national holiday in Bangladesh on this day, is held by many to be the occasion when God ordains all actions in the coming year.

mystic: Person who believes he or she can gain spiritual knowledge through processes like meditation that are not easily explained by reasoning or rational thinking.

nationalism: National spirit or aspirations; desire for national unity, independence, or prosperity.

oasis: Fertile spot in the midst of a desert or wasteland.

official language: The language in which the business of a country and its government is conducted.

Ottoman Empire: A Turkish empire that existed from about 1603 until 1918, and included lands around the Mediterranean, Black, and Caspian seas.

patriarchal system: A social system in which the head of the family or tribe is the father or oldest male. Ancestry is determined and traced through the male members of the tribe.

patrilineal (descent): Descending from, or tracing descent through, the paternal, or father's, family line.

pilgrimage: religious journey, usually to a holy place.

plantain: Tropical plant with fruit that looks like bananas, but that must be cooked before eating.

Protestant: A member of one of the Christian bodies that descended from the Reformation of the sixteenth century.

pulses: Beans, peas, or lentils.

Ramadan: The ninth month of the Muslim calender. The entire month commemorates the period in which the Prophet Muhammad is said to have recieved divine revelation and is observed by a strict fast from sunrise to sundown.

Rastafarian: A member of a Jamaican cult begun in 1930 that is partly religious and partly political.

refugee: Person who, in times of persecution or political commotion, flees to a foreign country for safety.

revolution: A complete change in a government or society, such as in an overthrow of the government by the people.

Roman alphabet: Alphabet of the ancient Romans from which alphabets of most modern European languages, including English, are derived.

Roman Catholic Church: Christian church headed by the pope or Bishop of Rome.

Russian Orthodox: The arm of the Eastern Orthodox Church that was the official church of Russia under the tsars.

Sahelian zone: Eight countries make up this dry desert zone in Africa: Burkina Faso, Chad, Gambia, Mali, Mauritania, Niger, Senegal, and the Cape Verde Islands.

savanna: A treeless or near treeless grassland or plain.

segregation: The enforced separation of a racial or religious group from other groups, compelling them to live and go to school separately from the rest of society.

Seventh-day Adventist: One who believes in the second coming of Christ to establish a personal reign upon the earth.

shamanism: A religion in which shamans (priests or medicine men) are believed to influence spirits.

shantytown: An urban settlement of people in inadequate houses.

Shia Muslim *see* Islam.

Shiites *see* Islam.

Shintoism: The system of nature- and hero-worship that forms the native religion of Japan.

sierra: A chain of hills or mountains.

Sikh: A member of a community of India, founded around 1500 and based on the principles of monotheism (belief in one god) and human brotherhood.

Sino-Tibetan language family: The family of languages spoken in eastern Asia, including China, Thailand, Tibet, and Myanmar.

slash-and-burn agriculture: A hasty and sometimes temporary way of clearing land to make it available for agriculture by cutting down trees and burning them; also known as swidden agriculture.

slave trade: The transportation of black Africans beginning in the 1700s to other countries to be sold as slaves—people owned as property and compelled to work for their owners at no pay.

Slavic languages: A major subgroup of the Indo-European language family. It is further subdivided into West Slavic (including Polish, Czech, Slovak and Serbian), South Slavic (including Bulgarian, Serbo-Croatian, Slovene, and Old Church Slavonic), and East Slavic (including Russian Ukrainian and Byelorussian).

sorghum: Plant grown for its valuable uses, such as for grain, syrup, or fodder.

Southeast Asia: The region in Asia that consists of the Malay Archipelago, the Malay Peninsula, and Indochina.

Soviet Union *see* **Former Soviet Union.**

subcontinent: A large subdivision of a continent.

subsistence farming: Farming that provides only the minimum food goods necessary for the continuation of the farm family.

Sudanic language group: A related group of languages spoken in various areas of northern Africa, including Yoruba, Mandingo, and Tshi.

Sufi: A Muslim mystic who believes that God alone exists, there can be no real difference between good and evil, that the soul exists within the body as in a cage, so death should be the chief object of desire.

sultan: A king of a Muslim state.

Sunni Muslim *see* Islam.

Taoism: The doctrine of Lao-Tzu, an ancient Chinese philosopher (c.500 **BC**) as laid down by him in the *Tao-te-ching.*

Third World: A term used to describe less developed countries; as of the mid-1990s, it is being replaced by the United Nations designation Less Developed Countries, or LDC.

treaty: A negotiated agreement between two governments.

tribal system: A social community in which people are organized into groups or clans descended from common ancestors and sharing customs and languages.

tundra: A nearly level treeless area whose climate and vegetation are characteristically arctic due to its northern position; the subsoil is permanently frozen.

untouchables: In India, members of the lowest caste in the caste system, a hereditary social class system. They were considered unworthy to touch members of higher castes.

Union of the Soviet Socialist Republics *see* Former Soviet Union.

veldt: A grassland in South Africa.

Western nations: General term used to describe democratic, capitalist countries, including the United States, Canada, and western European countries.

Zoroastrianism: The system of religious doctrine taught by Zoroaster and his followers in the Avesta; the religion prevalent in Persia until its overthrow by the Muslims in the seventh century.

Index

All culture groups and countries included in this encyclopedia are included in this index. Selected regions, alternate groups names, and historical country names are cross-referenced. Country chapter titles are in boldface; volume numbers appear in brackets, with page number following.

INDEX